D1218190

Breaking The Shakespeare Codes

THE SENSATIONAL DISCOVERY OF THE BARD'S TRUE IDENTITY

Robert Nield

C.C.Publishing
(Chester)

First published in 2007 by
C.C. Publishing, in conjunction with Park Manor Publishing,
Chester, CH3 7RX
Tel: 01829 741651

British Library cataloguing in Publication Data.
A catalogue record for this book is available from the British Library.

ISBN   978-0-949001-34-4

Origination by C.C.Publishing (Chester).
Printed and bound in the UK by
Livesey Limited, Shrewsbury.

www.cc-publishing.co.uk

To the memory of my parents

and

The restless spirits of the unquiet dead

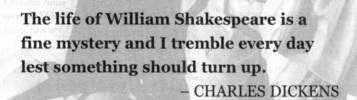

The life of William Shakespeare is a fine mystery and I tremble every day lest something should turn up.

– CHARLES DICKENS

I am ... haunted by the conviction that the divine William is the biggest and most successful fraud ever practised on a patient world.

– HENRY JAMES

Acknowledgements

I would like to extend warm thanks to all who helped in bringing this book to life.

I first want to recognise the very helpful contributions of Kate Vereker, my research assistant. After extracting hundreds of potential anagrams from tens of thousands of lines in the 1623 Folio and The Sonnets, she scoured the Elizabethan picture archives and identified several images of crucial importance: a miniature called 'Sir Arundel Talbot', a painting known as 'the Persian Lady', details in the sieve portrait of Elizabeth I and the portrait of an 'unknown courtier' dated 1583. It is certain that without Kate's commitment, enthusiasm and sharp eye for detail this book would have been much the poorer.

In fact, *Breaking The Shakespeare Codes* benefited in a variety of ways from the help and advice of several people: John Buckley who ploughed through an early draft and suggested three-quarters of the book's title; Geraldine Cooke who offered helpful editorial comments; Mary Hudson who kindly read through a rough draft; Alan Quinn who drew attention to the unknown knight in the painting 'Eliza Triumphans'; Jason Vereker who assisted with the dust jacket design and Emma Whitehead who typed hundreds of lines extracted from the 1623 Folio, and whose eagle-eyes spotted the insignia at Hampton Court.

I also want to commend the professional help and advice of Mark Bevan, whose expertise in the arcane techniques of printing and publishing, transmuted the base-metal of my manuscript into a finished product. My personal thanks also go to Linda Wraith, for the very kind assistance of a generous loan which helped to alleviate the pecuniary burden that self-funding of the project imposed.

Last – but very far from least – Joan Robinson, to whom I owe an incalculable debt of gratitude and to whom I want to convey my very special thanks. Were it not for her kindness, generosity, hard work and unstinting support through five long years, this book would never have seen the light of day. Above all, if she hadn't taken the trouble to drag her semi-reclusive neighbour to an antiques fair in Manchester, one rainy Saturday in June 2001, you would not be reading this now!

In accordance with custom, the author accepts responsibility for any errors.

Robert Nield

Contents

Illustrations
(in order of appearance)

Sketch of the 'Shakespeare birthplace' in Henley Street, Stratford.
Engraving after R. Green (1769).

Holy Trinity Church, Stratford – photograph.

Panorama of London (detail) from an engraving by Wenceslas Hollar (1647).

Bull-baiting and bear-baiting in the Fechthaus Nuremberg.
Woodcut from Curioser Spiegel (1689).

The Globe Theatre – after Jan Claesz Visscher's view of London (c 1616).

Anne Hathaway's cottage, Hewland's farm, Shottery.
Photograph © 2006, Kate Vereker.

The Earl of Southampton in the Tower of London (detail).
After John de Critz the Elder.

Title page of the 1623 Folio, with engraving of 'Shakespeare'.
by Martin Droeshout.

Michael Drayton – engraving by William Hole (1619).

The Stratford Monument – engraving based on William Dugdale's 1634 sketch.

Shakespeare Monument at Wilton House. Designed by William Kent (1743).

Sir Francis Bacon (detail) from an oil portrait after Paul van Sumer.

Delia Bacon – photograph.

Ignatius Donnelly – photograph.

Sir Francis Walsingham (detail) oil painting after John de Critz the Elder.
National Portrait Gallery.

'Christopher Marlowe' (detail). Oil painting, Corpus Christi Coll. Cambridge.

Edward de Vere, 17th Earl of Oxford (detail) by Marcus Gheeraedts the Younger.

William Stanley, 6th Earl of Derby (detail),
by Marcus Gheeraedts the Younger.

'Lost Portrait of Elizabeth I'.
Oil on canvas. Possibly by Marcus Gheeraedts the Younger.
© 2006, Robert Nield & Joan Robinson.

Elizabeth I, Armada Portrait c 1588 (oil on panel)
Attributed to George Gower (1540-96).
Woburn Abbey, Bedfordshire, UK. The Bridgeman Library

Robert Dudley, Earl of Leicester (c 1575-1580).
Oil painting. Artist unknown.
National Portrait Gallery.

Sir William Cecil, Lord Burghley (detail).
Oil painting attributed to
Hans Eworth (c 1565) Hatfield House.

Hampton Court Palace garden.
Photograph © 2006, Kate Vereker.

Henry Hastings.
Artist unknown.

St Giles Church and Hastings Chapel, Stoke Poges.
Photograph © 2006, Kate Vereker.

Stoke Park Manor House, Stoke Poges.
Photograph © 2006, Kate Vereker.

Initials at St Giles Church, Stoke Poges.
Photograph © 2006, Robert Nield.

Richard Tarleton with fife and tabor.
Woodcut on title page of Tarleton's Jests (1611).

Kenilworth Castle (remains) – photograph.

Graffiti at Chester Cathedral.
Photograph © 2006, Robert Nield.

Execution – woodcut (detail).
From Roxburghe Ballads 17th century.

Wilton House, near Salisbury.
Print 'Picturesque Views of the Noblemen and Gentlemen
of Great Britain and Ireland (1870), F.O.Morris.

Mary (Sidney) Herbert, Countess of Pembroke.
Engraving by Simon van de Passe (1618).
National Portrait Gallery.

Old Petworth House and gardens, from a map of Petworth (1610).

Sir Philip Sidney (detail). Oil painting attributed John de Critz the Elder.

Robert Devereux, 2nd Earl of Essex (detail).
Marcus Gheeraedts the Younger.

James I, oil painting attributed John de Critz the Elder. (c 1610).
National Maritime Museum, Greenwich.

Robert Cecil, 1st Earl of Salisbury. Detail from oil painting of
Somerset House conference 1604.
National Portrait Gallery.

John Florio – engraving by W. Hole (1611),
frontispiece of English-Italian dictionary.

Portrait of Elizabeth of England – Sienna, Pinacoteca Nazionale.
© Photograph SCALA, Florence.
Courtesy of the Ministero Beni e Attributed Culturali 1990.

'Unknown Courtier', 21 years old in 1583.
Oil painting possibly by Zuccaro.
Owner and present whereabouts unknown.

Queen Elizabeth I (1533-1603) in procession (Eliza Triumphans) (c 1601).
Oil (on canvas) attributed Robert Peake. (fl.1580-1626).
Private Collection. The Bridgeman Picture Library.

Ben Jonson (detail). Oil portrait after A. Blyenberch.
National Portrait Gallery.

Shakespeare Monument, Holy Trinity Church, Stratford.
Gerard Johnson (1616-1623).

Engraving by W. Marshall & Verse by J. Benson in
'Poems', written by: Wil. Shakespeare. Gent' (1640).

A miniature called 'Sir Arundel Talbot' (1596), by Isaac Oliver.
© V & A Images/ Victoria and Albert Museum.

Portrait of a Woman in Oriental Dress, Marcus Gheeraedts the Younger.
The Royal Collection © 2006, Her Majesty Queen Elizabeth II.
(Currently at Hampton Court).

Initials on external wall of Holy Trinity Church, Stratford.
Photograph © 2006, Robert Nield.

Insignia on staircase at Hampton Court Palace.
Photograph © 2006, Kate Vereker.

A note about nomenclature
In discussing the authorship of Shakespeare it is customary to refer to the traditional author, the Stratford man, as 'Shakspere' – the surname recorded, at his christening, in the register of Holy Trinity Church. In so doing the 'man' is distinguished from his alleged 'work' – which is denoted, in this book, by *Shakespeare* written in italics. Thus, Shakspere is the traditional author (also referred to as the 'Stratford man') and *Shakespeare* is the canon itself. In addition, 'Shakespeare' in quotes referes to the real author – in other words, whoever actually wrote 'the works'.

Introduction

Why pick on the Bard?

'Shakespeare' the pre-eminent writer, alone of all celebrated persons in the last 500 years, has long attracted intense scrutiny and doubt. Why?

A partial answer combines two factors:

Firstly, *Shakespeare* is one of the most famous names in history, so it is inevitable that the biography has been given very close attention.

Secondly, the known facts of the alleged author's life, yield no clues about his activity as a writer. That is to say, there is no contemporary documentary evidence that the Stratford businessman, William Shakspere, wrote *anything* (not even a letter) let alone the greatest collection of literary works in English.

The fact that 'Shakespeare' is regarded as the foremost writer in the language, yet the traditional author's *literary* biography is totally void, arouses deep suspicions and doubts – concerns enhanced by the observation that, in stark contrast to the absence of literary evidence, many of the Stratford man's business dealings and legal affairs are well documented. This conspicuous asymmetry in the biographical record is strange, especially for a prolific commercial writer, and is good reason to doubt the Stratford man's authorship claim. But of still greater significance is the fact that a few contemporaries left very strong indications in text alluding to the Bard's works, that the true author was hidden.

A curiously apt name

Even the name arouses suspicion. On fifteen of the thirty-three earliest publications, the surname included a hyphen: Shake-speare. In the sixteenth century the name was spelt in many different ways, although no other examples of the hyphenated form have ever been found. Furthermore, none of the author's literary contemporaries could boast of having such a dramatic and dynamic surname: Jonson, Drayton, Middleton, Beaumont, Fletcher, Marlowe, Mundy, Chapman, Spenser, Greene, Nashe, Peele, Ford, Webster, Weever, Davies, Holland, Digges, Kyd, Donne, Edwards, Hall, Marston, Warren, Haywood, Chettle, Dekker, Lodge, Massinger, Harvey, Daniel, Watson & Lyle.

All are comparatively 'ordinary' names, none has the striking 'theatrical' quality of Shake-speare – which 'stands out from the crowd'; indeed, it looks *and* sounds very much like a construct – a stage-name – especially in view of the fact that literary pseudonyms were common at the time.

Pen-names in literature
Throughout history many writers have used pen-names. Here are some famous examples:

The Bronte sisters: Anne, Charlotte and Emily called themselves, respectively: Acton, Currer and Ellis Bell. Cecil Day Lewis (Nicholas Blake); Boz (Charles Dickens); Lewis Carroll (Charles Dodgson); Elia (Charles Lamb); George Eliot (Mary Ann Evans); George Sand (Amandine Dupin); Maxim Gorki (Alexei Peshkov); spy novelist John le Carre (David Cornwell); Agatha Christie (Mary Westmacott); George Orwell (Eric Blair); Saki (Hector Munroe); Stendhal (Marie Henri Beyle); Mark Twain (Samuel Clemens); Anthony Burgess (John Wilson); the famous French philosopher and man of letters Voltaire (Francois-Marie Arouet) and the seventeenth-century French playwright Moliere (Jean Baptiste Poquelin).

With so many well-known nom-de-plumes in world literature it would cause little surprise to find that the rather contrived-looking 'Shake-speare' is just one more.

Concerns of the literati
Many writers and actors have seriously doubted the traditional attribution of the *Shakespeare* canon. A few quotations give an idea of the general concern:

Henry James: 'I am … haunted by the conviction that the divine William is the biggest and most successful fraud ever practised on a patient world'.

Walt Whitman: 'Beneath a few foundations of proved facts are certainly engul'd far more dim and elusive ones, of deepest importance – tantalizing and half-suspected – suggesting explanations that one dare not put in plain statement'.

Charles Dickens: 'The life of William Shakespeare is a fine mystery and I tremble every day lest something should turn up'.

Ralph W. Emerson: 'Other men have led lives in some sort of keeping with their thought, but this man was in wide contrast'.

Dr Blair Worden, Oxford scholar: 'The relationship between an artist's biography and his writing is always a difficult subject, but there can be no other important writer since the invention of printing for whom we are unable to demonstrate any relationship at all'.

As the last quotation shows, orthodox scholars acknowledge their complete failure to bridge the gulf between *Shakespeare* (the works) and the documented 'life' of the Stratford man. In view of the admission, it is very strange that the academics have not pursued the authorship question themselves; indeed, they have persistently *denied* the existence of any 'problem' with the traditional author – even though there are many powerful reasons, apart from lack of documentary material, to seriously doubt William Shakspere's authorship.

Personally, I am very glad that the professional academics have declined to address this most important issue, because it has given *me* the chance to put the record straight.

Shakespeare: The Enigma

A serendipitous discovery

Although I had long known of the controversy surrounding *Shakespeare's* authorship, the issue never seriously attracted my attention because, with a background in science, it was a matter beyond my professional concern. I therefore never imagined that the question of the Bard's identity would plunge me into the murky depths of a four hundred-year-old mystery – still less did I foresee that it would absorb every available minute for more than five years. But in summer 2001 everything changed dramatically with the chance discovery of an Old Master portrait at a Manchester antiques fair. Within hours of setting eyes on the painting, which is thought to be a lost portrait of Elizabeth I, a sensational resolution of the Shakespeare Authorship Controversy suddenly presented itself – an astonishing insight that inspired and motivated the research for this book.

Was 'Shakespeare' really two people?

William Shakspere, of Stratford-upon-Avon, was surely the most mysterious of all the Virgin Queen's subjects; his life was full of odd contrasts, apparent inconsistencies and mysterious contradictions, *viz*:

1. A prolific writer – but no text in his own hand survives.
2. Someone that Ben Jonson called 'Sweet Swan of Avon' – yet a ruthless merchant who hoarded grain in times of famine.
3. A self-deprecating poet who wrote 154 sonnets without seeking payment – but a greedy businessman who hounded petty debtors.
4. A playwright who used far more dialect words from the north of England than from Warwickshire – yet an individual whose formative years were spent in Stratford.
5. An author possessing the deepest insight, of any contemporary writer, into the mind-set of royalty – but a man who lived his life surrounded by commoners and yokels.

6. The writer who had by far the largest vocabulary of any contemporary author – yet a rustic with no known education.

7. A polymath and literary genius – but a witness in a lawsuit who was unsure of his age!

8. A playwright whose works were performed at Elizabeth's court more frequently than those of any other dramatist – yet no courtier ever referred to the brilliant writer from Stratford.

9. An author of whom contemporaries wrote: 'his hand and mind went together' – though someone who struggled to sign and spell his own name.

10. A writer famed for eloquence and wit – but nobody reported anything he ever said.

11. A sonneteer certain that his name would be buried with his body – yet the *Shakespeare* name appeared on published works and was well known long after his death.

12. A dramatist who set many of his plays in Italy – although a man raised in the heart of England.

13. An individual whose will failed to mention his prestigious patron, the Earl of Southampton – yet a snob who bought a coat-of-arms and titled himself 'gentleman'.

14. A very talented and successful playwright – although, in the dog-eat-dog world of the London theatres, an author who seems to have had no literary enemies.

15. A dramatist who wrote politically very dangerous plays – but, unlike many of his literary rivals, a playwright who never got in trouble with the authorities.

16. A man who earned his living by the pen – though never explicitly identified as a writer during his lifetime.

17. A dramatist who used obscure foreign sources for his plays – yet a man whose will made no mention of books.

18. A playwright who worked very hard for twenty years – but an author who made no attempt to save any of his manuscripts.

19. A famous writer – yet someone who let a legal clerk sign the most important of personal documents – his will.

20. A playwright lauded in 1623 as the 'wonder of our stage', 'soule of the age' and 'starre of poets' – but no theatrical colleague or member of the literati acknowledged his death in 1616.

With so many apparent inconsistencies in the biography, there is a very real possibility that 'Shakespeare' was not one person but *two*. It is therefore little wonder that, outside the cloistered confines of academia, the issue of 'Shakespeare's' identity has become the focus of much heated debate. Even a quick glance at the evidence shows that the traditional attribution of authorship is plagued by a host of unresolved problems and difficulties.

It is very strange that the dramatist himself left no 'paper trail'– not a single inadvertent clue – to show that he had been a writer, as though he had a pathological need to hide *everything* that pertained to his literary career. All the primary material, which might have provided incontestable proof of Shakspere's authorship, seems to have gone missing – yet, by contrast, many aspects of his life *other* than the writing are recorded in some detail. This surprising asymmetry in the biographical record is one of the strongest points against the Stratford man's claim to authorship.

However, although the total absence of primary evidence greatly undermines the case for orthodoxy, the most serious difficulty is that every line of inquiry, starting with William Shakspere, of Stratford, leads to a puzzle, mystery or anomaly. In what ought to be a plain and simple story about the life of a playwright from the sticks, nothing is plain and very little is simple. There are just too many problems and unanswered questions – that is the single most powerful reason to doubt the credibility of the traditional attribution. In other words, there is definitely a case to answer.

Does 'Shakespeare' hide a secret of historic proportions?

If the *Shakespeare* story is a hoax and the real author was concealed, four questions arise:
1. The London theatres were hot-beds of rumour and gossip – why were there no stories about a secret 'Shakespeare author' circulating at the time?
2. What kept 'the secret' completely secure, even after the author's death?
3. Why was it necessary to create a very elaborate hoax about a 'mere' playwright?
4. Why has the Authorship Controversy proven so difficult to resolve?

Whatever the answers, one thing seems certain: if 'Shakespeare' was a ploy, whoever constructed it went to great lengths to hide *something* very securely – something that, to warrant such deep secrecy, must have been of immense importance.

Doubts and misgivings

The recorded life of William Shakspere is entirely unrelated to his (alleged) writing career; documents retrieved from the archive offer no help in understanding how he, the Stratford man, came to write the works attributed to him. Nothing is known of the author's views, interests, friends or *modus operandi* and little can be said about his personality, except that he seems to have been rather greedy and uncharitable. It appears that the Warwickshire yokel was much more concerned about saving money, than saving anything he wrote. Indeed, one of the strangest facts about William Shakspere is that he made no attempt to preserve copies of any of the manuscripts on which he had (supposedly) worked very hard for twenty years.

Finding biographical evidence about 'Shakespeare' – the writer – has proven extremely difficult. The frustrating lack of primary evidence is a wellspring for speculation and a trap – a dream for the theorist, a nightmare for the honest biographer. So few are the facts about 'Shakespeare' the playwright, that no biography worthy of the name *can* be written. But, the human mind abhors a vacuum and so, just as artists are compelled to fill stark white canvases with paint, the Bard's biographers feel obliged to flood the empty pages of his life story with speculation and conjecture. Those tempted to sketch a 'life' are forced to assume the role of literary cartoonist, filling spaces and joining dots in a desperate attempt to flesh-out the almost featureless portrait of the Warwickshire yokel. That is why 'conventional' biographies are replete with digressions and padding – there just isn't enough reliable and relevant material to fill more than a few pages.

Of all the famous people in modern history, it is strange that a *writer* happens to be the most enigmatic and mysterious – an individual who has proven to be profoundly resistant to analysis. The alleged rustic author was a provincial merchant, a rapacious opportunist who hoarded grain while his neighbours starved, a bit-part actor, a tax dodger, a litigious skinflint, a shareholder in London theatres and a miserly husband who only thought fit to bequeath his wife, Anne Hathaway, the 'second best bed'. Among these rather dismal facts, it's hard to detect even the faintest glimmer of the genius who created such remarkable dramatic masterpieces as *Hamlet, Othello, King Lear, Macbeth and The Tempest*. Indeed, it is far from clear that the yokel who appears in the historical archive – the shadowy entrepreneur from Warwickshire – was the author of the literary works attributed to him by tradition. And it is difficult to imagine the grain-hoarding miser, relentlessly pursuing petty debtors, as the self-deprecating poet who toiled over one hundred and fifty-odd sonnets without seeking financial reward.

Above all, a positive attribution for works as culturally significant as *Shakespeare* requires much more than the mere similarity of a name – it demands an author with all the right attributes and credentials. In that respect, William Shakspere's education poses a serious problem. His parents were illiterate, he grew up in a home devoid of books, it is unclear if he went to school, he certainly never attended university and he lived amongst raw peasants for the first twenty-odd years of his life. Bereft of intellectual and cultural stimulation, sixteenth century Stratford was not an environment in which one might expect a polymath and literary genius to develop. Of the nineteen aldermen on the town council – surely Stratford's finest – only seven could sign their names. So it seems that the greatest writer in the English language, grew to adulthood in a cultural desert with mainly uncouth rustics for company.

Despite the deprivations of rural life, William Shakspere (by means unknown) acquired a huge vocabulary, variously estimated at up to 40,000 words – a personal lexicon several times that of any contemporary rival and about one hundred times that of a typical peasant. In the absence of an English dictionary, the accumulation of such a vast store of words would have required the resources of a major library, as well as huge commitment in time and effort. A monumentally difficult undertaking, achieved without leaving a single clue to show how it was done.

As elusive as a fleeting shadow, the playwright left no definite trace of himself in his writing. Unlike his contemporary Ben Jonson, whose plays are full of authorial opinions, the personal 'voice' of the playwright is entirely absent from his work. The author never explicitly reveals what he thinks. In view of the multitude of characters he created, and the sheer scale of the canon, it is curious that the most famous of dramatists appears as little more than a cipher.

Acclaimed for the eloquence with which they elucidate the human condition, the *Shakespeare* plays are a unique combination of poetry, drama and psychological insight. No other writer of the last five hundred years has made such a significant contribution to language, literature and culture. More than 17,000 books listed in the catalogue of the British Library are dedicated to the author and his works and, it is estimated, a new article about 'Shakespeare' is published on average every eight minutes. It is therefore unsurprising, in light of the Bard's accomplishments, that he was voted 'Man of the Millennium'.

Famous doubters

Although more has been written about 'Shakespeare' and his work than anyone else in history, the author's identity has long aroused deep suspicion. Since the middle of the nineteenth century, many have questioned whether the eldest son of an illiterate glover and farmer's daughter – a man with no known education – actually wrote the celebrated works attributed to him. Many have investigated the authorship issue with an open mind and have concluded that the Stratford man was probably not the true author. Nearly all the groups subscribing to these 'heretical' opinions, dubbed 'Anti-Stratfordians', share the view that William Shakspere was merely a front man – an impostor who sold works by the real author, or authors, under a *nom de plume* that was similar to his own name.

Over the years a number of prominent figures have added their voices to the chorus of unbelievers, including: Samuel Taylor Coleridge, Charles Dickens, Otto von Bismarck, Ralph W. Emerson, Henry James, Lord Palmerston, Benjamin Disraeli, Walt Whitman, Mark Twain, John Galsworthy, Thomas Hardy, Sigmund Freud, Charlie Chaplin, James Joyce, John Buchan, Helen Keller, Charles de Gaulle, Vladimir Nabokov, Orson Welles, Daphne du Maurier, Muriel Spark, Enoch Powell, Sir John Gielgud, Sir Derek Jacobi and Kenneth Branagh.

With so many famous doubters an obvious question suggests itself: if the case for the Stratford man is watertight, as orthodox scholars insist, why have all these members of the *cognoscenti* – many of them well-known writers and actors themselves – concluded that the traditional attribution is wrong?

Almost certainly, the answer is because the case for William Shakspere's authorship is nothing like as secure as the academics would have us believe.

Of more than sixty alternative authors that have been proposed, since the mid-nineteenth century, Sir Francis Bacon, Christopher Marlowe and Edward de Vere (17th Earl of Oxford) are probably the best known. However, there are serious flaws with all the contenders – so, the adherents of orthodoxy refuse to take the authorship debate seriously. Yet, although most scholars are adamant that there is no mystery about the author's identity, many admit that *as a writer* William Shakspere is an enigma. But if even the academics find something odd about the Stratford man's writing of 'the works', there must surely be a case to investigate. It is therefore somewhat surprising, at first sight, that they have failed to take up the challenge.

The names of many alternative authors, both individual candidates and members of various collaborations, are listed below:

Sole or principle authors (in no special order):

Francis Bacon	Edward de Vere	William Stanley
Roger Manners	Sir Walter Ralegh	Christopher Marlowe
Anthony Bacon	Michael Angelo Florio	Robert Devereux
William Butts	Sir Anthony Shirley	Henry Wriothesley
Robert Cecil	Cardinal Wolsey	Robert Burton
Sir John Barnard	Sir Edward Dyer	Charles Blunt

Queen Elizabeth	Sir William Alexander	John Richardson
Anne Whateley	John Williams	Henry Neville
Mary (Sidney) Herbert		

Members of potential collaborations: Barnabe Barnes, Richard Barnfield, Richard Burbage, Henry Chettle, Samuel Daniel, Thomas Dekker, John Donne, Thomas Sackville, Sir Francis Drake, Michael Drayton, Walter Devereux, Henry Ferrers, John Fletcher, John Florio, Robert Greene, Bartholomew Griffin, Thomas Heywood, King James, Ben Jonson, Thomas Kyd, Thomas Lodge, John Lyly, Thomas Middleton, Anthony Munday, Thomas Nashe, Henry Lord Paget, George Peele, Mary Sidney, William Herbert, Henry Porter, Elizabeth Sidney, Sir Philip Sidney, Wentworth Smythe, Edmund Spencer, Richard Vaughan, William Warner, Thomas Watson, John Webster, Robert Wilson.

A vast number of hypothetical groups could be assembled from these names, each one corresponding to a different 'Shakespeare'.

Every Anti-Stratfordian sect assumes that the real author's name is known to history, hence: Francis Bacon, Christopher Marlowe, the Earl of Oxford and the rest, are names familiar to historians of the Elizabethan period. However, it is possible that the real author's name is absent from the archives. If that is the case, it would help to explain why he has remained stubbornly elusive, and why the orthodox methodology of historical research – which relies almost entirely on the analysis of documentary material – has failed to resolve the authorship controversy. In seeking a more credible candidate than the Stratford man, many have naturally tried to find clues to the author's identity in 'the works' themselves. Unfortunately, all such attempts have proven inconclusive, because the *Shakespeare* texts are so rich in possible allusions, that 'evidence' can be found within them to support the claims of many authorial contenders.

Reasons for caution
Before accepting the assertion that a Warwickshire yokel with no known education wrote *Shakespeare*, it is necessary to take cognisance of a number of salient points:

- Intrigue, conspiracy and subterfuge were rife in Elizabethan and Jacobean times; hence, the 'Shakespeare story' might be a ruse – a conspiracy to hide the real author.
- Sixteenth century England has been compared to a police state; writers had to be very careful what they put in print – transgressors were usually punished severely.
- Codes, ciphers, acrostics and anagrams were methods of

encryption used by those with secrets to hide – hence, contemporary references to 'Shakespeare' might contain encoded messages.

- The use of pen names was common at the time, some authors even used 'shadow' writers as cover – a practice known as 'masking'.
- Contemporaries were strangely guarded when referring to the author of *Shakespeare*, perhaps because they were privy to a dangerous secret.
- The name Shake-speare was spelt with a hyphen on about 45% of the published works in the early years; there was no such surname, although pseudonyms were often hyphenated.
- The hyphenated version of Shake-speare – an especially dramatic and dynamic name – looks and sounds suspiciously like a code word, particularly in a theatrical context and by comparison with the name of every other writer.
- The quality and subject matter in the *Shakespeare* plays is very different, in general, to those of the author's contemporaries.
- Pallas Athena – goddess of knowledge, wisdom and truth – had the Latin epithet *hastivibrans*, which means 'spear shaker'; hence, 'Shake-speare' would have been an especially appropriate pseudonym for the author of works that incorporate knowledge, wisdom and truth about the human condition.
- Many characters in the plays assume disguises – the dramatist seems to have been obsessed with concealment, perhaps because he too was hidden.
- Although the name 'William Shakespeare' appeared on many of the published works, it does not *necessarily* follow that someone of that name was the author. In an age before copyright, the owner or vendor of an anonymous work was free to put his name on the title page.
- Verse on the monument in Holy Trinity Church, Stratford implies that something is hidden 'with in'. Lines 2/3: 'Read if thou canst whom envious death hath plast with in this monument Shakespeare'. However, the monument isn't large enough to hold a body and, in any case, Shakspere is (supposedly) buried in the adjacent grave.

Deep secrets in a dedication

A very important clue to the author's real name appeared in 1609, when the publisher Thomas Thorpe prefaced *Shake-speares Sonnets* with his dedication to a mysterious 'M^r. W.H.', a man identified by Thorpe as 'the onlie begetter' of the sonnets.

The precise meaning of 'begetter' – on which the dedication hinges – has probably caused more confusion than any other word in the English language, yet the only credible interpretation consistent with contemporary usage is that M^r. W.H. was, in fact, the author of the sonnets!

It was believed that verse was written with the help of a muse – a female spirit – and that poems were the 'children' of the poet and his muse; that is to say, the poet was thought of as the 'father' or 'begetter' of the poetry. Furthermore, the Latin meaning 'to beget' – *gignere* – is the origin of the English 'genius'. Since most writers in those days had an excellent knowledge of Latin, it's likely that Thorpe knew of the link between 'beget' and 'genius'; hence, the implication is that M^r. W.H. was 'the onlie genius' of *Shake-speares Sonnets*.

It has been suggested, however, that the 'H' resulted from a typographical error and that the initial should read 'S' – but, the probability of such a mistake, at the same frequency of error as in the sonnets themselves, is very low. Moreover, it was vital to get the initials right, so they would almost certainly have been checked before publication.

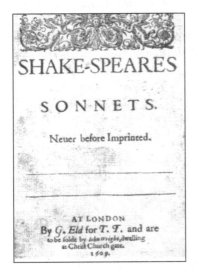
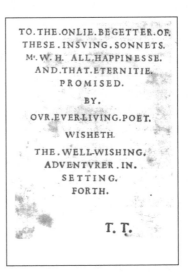

The title page and publisher Thomas Thorpe's enigmatic dedication in the first edition of 'Shake-speares Sonnets'. It is significant that the surname 'Shake-speare' – with hyphen – did not exist.

Taking all of the above into account, the balance of probability very strongly suggests that it was the mysterious M^r. W.H. who was the real author of *Shake-speares Sonnets*. Indeed, scrutiny of the first three lines of Thorpe's dedication provides confirmation:

TO. THE. ONLIE. BEGETTER. OF.
THESE. INSUING. SONNETS.
M^r. W.H. ALL. HAPPINESSE.*

Why did Thorpe reveal only the initials of the 'onlie begetter'? Bearing in mind that this was written in an age renowned for intrigue, secrecy, codes and ciphers it's a fair bet that the text contains encrypted information, probably concerning the 'onlie begetter'. In fact, the lines are a simple anagram which both names M^r. W.H. and identifies him as the 'unseen' poet of the sonnets viz:

Bringe help to William Hastings
the unseene poet of these sonnets *

The request 'Bringe help...' is clearly intended as a plea to the anagram solver to assist the 'unseene poet' by making his name known. Of course the question arises as to why someone with an apparently ordinary name, like William Hastings, would need to be hidden. What was so special about this man that necessitated a leak-proof conspiracy of silence amongst all those who knew of him?

Breaking the Shakespeare Codes provides the astounding answers and explains how and why the secret of William Hastings' authorship was kept permanently secure – even in an age seething with gossips, spies and rumourmongers.

But before examining Hastings' case, three fundamental questions must be addressed:

- Why are there very serious doubts about the traditional author?
- Who are the main challengers to orthodoxy?
- Why is it necessary to seek a new candidate?

* Footnote: i) the anagram solution does not include the superscript 'r' of M^r.
ii) 'bringe' and 'unseene' are spellings consistent with seventeenth century orthography.

The Acting Playwright

William Shakspere's background

To understand some of the reasons why serious doubts about William Shakspere's authorship have arisen it is helpful to examine his family background and the rather primitive rural environment in which he grew up.

Stratford-upon-Avon

The Stratford that William Shakspere knew was one of the oldest market towns in England. A sizeable conurbation for the time, significantly larger than villages like Liverpool and Manchester, with a population of 1,800-2,000, twelve streets, a fine thirteenth century church (Holy Trinity) and a grammar school. The town nestled in a wooded valley by the banks of the Avon where there had once been a ford. In 1490 Sir Hugh Clopton, a local man and former Lord Mayor of London, built a substantial stone bridge to replace the old wooden one – a construction which still stands – that carried the main highway to the great metropolis, a hundred miles to the southeast.

Stratford's prosperity depended chiefly on commodities such as wool, livestock, general farm produce and ale; in fact it was a fairly self-contained community and each week some of the excess produce was taken to the capital, in exchange for goods that were unavailable locally. On the muddy, rut-scored tracks that passed for roads in Elizabethan England the journey to London usually took at least four or five days.

So, out in the green cornfields of Warwickshire, far from the centre of wealth and power, sleepy Stratford was little more than an isolated rural backwater.

A shaky name

Shakespeare – the war-like surname, which readily lends itself to sexual innuendo and puns – had long been the butt of ribald jokes and tended to be associated with individuals of ill repute. There were a number of 'Shakspere' families living within the parish of Holy Trinity in the sixteenth century;

indeed the surname and its many derivatives were relatively common throughout Warwickshire. In those days orthography had not been standardised and words were spelt more or less phonetically; as a result, the surname appears in over eighty versions in contemporary text: Chacsper, Shaxberd, Shakspeyr, Shagspere, Saxspere and Shakispere are just a few of the more eccentric examples. It is worthy of note that none of the many variants was ever spelt with a hyphen.

Grandfathers: Richard Shakspere and Robert Arden

Richard Shakspere, William's paternal grandfather, was a tenant farmer on land owned by Robert Arden of Wilmcote, a village located four miles northwest of Stratford. It is not known when Richard was born, although the archives show that he died in 1561. His wife's name has been lost to posterity, but the records indicate that he had at least two sons: John and Henry. John, the older brother and father of William, was born in 1529 at Snitterfield, a small village perched on a hill four miles to the north of Stratford.

The maternal grandfather, Robert Arden, was a fairly well-to-do husbandman and the father of eight daughters – the youngest of whom, Mary, was the mother of William Shakspere. Robert died in 1556 leaving Mary the main benefactor, with a dowry of about £6 and a sixty-acre farm called Asbies, at Wilmcote. It would seem that in marrying Mary Arden, 'the boss's daughter', John Shakspere took his first step on the road to self-betterment.

Parents: John Shakspere and Mary Arden

Sometime around 1550, John Shakspere left brother Henry to the farming and moved to Stratford. Archives show that soon after arriving in Henley Street, in 1552, he was fined one shilling for making a muckheap in the street outside his house. In fact, John owned three properties in town, which comprised two adjacent buildings in Henley Street and a dwelling in Greenhill Street. It has been suggested that the latter was probably where John's children were born and raised.

Little is known about Mary Arden, except that she married John Shakspere, probably in 1557, was the mother of eight children by him and died in 1608. By contrast, the archives have quite a lot to say about her husband. It seems that he was principally a glover, or whittawer – dresser of white hides and skins – a skilled job that involved a seven-year apprenticeship and an occupation that might have combined with trade as a butcher. It appears that John also dealt in corn, malt and wool and that he engaged in the illegal and rather murky business of usury – money lending. In fact, he once stood accused of charging interest at the extortionate rate of 25%.

A man evidently fired by ambition, the erstwhile tenant farmer made rapid progress and, during the 1560s, climbed to the top of Stratford's social ladder. On joining the council in 1557, he was entrusted first with the job of ale-taster. In an age before tea or coffee, when water was often unfit to drink, ale of one sort or another was the main beverage – so the ale-taster had a very onerous though rather enjoyable occupation; but, unfortunately, all good things come to an end, and the following year John found himself in the less congenial role of constable. The appointment suggests he was a man with physical presence, since he would have been called upon to deal with the more unruly elements of the local populace; records show that drunken fights were a frequent cause of disturbance in sixteenth century Stratford.

In 1562, after just five years on the council, John Shakspere was appointed to the office of Chamberlain – a post of significant responsibility which involved overseeing the town's finances. Three years later he was promoted to Alderman, a position which gave the holder the right to educate his eldest son at the local grammar school, free of charge. Whether John took the opportunity to do so is unknown because the school records for that period no longer exist. Finally, reaching the pinnacle of his career in 1568, John Shakspere was installed as the bailiff (mayor) of Stratford-upon-Avon, a position he held until 1571.

However, within just a few years of leaving office, John's fortunes took a sudden nose-dive; the fall from grace was as rapid as the ascent. By 1577 – the year he made a tentative application for a coat of arms – his business was in decline; and so it is assumed that even if William *did* attend grammar school he left early – by the age of thirteen – to assist his struggling father in the

John Shakspere's business premises in Henley Street, Stratford – said to have been the birthplace of his eldest son, William.

13

shop. The financial difficulties became so acute that all the family properties had to be mortgaged. For reasons unknown, though probably due to the pressing circumstances, John ceased to attend council meetings and was expelled in 1586. At the same time, he repeatedly failed to attend church – a biographical detail which some have taken to mean that John Shakspere was a recusant Catholic, a plausible conjecture since Warwickshire was a bastion of the Old Religion.

Throughout his life William Shakspere's father signed with an 'X', so it's reasonable to conclude he couldn't write; however, since he had been Stratford's Chamberlain it's likely he could do basic arithmetic and financial accounts. John Shakspere died in 1601, turned seventy – a great age when it is estimated that less than one person in 500-1000 reached their sixtieth birthday, and only about 10% of the population were lucky enough to witness forty summers. Like the rest of England, the inhabitants of Stratford-upon-Avon consisted mainly of young adults and children.

William Shakspere: himself

The parish register of Holy Trinity Church, states that: 'Gulielmus filius Johannis Shakspere' (William son of John Shakspere) was baptised on April 26th 1564. The Protestant vicar who officiated, an M.A. of Christ Church College, Oxford was one John Bretchgirdle – a forty-year old bachelor who had recently moved to Stratford, having previously been employed as a master at Witton Grammar School in Cheshire (now Sir John Deane's College).

The precise date of William Shakspere's birth is unknown but, in an age when infant mortality was very high, the newborn were usually baptised in the first few days of life. So, it is assumed that since 'Shakespeare' is the National Poet, William Shakspere was born on the feast of St George – April 23rd – England's patron saint day.

The third of eight children, William was the first of his brood to live beyond infancy. Although nothing is known about his life up to the age of eighteen, that stark fact has not prevented some biographers writing entire books about his childhood! Similarly, nothing is known of his activities or whereabouts between 1585 and 1592 when the writer Robert Greene – in a notorious letter – alluded to the player 'Shake scene' (*thought* to be Shakspere) as a plagiarist. That particular gap in the biography is sometimes referred to as 'the lost years' – a description which could be applied to much of the Stratford man's life.

The various biographical voids have been filled with all kinds of imaginative speculation: for example, that the miscreant youth had to leave town after he was supposedly caught, poaching deer, on the land of Sir Thomas Lucy at Charlecote Park – although there was no deer park there at the time.

It has also been suggested that William Shakspere was employed as a schoolmaster 'in the country' and that in 1580, at the ripe old age of sixteen, he obtained a position as a tutor at Houghton Tower in Lancashire, home of the prominent Catholic Alexander Houghton. Evidence for the latter claim is a small bequest to one William Shakeshaft in Houghton's will of August 1581. It should be noted, however, that the surname was common in Lancashire, so it's possible that the Shakeshaft mentioned in the will was a local man.

Another intriguing conjecture maintains that, before heading to the capital, young William worked as a lawyer's clerk – which would explain how he acquired knowledge of the many legal terms that appear in the canon. However, diligent searches have failed to uncover any documents with the signature of a legal clerk named William Shakspere.

Site of Shakspere's grave and the poet memorial, Holy Trinity Church has stood amid rural tranquillity, by the banks of the Avon, since the thirteenth century.

Another thesis proposes that the youth from Warwickshire found his first employment in London as a printer's assistant. In fact, one of the best printers in the capital was Richard Field – a man who hailed from Stratford – and Field printed some of the *Shakespeare* works. So it is plausible that Shakspere got his first job in the metropolis as a printer's assistant. But then, according to the seventeenth century dramatist William D'Avenant, the youth from Stratford first found employment in London looking after the horses of theatregoers. Perhaps it is significant that, many years later, the lads who looked after the horses were called 'Shakespeare's boys'.

In fact, there is no firm evidence to support any of these stories, most of them are little more than myth and folklore. Indeed, John Aubrey and

Nicholas Rowe, two early biographers of the late seventeenth and early eighteenth centuries who recounted many of the tales, were writing more than one hundred years after the alleged events and, to make matters worse, neither Aubrey nor Rowe has a good reputation for accuracy or reliability.

How William Shakspere came to be employed in the theatres is a mystery, although the most credible explanation is that he joined one of the troupes of travelling players that occasionally performed at Stratford. The two most prestigious troupes, Lord Leicester's Men and The Queen's Men, visited the town in 1587. In an age when few people travelled more than thirty miles from their place of birth during an entire lifetime, the twenty-three year-old would-be actor might have enrolled with one or other troupe and thereby made his way to London.

In view of the failure of John Shakspere's business and the number of family dependants, it is very surprising that the eldest son was (apparently) allowed to wander off into a new life as an itinerant player. At the time that William Shakspere is thought to have left Stratford (~ 1587) his father was nearing sixty – well past the point at which he would have normally been considered the family's breadwinner. In the sixteenth century, the eldest son was usually expected to take over from his father as the main provider, often in the same line of work. A player's life, however, was one of the most precarious and insecure imaginable: of low status – one step up from vagrancy – and very badly paid; many actors had to take second jobs just to survive. With a very uncertain income that could barely support one, let alone a family of eight dependants, what William Shakspere did was either the height of folly or else there was more to his finances than appears in the records.

Against that background, it is remarkable that after (presumably) carrying the heavy burden of family provider for several years, he managed to find the money to buy the second largest house in Stratford – 'New Place' – at just thirty-three years of age, in May 1597. With regard to the timing, it is worthy of note that plays first appeared in print under the *Shakespeare* title the following year – an indication, perhaps, that Shakspere had already been paid a large sum to act as the real author's 'official' mask.

A stinking great metropolis

During the sixteenth century, the population of the capital underwent a tremendous expansion – tripling at least – and most of the inhabitants (about 150,000 by 1600) were crammed within the restrictive confines delineated by the city walls. London itself, the metropolis within the walls, was a constant hubbub of noisy activity, an overcrowded warren of filthy streets and stinking alleys strewn with animal and human waste. It was said that one could smell the city at twenty miles, and that the stench of the Fleet ditch, an

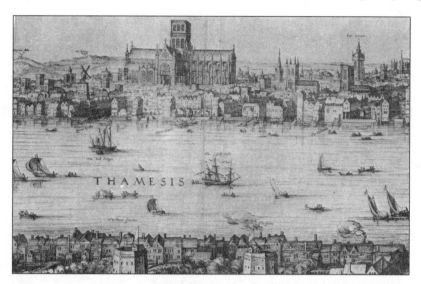

Part of a panorama of London (before the Great Fire of 1666) looking north, over the theatres and rooftops of Southwark, towards the vast bulk of the old St Paul's Cathedral (much larger than the present Wren building) which stood atop Ludgate hill. The Thames had doubled as the main thoroughfare and sewer of the city for hundreds of years, and in those days was far busier than it is now – partly because there was only one fixed crossing, the famous London Bridge.

open sewer near to St Paul's, was enough to make a grown man's gorge rise. For someone like *Shakespeare's* author, who seems to have had a particular dislike of noxious odours, such an environment would have been especially irksome.

There were many unpleasant and disagreeable aspects to life in the capital – most notably disease. Recurrent visitations of bubonic plague, which closed the theatres for months on end, took away thousands – while smallpox, malaria and syphilis claimed their share of victims too. Then there was the constant threat of crime: nimble-fingered cutpurses mingled freely amongst the jostling crowds and ruthless cutthroats lurked in dark ginnels, waiting to pounce on the unwary. To make matters worse, in the latter years of Elizabeth's reign, hoards of masterless men – vagabonds and beggars – roamed the streets, many of them erstwhile soldiers and sailors who remained unpaid by the queen for their contribution to the defeat of the Spanish Armada. In fact, the autumn of the Virgin Queen's reign abounded with social ills, including famine caused by bad harvests in the late 1590s, large numbers of unmarried mothers, the poor getting poorer, as usual, and a feeling of stagnation that arose from having had the same monarch on the throne for forty years. All of which engendered a sense of disquiet – a restive atmosphere catastrophically misjudged by the intemperate Earl of Essex, that contributed to his disastrous attempt at rebellion in 1601, and led to his downfall.

As a centre of burgeoning trade and growing international influence, London attracted hoards of travellers and merchants from the provinces and overseas; many of the visitors sought accommodation, food and drink at the old coaching inns in the city. In an attempt to attract custom, the more enterprising hostelries offered entertainments provided by troupes of players and musicians. It was in this dynamic environment, that the canny entrepreneur James Burbage spotted the commercial potential of providing theatrical performances for the paying public, in specially con-

Bull-baiting and bear-baiting were popular entertainments in Elizabethan England – even the queen enjoyed watching these barbaric spectacles; indeed, she had been known to laugh at distressed bears, set-upon by packs of specially trained mastiffs, as they foamed at the mouth with blood.

structed premises. And so in 1576 Burbage, a carpenter by trade and the manager of Lord Leicester's play troupe, built the first public playhouse – appropriately called The Theatre – at Shoreditch. Such were the humble origins of an enterprise that was to make London the international centre for theatrical entertainment.

The ever-expanding population of the capital developed an insatiable appetite for drama. It has been estimated that there were, on average, about one million individual visits to the theatre per year, so the pressure on dramatists to churn out new material was intense. In total, about 300 playwrights worked in the London theatres during the fifty years from 1590 to 1640 – there were probably ten times as many actors during the same period. However, the quality of much Elizabethan and Jacobean drama was poor, especially in comparison with *Shakespeare.*

The first public theatres were open to the elements and there was no artificial lighting – so the season was limited to spring and summer. Plays, which usually lasted about two hours, were performed in the afternoons while rehearsals took place in the mornings. Admission could be obtained for as little as a penny – if one was prepared to stand in 'the yard', amongst the malodorous common 'groundlings', at the foot of the stage. The relatively low cost meant that playhouses were often packed, even though the largest had capacities in excess of 3,000. But, in those less than hygienic times, nobody had thought to include lavatories on the premises – and playhouse doors were locked at the start of performances.

All the world's a stage

William Shakspere's name was first officially recorded, in a theatrical context, as an actor with the Lord Chamberlain's Men in 1595. Four years later, the name appeared in a list of players recently installed at the Globe – a newly built theatre in Southwark. One of about twenty playhouses in the capital at the time, the Globe was just yards from the south bank of the Thames, strategically located outside the jurisdiction of the city's puritanical authorities. Puritans regarded plays as a corrupting influence and the work of the devil.

In fact, the area south of the Thames was notorious for its dens of iniquity. All kinds of illicit diversions were to be found there, ranging from gaming rooms and bear-pits to bordellos. Indeed, some of the more enterprising theatre-owners like Richard Burbage, son of the pioneering James, ran brothels as well as theatres. The Stews, as they were called, were situated conveniently close to the playhouses – where prostitutes, of both sexes, advertised their wares amongst the heaving throngs of theatregoers. But with syphilis rife, any punter willing to take the risk on a few minutes of fun was literally dicing with death.

From 1603 onwards records show that William Shakspere was a player with the King's Men, the former Chamberlain's Men – re-titled on the accession of James I. Oddly, there is little more of interest in the archive about his remaining years in the theatre. He seems to have left London around 1610/11 with only occasional visits to the city thereafter. It's possible to be precise about the timing because in 1610 Thomas Greene, Shakspere's cousin, was living as a tenant at New Place, Stratford, when he was told to make preparations to leave – presumably because his landlord was intending to return to live there permanently. It was not until 1613 however, when The Globe burned down during a performance of *Henry VIII*, that the Stratford man's association with the London theatres was completely severed.

Apart from a handful of references placing Shakspere in London, most of the surviving records locate him at Stratford. His only known abode in the capital was as a lodger in 1604 with the family of Christopher Mountjoy, a Huguenot tire-maker who lived in Silver Street, Cripplegate. There is no evidence to suggest that the Warwickshire businessman had a permanent address in London, or that he owned a residence there whilst working in the theatres. It is curious that a man of considerable means, with long-term links to the capital, did not see fit to buy a property in the city (the Blackfriars Gatehouse) until 1613 when he was living in retirement, one hundred miles away at Stratford.

Shakspere's financial position is made still more mysterious, by the fact that there are no records of payment to him for *any* of his literary work, nor are there any records of his receipts of imbursement. Elizabethan archives tend to be quite

Richard Burbage's polygonal Globe Theatre was constructed in 1599 from the remains of his father's dismantled theatre. Built on derelict marshy land, near the present-day London Bridge, the new playhouse was about 100 feet in diameter and partially roofed with thatch – a feature which proved to be its undoing when the thatch was set alight by wadding from a theatrical cannon. The playhouse burned down in minutes, although the only recorded injury was a man's pride – when his breeches caught fire; luckily, a quick-thinking companion extinguished them with a 'pottle of ale'.

detailed, especially where money is concerned, so the *complete* absence of relevant documentation is surprising. As a result, it is unclear exactly how the Stratford man accumulated his wealth – one could not make a fortune acting, writing and managing plays – yet, with an estate of at least £1,200, William Shakspere died the second richest man in the London theatre world; only Richard Burbage, with his varied business interests, was wealthier.

Brothers and sisters
William Shakspere had four surviving siblings: Edmund, Gilbert, Joan and Richard. Three girls died in childhood: the 'first' Joan, Margaret and Anne – now, nothing more than names in a register. However, a little information

about those who reached adulthood has been preserved. Edmund (1580-1607) the youngest member of the family followed William to London, where he became an unsuccessful actor and fathered an illegitimate son. He died in the capital, aged twenty-seven, and was buried at St Saviour's Church, Southwark; his affluent older brother probably paid for the funeral. Gilbert (1566-1612) stayed in Stratford and became a glover, like his father; he never married and lived with his mother in Henley Street. Sister Joan (1569-1646) married a local man, a hatter called William Hart, had four children by him and continued to live in the Henley Street house with her mother and brothers. Finally, the almost anonymous Richard (1574-1613), like his elder brother Gilbert, remained unmarried and stayed in Henley Street with the rest of the family.

Wife: Anne Hathaway (1556-1623)
The record of William Shakspere's adult life begins in a state of confusion and mystery. It seems he was due to marry one Anne Whatley of Temple Grafton, the day before he married Anne Hathaway – a puzzling mix-up, the first of many anomalies in the Stratford man's story. Anne was the daughter of Richard Hathaway, a farmer from Shottery – a small village about one mile west of Stratford. She was eight years older than her spouse, an age difference that was rather unusual at a time when the bride was typically a couple of years younger than her groom. And, whereas the average age at which men wed in those days was about twenty-five, William Shakspere was only eighteen when he married in 1582. Since the age of majority was twenty-one, a special marriage licence had to be obtained from the Bishop of Worcester.

The archives imply that Anne was already three months pregnant with her first child (Susanna) when she married; it seems that young William was pressured by her relatives to do the decent thing. Two further additions to the family appeared in 1585, when the twins Hamnet and Judith were born – the children were almost certainly named after Shakspere's Stratford neighbours, Hamnet and Judith Sadler. It is unclear if the shotgun marriage was happy, though it appears doubtful. William Shakspere left his wife just the 'second best bed', and even that seemingly derisory item was only included in his will as an afterthought. Anne received no further mention in the document; there were no references to a 'loving wife', a common phrase in wills at that time – which might have betokened some vestigial trace of matrimonial affection. Indeed, the will gives a sense that the man who had it drawn up was not particularly warm-hearted; it is an impression supported by archival evidence which shows that William Shakspere never gave money to charity during his lifetime, and that he was nearly lynched by an angry mob for stockpiling grain during famines in the late 1590s. Anne Shakspere died at the age of sixty-seven in 1623, and was laid to rest in the chancel of Holy Trinity Church, in a grave adjacent to her husband's – a separation for all eternity that perhaps reflected a gulf dividing them in life.

Children: Susanna (1583-1649) Hamnet (1585-1596) and Judith (1585-1662)

Susanna, eldest of William Shakspere's three children, married Dr. John Hall in 1607. Hall, a Cambridge graduate, became well known throughout Warwickshire as a respected physician. The couple had one child, a daughter called Elizabeth. Susanna died in 1649 at sixty-six years of age. The only son, Hamnet, died in childhood – aged eleven, although his twin, Judith, who married Thomas Quinney, a local vintner, died at the relatively great age of seventy-seven in 1662. The Quinney's had three sons, though none of them lived beyond the age of majority.

Granddaughter: Elizabeth Hall* (Lady Barnard, 1609-1670)

Granddaughter Elizabeth, the daughter of Susanna Shakspere and Dr John Hall, was the last direct descendant of William Shakspere. In 1626 Elizabeth married Thomas Nash, owner of the Bear Inn in Bridge Street – now 'Nash House' which adjoins the site of New Place. Thomas died in 1647 and two years later his widow married John Barnard, who was later made a baron by Charles II. Elizabeth died in 1670 without issue. Of all the original Shakspere clan, only sister Joan left offspring whose descendants, through the Hart family, have survived to the present.

The immortal Bard

Probably nobody would guess, just by reading the works, that the author of *Shakespeare* was a Warwickshire yokel. Indeed, it is curious that a man nurtured in the heart of the English countryside, the 'Sweet swan of Avon' as Ben Jonson famously called him, focused relatively little on country folk and what might be called 'ordinary' people. It seems that the dramatist was much more concerned with writing about the nobility than writing about rustics. Moreover, it is very strange that someone who spent all his formative years living in a profoundly rural environment, acquired by far the deepest psychological insight of any contemporary writer into the mind-set of the ruling

---

*Many of the women in Shakespeare's plays are literate, yet William Shakspere – the affluent businessman – made no provision for the education of either his daughters or granddaughter. In fact, there is no evidence that anyone in his immediate family could write. It has been estimated that by 1600 about one third of Londoners could read, though far fewer were able to write – those that could were mainly members of the professions such as lawyers, clergy and teachers.

classes! By contrast, whenever the author wrote about yokels – the people he grew up with and knew best – he tended to portray them in sketchy outline, often as figures of fun.

Stratford-upon-Avon began to acquire its shrine-like status soon after the Shakespeare Jubilee was held there in 1769. The event was organised by David Garrick, the famous actor-manager and the man responsible for 'rediscovering' and popularising the *Shakespeare* plays which, after 150 years, had fallen into relative decline. The demise was partly due to closure of the theatres by the Puritans in 1642, and partly due to a radical change in theatrical taste after the restoration of the monarchy in 1660. But by the middle of the nineteenth century, with the British Empire fast approaching its apogee, 'Shakespeare' had been elevated to National Poet. The Warwickshire rustic had become a literary icon, patron saint of English culture, exported to every corner of the world just as his native tongue was becoming a global language.

In the years that followed, the emergence of a potent mix of myth and tradition gave a hero-worshipping public everything they could have wanted, in a literary genius and man of the people: the ramshackle Birthplace; the nameless gravestone and ominous curse; the monument with its cryptic inscription; the forlorn foundations of New Place – demolished by the owner in 1759; the quaint thatched cottage *said* to have been Anne Hathaway's and the pleasant river-side town of Stratford itself – all located in a beautiful English setting. It was, and still is, an absolute gift for the tourist industry.

Hewland's farm, Shottery – better known to generations of tourists as Anne Hathaway's cottage – presents a bucolic scene that fits perfectly with the image of 'Shakespeare' as a natural rustic genius.

Yet as the Bard of Avon's star climbed inexorably towards its dizzy zenith, many started to question the Stratford man's reputation as an untutored rustic genius. The questioning was not, in the main, the result of snobbery – as orthodox scholars claim – but because people genuinely found it very hard, if not impossible, to reconcile the known facts of William Shakspere's life with his (alleged) literary work. One of the chief reasons to doubt the Stratford man's authorship arises from the documented record. The archives contain nothing to suggest that the Warwickshire entrepreneur had ever been a writer.

The following is a selected chronology:

1564	April 26: Christened at Holy Trinity Church, Stratford-upon-Avon (the exact date and place of birth – unknown).
1582	November 27: granted licence to Wm Shakspere to marry Anne Whatley of Temple Grafton. November 28: marriage bond issued to William Shakspere and Anne Hathwey (Hathaway) of Shottery.
1583	May 26: Christening of daughter, Susanna Shakspere (at Stratford).
1585	February 2: Hamnet and Judith (twins) christened (at Stratford).
1589	William Shakspere named in legal action against John Lambert concerning land at Wilmcote.
1595	March 15: Shakspere's name appeared in accounts list of the Treasurer of the Royal Chamber.
1596	August 11: Hamnet Shakspere buried at Stratford aged 11 years. November 29 William Wayte petitioned for sureties against William Shakspere and others 'for fear of death'.
1597	May 4: Bought New Place – the second largest house in Stratford – for £60.
1598	October 1: Listed as a tax defaulter. October 25: Richard Quinney wrote to Shakspere requesting a loan of £40 – but, for reasons unknown, the letter was never sent.
1599	May 16: Sir Thomas Brend's inventory records that Shakspere along with others was in occupation at the newly-built Globe theatre. October 6: In default of tax payment.

1601	May 1: Paid £320 (a huge sum) for 107 acres of arable land near Stratford.
1603	Royal Patent issued naming nine actors, including Shakspere, who were authorised to stage plays at the Globe.
1604	Sued the Stratford apothecary Phillip Rogers for the price of some malt.
1605	July 24: Spent £440 (another huge sum) in a share of the lease of the Stratford parish tithes – as a result, became a lay rector.
1608	Started proceedings against John Addenbroke to recover a debt of £6. Took a seventh part share in the Blackfriars Theatre.
1609	June: settled the dispute with Addenbroke.
1610	Purchased 20 acres of land near Stratford from William and John Coombe. Told Thomas Greene, his cousin, to vacate New Place.
1612	May 11: Went to London to testify in the Belott vs Mountjoy lawsuit.
1613	March. Bought the old Blackfriars Gatehouse in London at a cost of £140.
1614	Involved in an attempt to enclose common land at Stratford that had been in use for centuries.
1616	January 25: Made first draft of the will, revised March 25. Most of the estate (about £1200) was left to the elder daughter, Susanna Hall. William Shakspere died on April 23rd and was buried three days later in the chancel of Holy Trinity Church.

Nothing in the foregoing or remaining archival record implies that William Shakspere was a writer, let alone that he was one of the leading poets and playwrights of the age. Scholars have combed the length and breadth of the country in an attempt to find evidence that refers to the putative writer from Warwickshire, but have failed to discover anything that identifies him as *Shakespeare's* author. In view of the number of documented references found to date – about 75 – it is statistically very surprising indeed that none of them hint at Shakspere's alleged writing career. For an individual who is assumed to have earned his living (at least in part) with what he penned, the *complete* absence of relevant evidence is highly suspicious.

— 3 —

Puzzles and Problems

The Walking Dictionary

One of the biggest puzzles in the 'Shakespeare story' is the issue of the author's huge vocabulary. Somehow, without use of a dictionary, William Shakspere – if he was the author – acquired a *working* vocabulary of about 29,000 words, the number of different words in the canon. How did he do it? There is no record of his employment in any of the big houses that possessed well-stocked libraries, where access to a wide range of books might have been possible. It would seem that only someone with plenty of free time and abundant literary resources – like an aristocrat or academic – could have achieved such a remarkable feat of scholarship in those days. Indeed, the author's personal lexicon is a fundamental problem with orthodoxy which has never been satisfactorily resolved.

Shakespeare's author rarely invented the plots or characters of his plays; instead, he used hundreds of sources, including some that were very obscure and some written in foreign languages. It seems that as well as acquiring an enormous vocabulary in his mother tongue, the author somehow found the time and resources to gain knowledge of French, Italian and Spanish – subjects not taught in Elizabethan schools – which he used to translate sources. Why he went to so much trouble simply to write entertainments is a mystery, since plays were not regarded as 'serious' literature. In any case, it wasn't necessary to raid obscure publications in foreign languages for new material, because there were plenty of translated sources already available in English.

Apart from a few inconsistently spelt and badly written signatures, it is strange that no text has survived in the hand of a prolific author who wrote well-over one million words. By contrast, fragments of the writings of many contemporaries, even those who did not live by the pen – such as Stratford businessmen – and who were nowhere near as prolific as *Shakespeare's* author, have survived to the present.

It is not known who owned the original play manuscripts from which the 1623 Folio was copied, nor is it known what became of them. Presumably, the owners sought their return after printing; whatever happened, the original manuscripts – in the hand of the dramatist himself – have not been seen in nearly four hundred years. Furthermore, it is not known who ordered publication of the Folio nor is it known who, if anyone, benefited from it financially.

A strange posthumous 'letter'

In 1592 the writer and reprobate Robert Greene penned a work entitled: *A groatsworth of wit bought with a million of repentance*. The publication included a malicious letter apparently directed against a player (not a writer) referred to as 'shake scene' which is thought to be a pun on Shakspere's name.

Supposedly penned whilst the author was dying, Groatsworth appeared in print more than two weeks *after* Greene's death, on September 20th 1592. The letter warns 'three ... men' of an 'upstart Crow beautified with our feathers' (a plagiarist)... an 'absolute *Johannes fac totum*' (Jack of all trades) ... a 'Tiger's heart wrapped in a player's hide' (alluding to lines in *Shakespeare's Henry VI*) ... and 'the only shake-scene in a country' (a pun on Shakspere's name). It seems that this invective is directed at the 'player' from Stratford.

The recipients of the warning were (almost certainly) Christopher Marlowe and (probably) Thomas Nashe and George Peele. The three were members of an elite group of writers that included Greene, known as The University Wits – graduates of Oxford and Cambridge, the only universities in England at the time. About three months after publication of *Groatsworth*, the writer Henry Chettle – publisher of Greene's work – penned an 'apology' in *Kind-Hearts Dream* responding to complaints from two of those alluded

---

To those Gentlemen his Quondam (sundry) acquaintance, that spend their wits in making plays...

Thou famous gracer of Tragedians... young Juvenal... and thou no less deserving than the other two...Base-minded men all three of you, if by my misery you be not warned: for unto none of you (like me) sought those burrs to cleave: those Puppets (I mean) that spake from our mouths, those Anticks garnished in our colours... Yes trust them not: for there is an upstart Crow, beautified with our feathers, that with his Tiger's heart wrapped in a Player's hide, supposes he is as well able to bombast out a blank verse as the best of you: and being an absolute Johannes fac totem, is in his own conceit the only Shake scene in a country.

This part of Robert Greene's notorious letter seems to contain the first reference in print to 'Shakespeare' – 'the only Shake-scene in a country'. The letter attacks an 'upstart Crow, beautified with our feathers', which appears to imply that the Stratford man was a plagiarist.

to in the original letter. However, Chettle did not make it clear to whom he was apologising, although Stratfordians would have us believe that, in the last five lines, he refers to William Shakspere:

'...*because myself have seen his demeanour no less civil than he excellent in the quality he possesses: Besides, diverse of worship have reported his uprightness of dealing, which argues his honesty, and his facetious grace in writing that approves his Art.*'

Chettle's deferential tone suggests it is more likely that he was apologising to one of the University Wits, since graduates were automatically accorded the status of gentleman. By contrast Shakspere, an unlettered yokel player, would probably not have warranted an obsequious apology of this kind, especially as he was only at the start of his career.

Injurious Imposters

Contemporaries were very guarded when referring to 'Shakespeare' the writer. In view of the fact that the author was (supposedly) a prominent member of the London theatre world for many years, the reticence is very curious. Friends and colleagues revealed no personality traits or characteristics and, on the rare occasions when they did pass comment, they either made cryptic remarks or wrote in vague generalities – as if there was a conspiracy to divulge *nothing* of personal significance about the author himself. Indeed, the only unambiguous references to the Stratford man, made *during* his lifetime, address him as 'player', 'fellow', 'master', 'countryman' or 'gent'. William Shakspere, the yokel from Warwickshire, was *never* identified as a 'poet', 'playwright', 'author' or 'writer' by *anyone* whilst he was alive.

Even in an age without copyright, it is surprising that Shakspere failed to voice complaint when 'his' works were mutilated by 'injurous impostors' – as Heminges and Condell claim in their prefatory letter to the 1623 Folio. Yet records show that the Stratford man strenuously pursued petty debtors through the courts. Furthermore, it is odd that, unlike the abundant records of his legal and business transactions, there is no written evidence of payment to the Warwickshire businessman for *any* of his literary work; yet Stratfordians claim that money was the chief motivation for his writing.

Shakspere's will

Shakspere's will makes no reference to books, poetry, plays or indeed any of the artefacts that might be expected from a long, professional writing career. It seems that he made no attempt to preserve either his original manuscripts or the notes he (presumably) made in the process of writing. Furthermore, it is very strange that the will makes no mention of an aristocratic patron – neither the Earl of Southampton nor the Earls of Pembroke and

Montgomery, to whom the 1623 Folio was dedicated.

Supposedly dictated by Shakspere himself, the will is typical of a businessman of the period and is generally agreed to be devoid of literary merit. It appears either that the writer's famous eloquence, and his knowledge of the law, failed him at the last or else he submitted to the help of a professional who penned the document – and probably signed it – on his behalf. It seems that William Shakspere, a commercial writer, didn't even sign his own will!

Stratfordians insist that Henry Wriothesley (pronounced Risley), the Earl of Southampton, was Shakspere's aristocratic patron – despite a total lack of documentary evidence and very powerful arguments to the contrary.

For a man who spent the first twenty-odd years of his life living in the sticks, it is odd that he knew a great deal about the chicanery and machinations of politics – as many of 'his' plays suggest. The author's astonishing insight is all the more remarkable in an age with no mass media, no free press and in view of the fact that there is no evidence the Stratford man had personal contact with politicians. Yet *Shakespeare* plays were performed at Elizabeth's court – the most politically savvy audience in the land – more frequently than the works of any other playwright.

Against that background, it is strange that neither the theatre-loving queen, nor any of her well-educated courtiers, ever referred to the specially favoured dramatist from Stratford. It seems that Shakspere himself – by contrast with 'his' works – made no significant impression, during a twenty-odd year career, on *any* of his brilliant contemporaries.

Patron – what patron?
Not a single letter *in the hand* of William Shakspere has survived, yet he was supposedly a writer and businessman who shuttled to and fro between London and Warwickshire for many years. It is therefore surprising that no missives have been found. However, someone calling himself 'William Shakespeare' dedicated two poems – *Venus & Adonis* (1593) and *The Rape of Lucrece* (1594) – in *printed* letters to the Earl of Southampton, apparently in the hope of obtaining patronage; but there is not a shred of evidence that the earl responded. Indeed, if Southampton had become Shakspere's patron, further dedications from the author would have been obligatory, yet 'William Shakespeare' never again referred to the earl.

Writer – what writer?

For many years John Chamberlain wrote to keep provincial friends informed about life in London. His letters made special reference to the theatres at the very time 'Shakespeare' was supposedly well known – yet, Chamberlain never referred to the famous dramatist. And Sir Henry Wooton, another contemporary correspondent, wrote about many actors and playwrights when the Stratford man is assumed to have been at the height of his fame – but he too never mentioned the 'soule of the age' and 'wonder of our stage', the great 'William Shakespeare'. In 1604, the writer Michael Drayton published his book *Worthies of Warwickshire*, including all the usual notables, but Shakspere's name was absent – a very curious omission, especially in view of the fact that Drayton came from a village near Stratford. And, in what seems to have been another strange oversight, the chronicler William Camden praised the work of *Shakespeare* in 1603 but failed to refer, in his *Britannia* of 1607, to the author as a Stratford inhabitant.

In a fairly comprehensive list, the anonymous writer of *Metamorphosis* (1600-1615) named over thirty contemporary poets and playwrights. In view of the fact that the author was very familiar with the world of theatre and that the list was extensive, it is extremely strange that he failed to include the famous name of William Shakspere. Moreover, the actors Edward Alleyn and Richard Burbage – central figures in the London theatre world – kept diaries and account books which referred to many writers of the time, although neither of them ever wrote of a dramatist called William Shakspere. Ben Jonson called *Shakespeare's* author 'starre of poets', 'the wonder of our stage' and 'soule of the age' in his commendatory verse in the 1623 Folio – and yet he waited seven long years after Shakspere's death before putting pen to paper! Why did Jonson take so long to make his views public, if he genuinely believed that the author was worthy of such high-flown praise?

Furthermore, it is most curious that a few years after having lauded the author as 'starre of poets', Jonson omitted the Stratford man's name from a list of five English poets that he considered 'the best to read' in *Timber, or Discoveries*. In fact Ben Jonson, who was supposedly the playwright's rival and drinking pal, never wrote of a 'William Shakspere' during the Stratford man's lifetime!

The author of *Shakespeare* appears fully formed at the start of his career; no clear evidence of a literary apprenticeship exists, no obviously juvenile works have been identified – although, it must be admitted, some of the plays are weak. In addition, the precise dating and sequence in which the works were written, has yet to be agreed upon by scholars. Several of the earliest plays attributed to 'Shakespeare' by the clergyman Francis Meres, in 1598, originally appeared *anonymously* – inconsistent, it might be thought, with a man who earned his living by the pen but to be expected of an aristocrat writing in secret. It is noteworthy that only about half of the plays in the canon had been printed by the time the First Folio appeared in 1623.

No contemporary writer in the 1590s identified the Stratford man as the author of plays that had been successful on the London stage. In that regard, it is odd that in the highly competitive, gossip-riddled world of the literati, nobody had anything good (or bad) to say about such a successful and talented individual – a silence made more remarkable by the fact that 'Shakespeare' seems to have been the queen's favourite playwright; surely the ultimate accolade... certain to arouse the envy of rivals, yet nobody ever passed comment.

Shakspere's signatures

In 1985 the graphologist Jane Cox said it was 'obvious at a glance' that the last two known signatures of Shakspere were not written by the same individual as the first four. Later, in a letter to *The Times*, Ms Cox went on to ask how a man who struggled to write his own name could have been the author of *Shakespeare*. The very poor quality of the first four signatures is particularly notable, especially in view of the fact that they appear on legal documents where legibility is important and where one would expect to find good examples of a person's signature. Moreover, the lack of fluency is entirely inconsistent with the claims of Heminges and Condell, in their prefatory letter to the 1623 Folio, that the author hardly ever blotted a line and that 'his hand and mind went together'. Furthermore, it is very surprising to find that a professional writer couldn't consistently spell his own name, yet the printers of his works had no such difficulty.

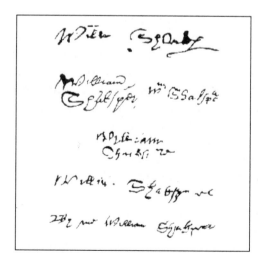

Six surviving signatures of William Shakspere. 1. Mountjoy deposition, 1612 (Public records Office) 2. Blackfriars conveyance, 1613 (Guildhall Library) 3. Blackfriars mortgage, 1613 (Guildhall Library) 4, 5 & 6. Shakspere's will, 1616 (Public Records Office).

The most elusive man in history

Throughout the many years that Shakspere was (supposedly) resident in London, his name never appeared in any of the parish registers – even those where notification of residence was compulsory. However, a record survives which shows that in 1604 he lodged in Silver Street, Cripplegate, with the Mountjoy family and that he was called by them as a witness in a lawsuit – a dispute about a marriage dowry – in 1612.

Illuminated by history's spotlight for a brief instant, the Stratford man appeared in the law court as himself. What sort of individual was revealed? A profoundly ignorant one, it seems. The forty-eight year old literary genius and polymath struggled to write and spell his own name on the legal deposition, had difficulty recollecting events in which he had taken an active part a few years earlier and incredibly – for someone assumed to have received a grammar school education – he was uncertain of his age! All of which stands in very stark contrast to the poet who wrote of '...my great mind...' in sonnet 114, and the dramatist who penned a play of the calibre of *The Tempest*, just two years before.

For a man who was apparently very careful not to make enemies, it is most strange that William Shakspere took professional liberties to a perilous extreme. *Richard II* is by far the most 'dangerous' play in the canon because it contains a notorious scene which explicitly depicts the deposition of Richard II by Henry Bolingbroke (Henry IV). To render the deposition of an English sovereign on stage was sedition, since there was a possibility that it might incite rebellion in the audience. In fact *Richard II*, with the deposition scene included, was *specially* performed at The Globe on the eve of Essex's rebellion in 1601, the intention being to engender an atmosphere in the capital conducive to insurrection.

Unsurprisingly, performances of the play angered the queen herself: 'I am Richard II, know ye not?' she exclaimed to the Keeper of the Tower of London, a few months after the failed uprising. In view of the queen's sharp reaction – and the fact that she knew the deposition of *Richard II* alluded to *her* – it is exceedingly odd that no action was ever taken against the author of the offending work. One would certainly have expected the playwright either to be sent to prison for life – or executed, for writing such material; yet William Shakspere wasn't even questioned in the ensuing inquisition! How the Stratford man managed to escape interrogation whilst aristocrats of the highest rank were sent to the block for their involvement in the rebellion, has never been explained.

The mystery is made more puzzling still by the fact that two years before the rebellion the queen sent Dr John Hayward to the Tower for life, simply for publishing a book dedicated to the Earl of Essex which referred to the infamous deposition scene. Elizabeth thought that Hayward was a front for someone more dangerous and instructed Francis Bacon to investigate. Such determined action by the queen herself significantly adds to the puzzle of how the lowly rustic playwright managed to escape without so much as being questioned. However *Richard II* isn't the only *Shakespeare* play that has dangerous undertones: *Hamlet, Macbeth, Julius Caesar, King Lear* and *The Tempest* all contain material that 'ought' to have caused offence to the monarch – yet the playwright was never called to account for any of it!

But then the merchant from Warwickshire escaped all kinds of trouble, as if protected by a 'higher power'; even tax defaults were paid anonymously on his behalf, though he was perfectly able to pay them himself. Indeed, Shakspere accumulated considerable wealth – but by seemingly 'invisible' means. In 1601, he spent £320 on 107 acres of arable land near Stratford, and in 1605 purchased a share in Stratford tithes for £440. By the standards of the time, these were huge sums – £440 was more than twice the market value of all the plays in the canon. It has been estimated that a playwright's income, writing an average of three or four plays a year, was comparable to that of a teacher – yet in just four years, Shakspere spent the modern equivalent of several hundred thousand pounds (assuming £1 then is about £1,000 now).

For the Stratford entrepreneur to have expended the time and energy required to write a play with the scope and depth of *Hamlet*, seems rather out of character – especially as he would have been paid only about five or six pounds for his pains. Furthermore, at a time when the duration of a play was normally about two hours, this 'monster' work – at 4 1/2 hours – was too long for the public stage. Why did the money-motivated, shrewd businessman write a work of such inordinate length for the commercial theatre? More importantly, *why* was Prince Hamlet – much the largest part in the canon – singled-out for special treatment? Why was that particular role of such concern to the Stratford man?

One of the earliest plays, *Loves Labours Lost* – the first to appear in print under the *Shakespeare* title in 1598 – involves aristocratic students. The play is based on real people at the court of Navarre, in France – a rather unexpected choice of subject for a yokel playwright especially as an early work, since the court of Navarre was far removed from the experiences of a non-graduate, English rustic. Indeed, in his 1970 biography *Shakespeare*, Anthony Burgess called the work 'almost painfully aristocratic'.

Titus Andronicus – the play most popular at the time, with its bloody mutilations, rape and cannibalism – probably made Shakspere more money than any other work; yet it is strange that, having hit on a highly successful formula, the canny Stratford entrepreneur never used it again. Instead, he wrote difficult 'academic' works like *Troilus and Cressida, Timon of Athens* and *Coriolanus*, plays that were way over the heads of the vast majority of theatregoers. A commercial playwright did not make money writing work like that – yet, according to orthodoxy, money was the *only* reason the Warwickshire businessman wrote.

The constant demand by the public theatres for new drama meant there was unrelenting pressure on playwrights to pen fresh material. Against that background of frenetic activity it is curious that, unlike almost all of his contemporaries, the Bard collaborated very little. It is also rather strange that he never wrote commendatory verse – customary in those days – about any of his literary colleagues. However if *Shakespeare's* author was a concealed nobleman, the absence of commendatory verse would be expected, since no aristocrat would deign to commend a commoner's work.

When Shakspere applied for a coat of arms in 1596, the Garter King – William Dethick – referred to him as a 'player' even though two very well known poems, *Venus & Adonis & The Rape of Lucrece* were already in print under the *Shakespeare* title. It seems Dethick did not know that the Stratford man was an acknowledged poet – an occupation of much higher status than a mere player. The question is: why did Shakspere, especially in seeking the kudos of a coat of arms, identify himself only as a lowly actor when he could have claimed to be a successful poet?

In the play *Every Man out of his Humour* (1599) Ben Jonson appears to satirise his rival's pretension to gentility through the risible buffoon Sogliardo. A bumbling country bumpkin, the conceited Sogliardo is laughably proud of his newly acquired coat-of-arms, which displays a headless boar and the motto: *Not without mustard*. In choosing that particular epithet, Jonson seems to have been taking a satirical swipe at Shakspere, whose family motto boldly declared: *Non sanz droict* which means 'Not without right'. It seems that Jonson – who delighted in exposing folly through satire – was making a parallel between the ridiculous Sogliardo and the snooty parvenu from Stratford.

It is curious that the man who supposedly wrote 'the works' spent his money exclusively on land, property, tithes and commodities – behaviour to be expected of a merchant trader, but rather surprising for someone whose plays give the impression of a writer not overly concerned with money. It is also very strange – judging by the content of his will – that the Stratford man seems never to have bought a single book, painting or musical instrument – yet the works suggest that the author read a great deal, was interested in art and was very fond of music. In fact, Shakspere's will makes no mention of *any* of the kind of cultural bric-a-brac, collected over a lifetime, that would normally be expected in the personal inventory of an affluent writer.

Deafening silence at Stratford

'Will. Shaxper. gent' is all that the register of Holy Trinity recorded when William Shakspere was buried there in April 1616. Even in death, there was no local recognition of a writing career. And many years later, when the 'Shakespeare' name was well-known nationally, the locals were very slow to claim him as the town's most famous son. It seems as if the good people of Stratford were either completely ignorant of the Bard's fame or else, for some mysterious reason, the eponymous author was taboo. Furthermore, it is curious that the gravestone in Holy Trinity has been inscribed not with an eloquent elegy (as might be expected) but with an unworthy bit of doggerel; hardly the most appropriate epitaph for a writer lauded by Jonson as 'the starre of poets'.

According to the Rev. John Ward, an Oxford graduate who went to Stratford in 1662 to practise medicine, the playwright died from a fever (during the night) after a 'merry meeting' with his former colleagues Ben Jonson and Michael Drayton – who just happened to pay a visit. If the story is based in fact, William Shakspere's sudden death immediately after a 'merry meeting' with professional associates is highly suspicious.

The Stratford businessman probably thought he was safe – a hundred miles from the capital – telling friends and relatives of

Martin Droeshout's engraving, which appears on the title page of the 1623 Folio, is the best attested of all the images purportedly of 'Shakespeare'. Indeed, the portrait was extolled by Ben Jonson as an excellent likeness in his folio verse To the Reader – yet the engraving contains curious technical flaws. Moreover, the image was almost certainly not made directly from life, since Droeshout was only fifteen years old when William Shakspere died.

his exploits, boasting about how he had been well paid to pass off another man's plays under his own name. But Shakspere seriously miscalculated and the stories found their way back to London – probably via Drayton, who retained links in the Stratford area.

It presumably came to the attention of the authorities that Shakspere was revealing secrets, in the public domain. It was clear that although he had served his purpose well, as a mask for the real author, he knew too much and had to be silenced – permanently. His highly suspicious demise was intended as a stark warning to all those in Stratford who knew the secrets. That is why, long after his death, none of the townsfolk referred to the famous author and why even his relatives remained silent.

It is strange that Michael Drayton, an author from near Stratford, made no mention of fellow writer William Shakspere.

Shakespeare's vacant mask

Unlike the engravings of other contemporary writers e.g. Michael Drayton, the portrait by Martin Droeshout (page 35) contains nothing either visual or textual (laurel leaves or inscriptions) to indicate that the sitter is a man of letters. In addition, the head is too large for the body and, as the *Tailor & Cutter* magazine observed in 1911, the tailoring of the doublet – which has a flat, unnatural appearance – is completely awry. Furthermore, compared with the realistic 'lived-in' features of Drayton, the unlined face has a curiously mask-like appearance that presents an inscrutable cipher to the viewer. It seems that the rather vacant expression depicted here – like that on the effigy in Holy Trinity Church – reflects the banality of the Stratford man's unexceptional existence.

If Droeshout couldn't even draw the anatomical proportions and doublet correctly, it is unlikely he was capable of making a decent job of the face – by far the most difficult part of a portrait to get right – yet Ben Jonson's verse suggests very clearly that it is an excellent likeness. With so many curious aspects to the engraving, it would appear that Jonson's over-the-top praise is a tongue-in-cheek attempt to arouse the reader's curiosity. That is to say, *To the Reader* paired with Droeshout's engraving is a 'send-up' and we the readers are meant to take, from the inconsistencies, the hint that 'Shakespeare' is not what he seems to be.

An engraving, based on William Dugdale's sketch of 1634, illustrates the Stratford Monument just a few years after it was installed in the chancel of Holy Trinity. It is striking that although relatively 'insignificant' details have been included, the image contains nothing to suggest that the monument represents a writer; indeed, it is odd that *both* items indicative of a man of letters – the quill pen and parchment that appear on the present monument – are absent.

Dr. John Hall, the Cambridge-graduate son-in-law of the alleged playwright, and husband of his eldest daughter Susanna, was a well-known physician in Warwickshire. Like every good medical practitioner, Dr. Hall kept casebooks of his patients and their treatments; however, the notes covering his father-in-law's life

---

To the Reader

This figure, that thou here seest put,
It was for gentle Shakespeare cut;
Wherein the graver had a strife
with Nature, to out doo the life:
O, could he but have drawne his wit
As well in brasse, as he hath hit
His face, the Print would then surpasse
All, that was ever writ in brasse.
But, since he cannot, Reader, looke
Not on his picture, but his Booke.

B.I.

This rather odd verse by Ben Jonson (subscribed B. I.) appears opposite the Droeshout engraving and title page of the 1623 Folio – the first collection of Shakespeare's plays published in book form, known as the 'First Folio'. There were four folio editions altogether, the last one appeared in 1684.

---

are missing. In view of the fact that the surviving casebook began in 1617, the year after Shakspere's death, the loss appears somewhat suspicious. It is also rather curious that, in the years following his death, neither the well-educated Dr. Hall nor any other relative mentioned the celebrated writer who had lived amongst them. In addition, there is no evidence that any family member owned a copy of the 1623 Folio* – a measure, perhaps, of just how little they cared about their famous kinsman, or an indication that they knew he *wasn't* the real author!

Poet-Ape

The epigram *On Poet-Ape* was No 56 in a series published by Ben Jonson in 1616 – the year of Shakspere's death – although it was written some years earlier, so the publication date might be just coincidence. Nevertheless, many

---

* 500 editions of the First Folio were published in November 1623 at a cost of £1 each – bound. 228 copies still exist, though almost all are now in major libraries; the largest collection is at the Folger Library in Washington. The term 'folio' refers to page size: a single page folded once. The earliest printed versions of the plays, many of them so-called 'bad' copies, appeared in 'quarto' size – a single page folded twice.

people have come to the view that the 'shake-scene' in Robert Greene's letter and Jonson's *Poet Ape* probably refer to the same person.

The first line of *Poet Ape* sounds like an implicit reference to Shakspere: 'Poor Poet Ape, that would be thought our chief,'. The question is: who, other than the Bard, would have considered himself 'our chief'? The verse clearly

---

On Poet-Ape

Poor Poet Ape, that would be thought our chief,
Whose works are e'en the frippery of wit,
From brokage is become so bold a thief,
As we, the robbed leave rage, and pity it.
At first he made low shifts, would pick and glean,
Buy the reversion of old plays; now grown
To a little wealth, and credit in the scene,
He takes up all, makes each man's wit his own.
And told of this, he sleights it. Tut, such crimes
Themy good one out. sluggish gaping auditor devours;
He marks not whose 'twas first and after-times
May judge it to be his, as well as ours
Fool, as if eyes will not know a fleece
From locks of wool, or shreds from the whole piece?

Just as Robert Greene's notorious letter alludes to 'shake-scene' as a plagiarist, so Ben Jonson's epigram accuses 'Poet Ape' – 'that would be thought our chief' – of literary theft.

identifies Poet Ape as someone who steals the work of others '...is become so bold a thief' (line 3) and '...makes each man's wit his own' (line 8) – criticisms reminiscent of Greene's letter in which 'shake-scene' is referred to as 'an upstart crow, beautified with our feathers'. It seems that both Jonson and Greene were alluding to Shakspere as a plagiarist.

Shakespeare – European linguist

The *Shakespeare* works encompass a vast spectrum of subject matter; so the question arises as to how William Shakspere found the time and resources to acquire a great deal of information. The range of specialist knowledge exhibited in the works is very surprising for a rustic entrepreneur, especially one whose intention was simply to make money writing plays. One could be a perfectly successful dramatist without possessing the knowledge of a polymath.

It is also very remarkable that the author took the time and trouble to learn French, Italian and Spanish in an age when few people, with the

Stratford man's background, learned to read even one modern language let alone three! Moreover, the French literary scholar Professor Abel Lefranc, having studied the *Shakespeare* works for thirty-five years, thought he discerned an author who understood *both* cultured and colloquial French – yet the Stratford man, had no known connection with France and no obvious reason to learn the language.

Subjects alluded to in the Shakespeare plays:

Acting techniques and the theatre, manners and protocol of court, the aristocracy, heraldry, sports of the nobility: falconry, royal tennis, archery, angling, hare coursing and deer hunting; horses and dogs; state craft and statesmanship; the Law and legal terminology; languages: Latin, French, Italian and Spanish; the geography of Italy; the court of Navarre; Danish terms and customs; horticulture and the design of gardens; music and musical terms; painting and sculpture; mathematics, astronomy and astrology; medicine and human anatomy; military life – warfare and battlefield conditions; exploration of the New World; navigation and seamanship; printing; natural history; Biblical scholarship; various forms of mental illness; Cambridge University jargon; cryptography and the secret service.

For an individual who spent his formative years living in an isolated rural environment, these esoteric and eclectic topics span an astonishingly broad spectrum – reflecting a range of interests more in keeping with a highly educated nobleman than a Warwickshire entrepreneur. According to *Shakespeare* devotees with professional backgrounds such as doctors, lawyers, mariners and soldiers the author possessed a depth and precision of specialist knowledge superior to any contemporary writer. It seems that whoever wrote the works was a walking dictionary and encyclopaedia, in an age when encyclopaedias and English dictionaries did not exist.

Shakespeare's reading list

In view of the breadth of his interests, it is not surprising that the dramatist's reading list was very extensive and included obscure foreign texts. The list of authors, identified as sources used in the canon, gives an idea just how wide-ranging his reading was:

Achilles, Aelianus, Alberti, Alciatus, Ammianus, Appian, Apuleius, Aretino, Ariosto, Athenaeus, Aurelius Antoninus, Averell, Bandello, Barnes, Belleforest, Boaistuau, Boccaccio, Boiardo, Bright, Brooke, Camden, Cardano, Castiglione, Catullus, Caxton, Cecchi, Cervantes, Chapman, Chaucer, Cinthio, Claudianus, Constable, Creton, Daniel, Day, Dolce, Drayton, Eden, Edwards, Eliot, Elyot, Fabyan, Florio, Foxe, Froissart,

Gallus, Gascoigne, Geoffery of Monmouth, Giovanni Fiorentino, Golding, Goslicius, Gower, Grafton, Grammaticus, Greene, Groto, Guazzo, Hakluyt, Hall, Harington, Harsnett, Heliodorus, Henryson, Heraclitus, Hesiod, Holinshed, Homer, Hooker, Hurtado de Mendoza, Isocrates, James I, Jonson, Jourdain, Kyd, LeFevre, Leo Africanus, Leslie, Lewkenor, Lodge, Lucretius Carus, Luscianus, Lydgate, Lyly, Marianus, Marlowe, Marston, Martire, Massuccio, Mexia, Montaigne, Montemayor, More, Mouffet, Mundy, Nashe, Ovid, Painter, Paracelsus, Peele, Pescetti, Petrarch, Pettie, Philostratus, Plato, Pliny the elder, Plutarch, Porto, Preston, Proclus, Puttenham, Quintus, Rabelias, Raleigh, Riche, Ronsard, Sabie, Savolio, Scot, Segar, Sidney, Silva, Silvayn, Skelton, Spenser, St Bernard of Clairvaux, Sterling, Stow, Strachey, Straporola, Surrey, Susenbrotus, Swinburne, Tacitus, Tasso, Theocritus, Thomas, Twine, Vega, Vespucci, Warner, Watson, Whetstone, Wyatt.

It is difficult to see how Shakspere gained access to works by all these writers – and found time to read them – especially as there is no reference to his employment in the household of an aristocrat, where there might have been a very well stocked library. Apart from two poems (*Venus & Adonis* and *The Rape of Lucrece*) none of the works in the canon was dedicated to anyone, which is very strong evidence that the author, if he was a commoner, was never employed by a nobleman. Quite simply, if the Stratford man had made use of the literary resources of an aristocrat, he would have been duty bound to recognise his patron with special dedications. No such dedications exist.

In this early engraving of the Shakespeare Monument at Holy Trinity Church, both of the crucial details representing a writer – quill pen and parchment – are missing.

Shakespeare's special interests

It is almost impossible for someone to completely hide their personal interests when they write extensively. Thus, an examination of the frequency at which certain topics appear in the plays should give an insight into the mind and background of the person who wrote them. The analysis, which was carried out separately by Caroline Spurgeon and Pierre Porohovshikov, found the following: Classics and mythology came top with 260 allusions, second sport & games with 196 references, third war and weapons which were alluded to on 192 occasions, the sea and ships came fourth with 172 references, fifth was law with 124 allusions and drama appeared sixth with 74 references.

The profile reveals a man with a very strong classical education, having a very keen interest in sport, very knowledgeable about military affaires and seafaring, someone well versed in law and very familiar with acting and the theatre. With its heavy bias towards military and maritime matters, the profile does not immediately bring to mind the civilian landlubber William Shakspere of Stratford-upon-Avon. Furthermore, the numerous legal references suggest an aristocratic author.

Shakespeare's unique insight

But it isn't just the huge vocabulary, vast range of knowledge and breadth of reading that makes *Shakespeare's* author special: an uncanny perception of the human psyche sets him apart from almost every other writer in history. In fact, one of the fundamental problems facing orthodoxy is how the rustic from Stratford acquired such penetrating psychological understanding of *everyone* – from the lowest stratum of society to the highest. It is very difficult, for example, to see how he gained a profound insight into the mind-set of royalty and the nobility, without drawing attention to himself in the process. Like Sir Walter Raleigh with his west-country burr, William Shakspere and his thick Warwickshire accent would have been especially noticeable at court – yet no courtier ever mentioned him. Moreover it seems that the author was an omni-present, invisible observer who had access to highly obscure information, which very few people in England *could* have known.

Shakespeare's obscure knowledge
- Details of Hamlet's castle and its environs.
- The names of families living in Venice in the 1590s, that appear in *The Merchant of Venice*.
- The names of Rosencrantz & Guildenstern, two Danish students enrolled at Padua University in 1596 and two students who appear in *Hamlet* (1601).

- Details of Correggio's *Io and Jupiter* described in *The Taming of the Shrew* – a painting on public display in Milan from 1585 to 1600.
- Details of Giulio Romano's painting of the Trojan War in the *Palazzo del Te, Mantua* – referred to in the *Rape of Lucrece*.
- People at the court of Navarre – models for characters in *Loves Labours Lost*.
- Circumstances of the wrecking of the *Sea Venture* in a storm off the Bermudas in 1609 – alluded to in *The Tempest*; information not made public until long after the play was written.
- Obscure references to the interrogation of the Jesuit priest Edmund Campion, in *Twelfth Night*.
- An allusion to Christopher Marlowe's death: the 'reckoning', a word used in the coroner's *unpublished* report, that also appears in *As You Like It*.
- An allusion in *A Midsummer Night's Dream* to one of the displays at Kenilworth Castle, in summer 1575.
- Detailed knowledge of falconry, a sport exclusively associated with the aristocracy. No other writer of the age referred to falconry as frequently and knowledgeably as *Shakespeare's* author.

It seems extremely unlikely that the yokel William Shakspere was the unique individual (the true author of the works) who was privy to all of these obscure pieces of information. Shakspere's (assumed) knowledge of these details is even more puzzling in view of the fact that there is no evidence he ever left the land of his birth, let alone that he travelled far and wide to Denmark, Italy and the New World. In fact, foreign travel in those days was very expensive, rarely undertaken by someone of Shakspere's status, and almost never embarked upon alone.

4

'Adon deftly masking'

The issues of authorial concealment and biographical anomaly, which are central to the authorship controversy, prompt two key questions:

1. Do contemporary texts exist which indicate that the author of *Shakespeare* was hidden?

2. Are there anomalies, irregularities or inconsistencies associated with the author by contemporaries?

It turns out that the answer to both questions is 'yes'.

Aristocratic Adon

In 1595 Thomas Edwards published his poem *Narcissus*. The poem was followed with an envoy in which Edwards praised a number of poets, referring to them by pseudonyms. Edmund Spenser, for example, was identified as 'Colin' after his poem *Colin Clouts comes home again*. One of the poets is dubbed 'Adon' – a name which almost certainly alludes to the author of *Venus & Adonis*, supposedly William Shakspere.

Line 1: 'Adon deftly masking through'. In those days, 'masking' referred specifically to an author's

> Adon deafly (deftly) masking through
> Stately tropes rich conceited,
> Shewed he well deserved to.
> Loves delight on him to gaze,
> And had not love her self entreated,
> Other nymphs had sent him bays.
>
> Eke in purple robes distained,
> Amidst the Centre of this clime,
> I have heard say doth remain,
> One whose power floweth far,
> That should have been of our rhyme
> The only object and the star.
>
> Well could his bewitching pen,
> Done the Muses objects to us,
> Although he differs much from men,
> Tilting under Friaries,
> Yet his golden art might woo us,
> To have honored him with bays.

Certain lines in Edwards' verse attract attention because they imply gross inconsistencies with Stratfordian orthodoxy.

use of a decoy – a front-man. The assertion that *Adon* is 'deftly masking' is a clear contradiction of orthodoxy, since William Shakspere – with his name on the published poem – cannot have been a decoy for himself! That is to say, Edwards implies that Shakespeare is the name of the real author's mask.

Line 7: 'Eke in purple robes distained' links *Adon* with the nobility – who traditionally wore purple – an association totally at odds with a commoner like Shakspere!

Lines 9, 10 & 11: 'One whose power floweth far, / That *should have been* of our rhyme/ The only object and the star.' – implies that Adon, an important person, could not receive explicit recognition (my italics). A strong hint that the poet is a 'masked' aristocrat.

Line 15: 'Although he differs much from men' – a very strange statement indeed, hardly consistent with the traditional image of the playwright as a man of the people! How did Shakspere *differ much from men*? And if he did, why did nobody else mention it?

Line 16: 'Tilting under Friaries,' – another very puzzling phrase which does not seem to relate in any way to the Stratford man, although it is clear that whoever Edwards was alluding to as *'Adon'* was a highly mysterious individual.

Two more contemporaries of *Shakespeare's* author – John Marston and Joseph Hall – published works implying that whoever wrote the poems *Venus & Adonis* and *The Rape of Lucrece* was a 'hidden' poet. Marston and Hall referred to the author by the pseudonym Labeo – which was, in fact, the name of an aristocratic Roman lawyer. Hall identified *'Labeo'* as *Shakespeare's* author by satirising him for his over-use of 'But' and 'Oh' at the start of verses in *The Rape of Lucrece* – and made fun of the poet for using too many hyphenated epithets. Through these hints Hall identifies *Labeo* as the author of poems published under the *Shakespeare* title.

What do contemporary references reveal about Labeo-Shakespeare?

The fourth book of Joseph Hall's *Satires* (1598) refers to *Labeo* in the first satire:

Lines 5 & 6 compare *Labeo* to a 'craftie cuttle' (cuttlefish) that 'lieth sure in the black cloud of his thick vomiture'. Cuttlefish are known as chameleons of the sea, because of their ability to change colour and appearance; they also spray a dark inky substance

> Labeo is whip't, and laughs me in the face.
> Why? For I smite and hide the galled place,
> Gird but the Cynick's helmet on his head,
> Care he for Talus or the flayle of lead?
> Long as the craftie Cuttle lieth sure
> In the black Cloud of his thick vomiture;
> Who list complaine of wronged faith or fame
> When he may shift it to anothers name?

(sepia) to hide from predators. Just as the 'craftie cuttle' conceals itself in thick clouds of ink, so *Labeo* too hides himself. In using this metaphor, Hall clearly implies that *Labeo* is a concealed writer. And so, having previously identified *Labeo* as the author of works published under the *Shakespeare* title, one is led to the conclusion that the author of *Shakespeare's* poems was hidden – which clearly rules out the Stratford man.

In 1598 John Marston hinted at the identity of *Labeo* in *Pigmalions Image* – a poem which he wrote in the style of *Venus & Adonis*. The appendix contains the following:

> So Labeo did complain his love was stone,
> Obdurate, flinty, so relentless none;
> Yet Lynceus knows that in the end of this
> He wrought as strange a metamorphosis.

The first two lines paraphrase lines 199 & 200 in *Venus & Adonis*:

> Art thou obdurate, flinty hard as steel –
> Nay, more than flint, for stone at rain relenteth?

By using the same words (flinty, obdurate & stone) Marston implies that *Labeo* is a pseudonym for the author of *Venus & Adonis*. These examples show that both Hall and Marston identified *Labeo* with the author of poems published under the *Shakespeare* title. Of course, they might have been referring to the Stratford man as *Labeo*; but, if that was the case, why would Hall indicate that *Labeo* is a *hidden* author? With his name emblazoned on the work, William Shakspere could not have been a concealed poet!

Summary

- Edwards implies that Adon – the author of *Venus & Adonis* – is a 'masked' aristocrat who cannot be given public recognition for his work and who, in some mysterious sense, 'differs much from men'.
- Hall and Marston identify the author of Shakespeare's poems *Venus & Adonis* and *The Rape of Lucrece* with the pseudonym *Labeo*.
- Hall associates *Labeo* metaphorically with a cuttlefish. As the text makes clear, cuttlefish expel thick clouds of ink for the purpose of concealment. Hence, the cuttlefish metaphor implies that *Labeo*, the author of two 'Shakespeare' poems, is a hidden poet.

In the last two lines of his verse, Hall asks a question which hints at mystery concerning the attribution of work: 'Who list complaine of wronged faith or fame / When he may shift it to anothers name?' This suggests name changing and, hence, an anomaly or 'irregularity' associated with the author of *Shakespeare* – which clearly should not be the case if the traditional attribution is correct.

It is evident that neither Edwards, Hall nor Marston had the Warwickshire rustic in mind when referring to the author of poems published under the *Shakespeare* title; indeed, analysis of their texts very strongly implies that they were alluding to a hidden member of the nobility.

A catalogue of failures

One of the most serious difficulties facing Stratfordian orthodoxy, arises from the failure of many contemporaries who 'ought' to have referred to William Shakspere as a writer, but did not do so:

- Failure of Ben Jonson, supposedly a friend and rival for many years, to write anything about William Shakspere *during* the Stratford man's lifetime.
- Failure of theatre fans, John Chamberlain and Henry Wooton, to refer to Shakspere in their letters – at a time when the dramatist was supposedly famous.
- Failure of William Camden, the chronicler, to mention the well-known author in his descriptions of Stratford in 1607.
- Failure of Michael Drayton, the writer who came from a village near Stratford, to refer to William Shakspere in his book *Worthies of Warwickshire*, even though the playwright was well known to him.
- Failure of the anonymous author of *Metamorphosis* – who compiled a list of more than *thirty* leading poets and playwrights – to include William Shakspere's name.
- Failure of the accounts book of Richard Burbage to refer to the man from Stratford, even though many of the Shakespeare plays were performed at the Globe and Burbage himself was a leading actor and the theatre owner!
- Failure of the diary of the famous actor Edward Alleyn to mention William Shakspere, even though Alleyn had played leading Shakespearean roles.
- Failure of Ben Jonson to name 'Shakespeare' as one of the five best English poets in his *Timbres or Discoveries* –despite having earlier called him 'starr of poets' in the 1623 Folio!

- Failure of courtiers to refer to the remarkable Warwickshire playwright, whose works were shown more frequently at Elizabeth's court than any other dramatist.
- Failure of Dr John Hall, Shakspere's well-educated son-in-law, to make any mention of his famous relative.
- Failure of Shakspere's closest kin to refer to the celebrated writer in the family.
- Failure of friends and business associates, in Stratford-upon-Avon, to identify the renowned poet and playwright who lived in the town.
- Failure of actors in the London theatres, who worked with Shakspere for many years, to identify him as a writer *during* his lifetime.
- Failure of William Shakspere himself, to make any mention of his writing career!
- Failure of the Earl of Southampton – supposedly Shakspere's patron – to identify the illustrious poet and playwright in his employ.
- Failure of the entire *cognoscenti*: Bacon, Raleigh, the Cecils, Queen Elizabeth, James I etc to refer to the brilliant dramatist – who was surely a familiar face at court.
- Failure of the Garter King to identify William Shakspere as a poet or playwright in 1596 when the 'Shakespeare' name was already associated with a very famous poem, *Venus & Adonis* (1593), the most popular literary work of the age.
- Failure of Philip and William Herbert, the Earls of Pembroke and Montgomery, to refer to the Stratford man even though the book of his plays – the 1623 Folio – was dedicated to them.

It is highly improbable that the loss of *all* the 'evidence' for authorship, which these 'failures' represent, was due to accident, oversight or negligence. A few gaps in the record might be expected, especially after 400 years, but it is highly suspicious that so many logical opportunities to refer to William Shakspere as a *writer* were missed. Moreover, it is very difficult to see how the Warwickshire entrepreneur could have been an important figure in the London theatre world and yet none of the many people who knew him and worked with him, had anything to say 'on record' about a man described in 1623 as the 'wonder of our stage'.

Missing literary references

In her book *Shakespeare's Unorthodox Biography*, Diana Price presented what she called a 'literary paper trail' – an authorship test consisting of ten categories of evidence (literary 'markers') that measure the strength of an alleged writer's claim to authorship. Of twenty-five writers contemporary with *Shakespeare's* author to whom the test was applied, Ben Jonson came top with full marks while the Stratford man was bottom with zero. Clearly, a very embarrassing result for the Warwickshire yokel, especially in view of the fact that even relatively obscure writers, with the weakest attributions, managed to score at least three out of ten.

Shakespeare's SHADOW at Wilton

A fine memorial to 'Shakespeare' stands in the entrance at Wilton House. The monument was designed by William Kent and completed in 1743 for Henry Herbert, 9th Earl of Pembroke – a descendant of Mary (Sidney) Herbert. The monument is inscribed with a famous quotation from *Macbeth*, although the original folio lines have been altered. An almost identical monument, with a misquotation from *The Tempest*, was installed, in 1740, at Poet's Corner, in Westminster Abbey. The Wilton Monument commemorates a tradition that the author spent time at the house, during the tenure of Mary (Sidney) Herbert.

Shakespeare's statue points to the first line of the inscription which reads: 'Life's but a walking SHADOW'. However, the corresponding line in the 1623 Folio is: 'Life's but a walking shadow, a poore player,'. The differences prompt a number of questions:

- Why was the original line altered – what motivated the change?
- Why is the statue pointing to the first line?
- Why is the word 'SHADOW' – directly beneath the statue's finger – inscribed in capitals?
- Why are LIFE, PLAYER and STAGE also capitalised?

The alterations look suspicious, especially as SHADOW is directly beneath the statue's finger. The special significance of 'shadow' in this context is that it can mean 'ghost' – an interpretation which suggests that 'Shakespeare' was not the *real* author of the works. Furthermore, it is noteworthy that 'shadow' is used in a very similar sense in a verse by John Benson (1640) which questioningly addresses William Marshall's engraving of Shakespeare: 'This shadowe is renowned Shakespears?'. (A text which will be discussed later.)

Shakespeare's Monument at Wilton commemorates a tradition that the author spent time at the house during the tenure of Mary (Sidney) Herbert. Curiously, the statue points to the capitalised word SHADOW in a famous quotation from Macbeth.

The monument inscription, with its deliberate alterations, strongly suggests that 'Shakespeare' is *only* a 'shadow' and that the real author has been hidden; it also implies, of course, that some people in the mid-eighteenth century knew the secret.

Summary of key points against Stratfordian orthodoxy

- The total absence of documentary evidence *during* William Shakspere's lifetime specifically and unequivocally identifying him as a writer.
- Nothing in Shakspere's will that hints at a career as a professional playwright or poet – no mention of books, manuscripts or any other literary artefacts.
- Thorpe's dedication in *Shake-speares Sonnets* to the 'onlie begetter' of the sonnets (the author) M^r. W.H.
- The author of the sonnets states that once dead he must be lost to the world and that his name will be buried with his body.
- The non-existent, hyphenated surname that appears on a number of the early publications.
- The astonishing failure of contemporaries to refer in works to 'Shakespeare' where his name would be expected to appear.
- The huge vocabulary, very extensive academic reading and encyclopaedic knowledge of the author – acquired at a time when there were no English dictionaries, no encyclopaedias and no public libraries.
- The question of how a commoner gained the deepest insight into the highest echelons of society – and without drawing attention to himself in the process.
- The fact that none of the highly educated *cognoscenti*, such as the Queen, Bacon, Cecil, Raleigh, James I etc – who saw the *Shakespeare* plays at court – ever referred to the brilliant playwright from Stratford.
- The notorious play *Richard II* with its infamous deposition scene – the author took a literally suicidal risk in writing it, yet the Stratford man was not even questioned in the aftermath of the rebellion that the play helped to incite.
- *Hamlet* is concerned, in part, with the issue of royal succession – a very dangerous subject for any playwright to deal with, especially in the twilight years of Elizabeth's reign.
- The question of Hamlet himself: why was the prince of *such* importance that the dramatist felt compelled to write a vast and complex play about him?

- The complete absence of commendatory verse from 'Shakespeare' to any of his contemporaries.
- *Macbeth* – written specially for James I – contains a great deal of material certain to perturb the nervous Scottish king. Why would the Stratford man have penned such a disturbing play for the new monarch – how dare he do so?
- *The Tempest*, like *Macbeth*, a play deeply concerned with the occult – was written and performed for the court. Again, what dramatist would be foolish enough to write such a play for a king, fanatically opposed to magic, spiritualism and the supernatural?
- Very strong hints by contemporary writers that *Shakespeare* was a pseudonym and that the true author was a concealed member of the nobility.
- The large number of legal terms and references – suggesting an aristocratic author.
- The curious fact that, in a highly competitive profession, nobody paid the slightest attention to such a talented and successful individual.
- The author's knowledge of highly obscure information that was available to very few people in England at the time.
- The astonishing fact that William Shakspere, supposedly grammar school educated, was unsure of his age in a lawsuit in 1612 and struggled to sign his name on the deposition.
- The total absence of customary eulogies, from former colleagues, when Shakspere died in 1616.

In conclusion

The more one finds out about William Shakspere of Stratford-upon-Avon, the less one understands how he came to write the works. In view of the fact that every line of inquiry ends in a mystery; in view of the evasiveness of academics; in view of all the excuses and special pleading that belief in orthodoxy requires, and in view of the strange reticence of Shakspere and his contemporaries to reveal anything of personal significance, it is unsurprising that many have felt compelled to look elsewhere for the real author.

5

Seven
Shakespeares

The following are brief outlines of the cases against six of the most frequently cited contenders for *Shakespeare's* laurels: Sir Francis Bacon (Lord Verulam), Christopher Marlowe, the Earl of Oxford (Edward de Vere), the Earl of Derby (William Stanley), the Earl of Rutland (Roger Manners) and Queen Elizabeth. Finally, the case against a seventh 'Shakespeare', so-called 'group authorship', is examined.

Sir Francis Bacon (1561-1626)

Not unnaturally, many nineteenth century doubters of orthodoxy saw in Sir Francis Bacon a man who had the right connections and intellectual capabilities to be the author of *Shakespeare*. In fact, many wise saws and instances in 'the works' were found to be similar to aphorisms in Bacon's notes — similarities that became known as 'parallelisms'.

At first sight, the parallels appear to provide good evidence that Bacon had a hand, at least, in writing *Shakespeare*. However, very similar parallels can be seen in the writings of other authors of the period — so, unfortunately, the parallelisms do not represent a *unique* link between Bacon and 'the works'. It is perhaps unsurprising that this is the case, since teachers taught the same subjects in accordance with a very rigid methodology and syllabus. There was a lot of rote learning, especially when it came to Latin, Greek and the Bible. In that respect, pupils received a rigorous but standardised education. It is therefore hardly surprising that the parallelisms in Bacon's notes, resemble quotations and aphorisms in texts of contemporaries who received similar schooling.

Brilliant though he was, Francis Bacon's known writings seem rather too prosaic for the author of *Shakespeare*. It is not easy to imagine the well-known philosopher and serious-minded academic, penning comedies replete with the kind of bawdy jokes that appear in the plays. It seems his mind-set was rather too high-brow to entertain anything as 'common' as low comedy. But above all, the style of *Shakespeare* is entirely absent from Bacon's acknowledged works — critics agree that there is little literary merit in the poetry he wrote late in life. And, although Francis Bacon was perhaps a better, or more original, philosopher than *Shakespeare's* author, he admitted himself that he was not a poet. Moreover, much of the 'philosophy' in the plays is second-hand, which is hardly what one would expect from a thinker of Bacon's class. So, it seems that the poetry is 'too good' and the philosophy too much like 'received wisdom' for Francis Bacon to have been the author of *Shakespeare*.

Furthermore, whereas Bacon was a systematic thinker who sought to construct a vast intellectual scheme — *The Great Instauration* — *Shakespeare's* author gives the impression of a pragmatist uncon-

Generally acknowledged as one of the cleverest men in England, Sir Francis Bacon (Lord Verulam) was a courtier, lawyer, philosopher, spy, statesman and scientist — the polymath's polymath.

cerned with attempts to devise grand, over-arching theories. In that respect, Hamlet's famous line comes to mind: 'There are more things in Heaven and Earth, Horatio, than are dreamt of in our philosophy' — a neat riposte to systematic thinkers of Bacon's ilk. Indeed, if there is an over-all 'philosophy' in the *Shakespeare* plays it is that there is no 'philosophy' — only an attempt to show life as it is, to hold the mirror up to nature.

In addition, Sir Francis Bacon was neither the 'sporty type' nor was he particularly interested in military matters and seafaring — unlike the Bard, who certainly was. As a person, he appears to have been a bit of a cold fish, a man who seems to have been somewhat detached and aloof — so it's difficult to imagine him as the author of a play like *Romeo and Juliet*. And, it's not at all easy to believe that Francis Bacon would have written the explicitly heterosexual 'Dark Lady' sonnets in view of the fact that he was a life-long homosexual, like his older brother Anthony. In fact, his mother wrote to Anthony concerned that Francis was going to bed with 'disreputable' men — it seems he had a predilection for Welsh servants. With such a private life, it is difficult to imagine Francis Bacon being involved with any mistress, dark or otherwise; indeed, his marriage to Alice Barnham, at the age of forty-five, proved less than happy.

A pivotal fact arguing against Bacon's authorship of *Shakespeare*, was his role in the prosecution of the Earl of Essex over the latter's attempted rebellion in 1601. Sir Francis himself drew attention to a performance of the seditious play *Richard II*, which took place the day before the uprising. It's hardly credible, if he was the author, that he would have focused on such self-incriminating evidence — and put himself at serious risk of prosecution. Anyone defending Essex, who knew of Bacon's secret authorship, would surely have pointed out that it was he, Sir Francis, who had written the offending play. But in any case, it is extremely difficult to believe that a highly intelligent lawyer would have placed himself in serious jeopardy by writing seditious material.

Of huge importance in the case against Bacon's authorship claim, is the fact that Heminges and Condell, the actors who collated and edited the *Shakespeare* plays for the 1623 Folio, tell us in the preface that they had to carry out the work on the author's behalf because he was dead — yet Bacon was still very much alive; indeed, his death did not occur until three years after the folio was published.

The question arises as to why any playwright would entrust 'mere' players to carry out such a technically demanding task. The author would surely want the work to be executed perfectly, and the only way to be certain of getting it right would be to do it himself. Yet, the folio contains many errors — it isn't a perfect copy of the original text; why would the dramatist have allowed a lot of mistakes to appear in his great work if he was in a position to oversee the editing?

Finally, an important point which argues very strongly against Bacon's authorship is the fact that, ever since the debate entered the public domain in the mid-nineteenth century, each generation of Baconian scholars — with no axe to grind as far as the authorship controversy is concerned — has vehemently denied the claim that Sir Francis Bacon wrote *Shakespeare*.

Brief chronology

1561   Born January 22 at York House in the Strand, London. Youngest son of Sir Nicholas Bacon and his second wife Anne Cooke. A sickly child, Francis was reared and educated at his father's house, Gorhambury, near St Albans.

1573   Attended Trinity College Cambridge, with his brother Anthony.

1576   Admitted to Gray's Inn to study law. Visited Paris and studied politics.

1579	Sir Nicholas Bacon died leaving Francis without inheritance — the cause of much financial distress.
1582	Became a barrister.
1584	Entered Parliament as MP for Melcome, Dorset — later represented various constituencies: Taunton, Southampton, Liverpool, Ipswich & St Albans.
1591	Robert Devereux, Earl of Essex, became Bacon's pupil and patron. Bacon indicated his wish to give up the law and study philosophy.
1598	Arrested for debt.
1601	Took part in the prosecution of his former patron, the Earl of Essex.
1603	Knighted on the succession of James I.
1604	Took part in negotiations on the union of England and Scotland.
1606	Married Alice Barnham.
1607	Made Solicitor General.
1613	Became Attorney General.
1616	Appointed to the Privy Council.
1617	Created Lord Keeper.
1618	Made Lord Chancellor — titled Baron Verulam.
1621	Created Viscount St Albans. Accused of bribery and corruption. Sent to the Tower. Subject to a large fine. Later released and granted limited pardon.
1626	Died at Highgate from an infection that, according to one account, was caught while performing an experiment to freeze a chicken with snow. Buried at St Michael's Church, St Albans.

Points against Bacon's authorship claim

- Bacon was alive in 1623 when the first folio was published — yet, in their prefatory 'letter', Heminges and Condell state that the author is dead.
- Why would Bacon have sanctioned Heminges and Condell to collate and edit his 'great work' — why would he have allowed many mistakes to appear in the 1623 Folio, when he was able to oversee the editing?
- Every Baconian scholar of the last 150 years has rejected the claim that Francis Bacon was Shakespeare's author.
- No record exists of Bacon visiting Italy — scene of many *Shakespeare* plays.

- Bacon is not known to have visited Elsinore (Hamlet's Castle) in Denmark.
- Bacon lived in the south of England, so how and why did he acquire knowledge of Yorkish dialect?
- The author of the sonnets calls himself Will — not Francis.
- Francis Bacon's initials are not the same as the 'onlie begetter' of the sonnets.
- Bacon had no known association with seafaring — a recurrent theme in the *Shakespeare* plays.
- Bacon was not the sporty type — unlike the author of *Shakespeare*, who refers in detail to many kinds of sports and games.
- How and why was Bacon's 'authorship' kept perfectly secret long after his death?
- Why would a man as well known as Bacon state in sonnet 81: 'Though I (once gone) to all the world must die' and 'The earth can offer me only a common grave'?
- In view of the fact that Bacon was a confirmed homosexual, it's difficult to believe he would have written the explicitly heterosexual 'Dark Lady' sonnets.
- Why would an ambitious man such as Bacon, seeking preferment and thinking of his career, write a very disturbing play like *Macbeth* for James I?
- Bacon had never been anywhere near a battle — he was not a soldier — yet *Shakespeare's* author knew precise details of battlefield conditions.
- Bacon himself stated categorically in Apology... *concerning the late Earl of Essex, 1604*: 'Although I profess not to be a poet'.
- Poems by Bacon, late in his career, are considered by critics to be of little merit.
- Bacon was highly intelligent and a lawyer; it is inconceivable that he would have been so foolish as to write *Richard II* with a seditious deposition scene.
- Acting for the prosecution at the trial of Essex in 1601, Bacon himself raised the issue of the performance of *Richard II* — a very dangerous thing to do if he was the secret author of the play.
- *Shakespeare's* author was a natural comic writer with a bawdy sense of humour — attributes which seem very alien to Bacon's rather sober temperament.

- Like all talented and influential men Bacon had enemies. If he was secretly writing plays under a pseudonym, why did none of his adversaries ever 'embarrass' him — as they had over his sexual orientation — by making his secret authorship public?

Collectively, these points very strongly argue against Bacon's authorship of *Shakespeare*.

Two early heretics
Delia Bacon (1811-1859)

In the late eighteenth century the Rev. James Wilmot, a distinguished scholar, scoured Warwickshire in an attempt to find evidence supporting William Shakspere's claim to authorship. Much to his surprise and disappointment the quest was a total failure and, in an attempt to find a more credible author, he eventually came to the conclusion that Bacon secretly wrote *Shakespeare*. Probably for fear of ridicule Wilmot refrained from making his beliefs widely known.

Having no such inhibition, the eccentric American Delia Bacon, namesake but no relation of Sir Francis, was the first to make a public presentation of an alternative to the alleged author. The debut of her thesis came in 1856 in an issue of Putnam's monthly magazine; a year later it was followed by her book *'Philosophy of the Plays of Shakespeare Unfolded'*. In the latter work she expounded the theory that *Shakespeare* was written by a secret cabal of thinkers led by Francis Bacon — a group of intellectuals she called 'Raleigh's school'. In other words, Delia was not a 'pure Baconian' but the first promulgator of 'group authorship' — the hypothesis that the works of *Shakespeare* were a collaborative effort.

Delia Bacon was the first person, in print, to seriously question Shakespeare's authorship.

A lone and rather tragic seeker after truth, Delia convinced herself that the ultimate proof for her theory lay hidden beneath the gravestone in Holy Trinity Church. She even tried, under cover of darkness, to remove the stone herself — though, needless to say, the rather audacious and impractical attempt was quickly abandoned. Sadly, soon after failing to unearth the dark secrets of the grave, Delia was stricken with mental illness and committed to an asylum in the United States where she died two years later. It seems that the gravestone curse had claimed its first victim!

Ignatius Donnelly (1831-1901)

In 1888 the American heretic Ignatius Donnelly published a huge book entitled *The Great Cryptogram*, which purported to explain how Francis Bacon had concealed messages, asserting his secret authorship of *Shakespeare*, within the works. Donnelly went on to claim that Bacon had also written the plays of Christopher Marlowe, Montaign's essays and Robert Burton's *Anatomy of Melancholy*. The claims were so extravagant it is perhaps little wonder they provoked a hostile reaction from orthodox scholars and that, as a result, Donnelly found himself castigated as a crank. As it so happens, the eccentric cryptographer set a precedent and everyone who has since taken up the code-breaking challenge has been cast, perhaps unfairly, in a similar light.

Through increasingly offbeat schemes to demonstrate Bacon's authorship, based on implausibly elaborate cryptograms in the Shakespeare text, Donnelly inadvertently did much to discredit the search for hidden codes and ciphers.

Cryptography: national security and state secrets — a matter of life and death

It would be very unwise, however, to dismiss all cryptographers as obsessive oddballs on the lunatic fringe. After all, Francis Bacon himself invented a method of encryption — the bi-literal cipher — and even wrote a book about code-making. Indeed, cryptography assumed an increasingly important role in issues of national security, as the well-known case of Mary, Queen of Scots demonstrates.

In 1567 Mary — the Catholic Queen of Protestant Scotland who grew up in France — found herself, after a long and circuitous route, in self-imposed exile in England. Having lived under house arrest as a 'guest' of Elizabeth for nineteen years, she became involved in a treacherous conspiracy — the Babbington plot — which was intended to overthrow the Virgin Queen, put Mary on the throne and return England to Catholicism. But, by intercepting encoded messages between the Scots Queen and the conspirators, spy-chief Sir Francis Walsingham entrapped her and foiled the alleged plot.

Spy-master Sir Francis Walsingham vied with Lord Burghley and the Earl of Leicester to provide the queen with the most up-to-date intelligence. Unswervingly loyal to his sovereign — although Elizabeth never really cared for him — Walsingham was one of the leading Protestants in England. Devious and ruthless, he organised a highly effective network of spies that spanned the whole of continental Europe — he even paid the agents and informers out of his own pocket — and ended up owing a fortune since, as usual, the queen did not provide financial assistance. Plagued with boils throughout his life, he died a very painful death from testicular cancer. His burial took place at night, to prevent creditors taking the body for ransom.

The debate continues as to whether Mary really was guilty of treason, or whether Walsingham manufactured the evidence and framed her. Be that as it may, she was found guilty and, after much hand-wringing by Elizabeth, was executed at Fotheringay Castle in February 1587. It was an event of historic proportions — a Catholic queen executed by her host and 'protector' a Protestant Queen – a politically seismic shock that helped to trigger (or at least give a pretext for) the Spanish Armada in the following year. Crucially, it was an episode which showed just how important cryptography had become, in the latter part of the sixteenth century.

Secret knowledge is the key to power

Owing to the need for governments and individuals to retain their own secrets, and learn the secrets of others, much effort went into code-making and code-breaking. Hence, the idea that information might have been encrypted in the *Shakespeare* works themselves — and in contemporary texts referring to the author — is certainly not ridiculous. Indeed, it is well-known that many authors hid secrets in their writings by using a variety of methods, including anagrams, acrostics, codes and ciphers. It is therefore virtually certain that if 'Shakespeare' is a hoax, encrypted information has been incorporated in appropriate texts, by the author himself and contemporaries privy to the secret.

Christopher Marlowe (1564-1593)

Many of the alternative authorial candidates were of noble or high birth, but it was the commoner Christopher Marlowe whose writing talent was of the same order as the author of *Shakespeare*. Indeed, Ben Jonson wrote of his ability to pen a 'mighty line'. Some doubters of orthodoxy have detected a strong similarity with The Bard, because 'Shakespeare' and Marlowe deal with similar 'heroic' themes; however, literary critics point out the fallacy of supposing that Marlowe's *style* of writing and the style found in *Shakespeare* are one and the same. Whilst it is likely that Marlowe had a powerful influence on *Shakespeare's* author in the late 1580s and early 1590s, the use of language and exploration of character in the plays penned by the two dramatists appear quite distinct to experts. And Marlowe — unlike The Bard — did not write comedies.

The son of a prosperous shoemaker, eldest in a family of four boys and five girls, Kit Marlowe was born in Canterbury in 1564. The boy showed signs of academic promise, gaining a scholarship at the King's School, Canterbury in 1578 and going on to win a scholarship at Corpus Christi College, Cambridge in 1581. He remained an undergraduate at the college for six years, supposedly studying divinity. However, it seems that whilst a student he came to the attention of the secret service and was recruited into the murky world of Elizabethan espionage. In fact, records show that Marlowe spent a lot of time away from college — in all likelihood on clandestine government busi-

This picture allegedly of Christopher Marlowe, dated 1585, was found by an undergraduate among builder's rubbish, in a bad state of repair, outside the Master's Lodge at Corpus Christi College, Cambridge in 1953. Although the age of the sitter is right (twenty-one) and Marlowe was a student at Corpus Christi, it is far from certain that this really is the dramatist's portrait.

ness — and that he was specially awarded a degree, probably for services rendered.

Once in London, Christopher Marlowe soon established himself as a brilliant but unconventional individual, an iconoclast who delighted in challenging received wisdom and the accepted norms of behaviour. Openly homosexual, he is alleged to have said that: 'all they that love not tobacco and boys are fools' — yet there is no mention of tobacco or smoking in the *Shakespeare* canon — that 'Christ was a bastard and his mother dishonest', that 'Moses was but a juggler' and that 'St John the Evangelist was bedfellow to Christ'. How much of this Marlowe really did say is difficult to know because there were those who wouldn't have hesitated to besmirch his reputation and character with attributed blasphemies. However, the scant record does suggest that he was a colourful, boisterous character and that perhaps, like Lord Byron, he was 'mad, bad and dangerous to know'. Nevertheless, in his six-year career as a writer (1587-1593) the young genius transformed English drama — the first playwright to pen tragedies in blank verse and the first to write those 'mighty lines'. It is a measure of his precocious talent that the masterpieces *Doctor Faustus, Tambourlaine the Great* and *The Jew of Malta* were all written before his twenty-ninth birthday.

Unfortunately, much of Marlowe's tragically short life is a mystery because little documentary evidence has survived. But the very suspicious circumstances attending his death in a brawl at a Deptford hostelry — a safe house of the secret service — supposedly over payment of the bill (the 'reckoning') are the most mysterious of all. Indeed, it has been suggested that the death was faked, so as to enable the dramatist-spy to escape from a dangerous situation that seriously compromised his superiors in the secret service.

In 1895 Wilbur Ziegler, an American lawyer, was the first to claim that Kit Marlowe wrote *Shakespeare*. Sixty years later another American, the publicist Calvin Hoffman, revamped the theory in his book *The Murder of the Man who was Shakespeare*. Hoffman linked Marlow's supposed 'faked death' to Thomas Walsingham, brother of the deceased spy chief Sir Francis. According to the Ziegler-Hoffman conjecture, the ruse allowed Marlowe to continue writing, hidden away in Europe, while the actor-manager William Shakspere sold the works under his own name on the author's behalf. In 1956 Hoffman obtained permission to open the Walsingham family vault at Chislehurst Church in the hope of finding the crucial evidence that would prove Marlowe's authorship, but the search yielded nothing of significance.

There are two serious difficulties with the theory:
- The *Shakespeare* name first appeared on work *(Venus & Adonis)* shortly after Marlowe's 'death' in 1593. The question

is: Would Thomas Walsingham, after going to the trouble of spiriting the dramatist away to the continent, allow him to publish works — even under a false name — immediately afterwards, especially as the reason for staging the 'murder' was to protect Walsingham himself?

- If Christopher Marlowe was so afraid of his enemies that *he* himself went to the trouble of staging a phoney death, would it make sense for him to write plays for the public theatre — a short time later — even under a pseudonym? Perceptive enemies would almost certainly have recognised Marlowe's work by his distinctive signature, the 'mighty line', and would have realised that the erstwhile spy was still alive.

A further key question is why no contemporary 'outed' Marlowe as *Shakespeare's* secret author? In an age of gossips when it was difficult to keep anything secret for long — especially among theatre folk and the *literati* — it is strange that there were no stories circulating *at the time* that the killing had been faked and that the dramatist was writing under a false name. After Marlowe's 'actual' death (whenever that was) nobody revealed 'the truth' about his secret authorship of *Shakespeare*, even though he was beyond the reach of any who sought to do him harm. Why would those who knew the secret continue to hide it, long after the ruse had served its original purpose? Friends and colleagues would surely have wanted the world to know what had happened — yet Marlowe's name was only linked with *Shakespeare's* authorship, for the first time, three hundred years after his death.

Brief chronology

1564	February 26. Christopher Marlowe was born. Christened at St George the Martyr, Canterbury.
1578	Entered the King's School Canterbury on a scholarship.
1581	Attended Corpus Christi College, Cambridge to study divinity.
1587	At some time in the previous six years, almost certainly whilst at Cambridge, he was recruited by the Secret Service. Worked as a dramatist in London under the patronage of Thomas Walsingham, brother of the spymaster Sir Francis Walsingham. Admitted to Sir Walter Raleigh's secret group, The School of Night.
1589	Arrested for involvement in a street fight in which a man was killed. Bound over to keep the peace.
1592	Fought a bloodless duel with William Corkine.

1593   May 20 Arrested at the house of Thomas Walsingham
       and taken before the Court of Star Chamber — released
       on bail. Denounced for blasphemy and atheism.

1593   May 30: Stabbed in the head and killed by Ingram
       Friser during an alleged brawl at a Deptford hostelry —
       the establishment of Widow Bull — a safe house used
       by the secret service. Friser, a low-life who worked for
       Thomas Walsingham, was found not guilty of
       Marlowe's murder, on grounds of self-defence, and was
       soon given a royal pardon.

Points against Marlowe's authorship claim

- Christopher Marlowe was killed in highly suspicious
  circumstances, at a Deptford hostelry, on May 30th 1593. If
  his 'death' was a ruse and he went to live in Europe, his
  enemies — and it seems he made many during his brief life —
  would probably have found out. Yet, in the years that
  followed there were never any rumours that he was still alive,
  writing plays under a false name.
- Literary critics of *Shakespeare* and Marlowe insist that the
  writing styles are quite distinct and that the authors were
  definitely not the same person.
- Marlowe's forename was Christopher ('Kit') — unlike the
  author of *The Sonnets* who indicates that his name is 'Will'
  (sonnet 136).
- Christopher Marlowe's initials are inconsistent with Thorpe's
  dedication to 'the onlie begetter' of *Shake-speares Sonnets*
  — M^r. W.H. (assuming that 'begetter' means 'author').
- Friends and colleagues must have known the truth about
  Marlowe's secret authorship — what prevented them 'telling
  all' when he was dead and there was no longer any need for
  secrecy?
- Having gone to the trouble of concocting an elaborate cover
  story, and being spirited away to Europe after his 'murder',
  why jeopardise security by staging plays in England that
  enemies might recognise as work by Christopher Marlowe?
- In view of his reputation for causing trouble and making
  enemies it seems very likely that Marlowe would have
  eventually made a nuisance of himself whilst in
  hiding. It's difficult to believe that such a brilliant misfit
  could have remained totally silent and 'invisible' for the rest

of his life — yet it seems he was never seen alive again after May 30th 1593.

- Why would Marlowe publish his '*Shakespeare*' plays anonymously in the late 1580s and early 1590s yet — at the same time — allow other plays like *Doctor Faustus, Tamburlaine the Great* and *The Jew of Malta* to appear under his own name? It seems totally inconsistent with Marlowe's temperament that he would fail to put his name on works *he* had written.
- How did Robert Greene — or the real author of the *Groatsworth* letter of 1592 — happen to allude to the code name that Marlowe was *going* to use in exile ('shake scene') long *before* Marlowe used it himself?
- Marlowe had no known connection with the north of England. How and why did he gain knowledge of Yorkish dialect?
- Why would a confirmed homosexual like Marlowe encourage the fair youth of the sonnets to marry and have children?
- Why would Thomas Walsingham have allowed Marlowe to risk breaking cover by writing under a false name — especially as Walsingham himself wanted people to believe that the playwright was dead?
- All the plays that appeared under Marlowe's name were tragedies, yet almost all the *Shakespeare* plays written during the 1590s were comedies or histories. There is no evidence Marlowe was a comic playwright.
- How did the eleven-year-old Christopher Marlowe, living in Canterbury at the time, know details of the pageant at Kenilworth Castle in summer 1575, as alluded to in *A Midsummer Night's Dream*?
- There is some evidence, notably the quality of writing, that Shakespeare's author worked on the 'King James' version of The Bible. Why would an atheist, like Marlowe, have been invited to help on that project?

Collectively, these points very strongly suggest that Christopher Marlowe was not the secret author of *Shakespeare*.

Edward de Vere — 17th Earl of Oxford (1550-1604)

A humiliating story, often recounted by detractors, relates to an occasion when the Earl of Oxford was presented to the queen. It was said that, as he bowed low before Her Majesty the flatulent nobleman let-off an extremely loud fart. Mortified by the embarrassing out-burst, the shame-faced earl scurried away from court and spent several years wandering round Europe in self-imposed exile. On returning to England, he summoned up courage and presented himself once more to Elizabeth. Knowing how long the itinerant earl had been away, the waspish queen immediately exclaimed: 'My Lord Oxford, we had quite forgot The Fart!'.

Oxford's authorship claim was first made public in 1920, by the amusingly named school master J. Thomas Looney, in a book entitled *Shakespeare Identified.* Looney (a Manx name pronounced 'Loney') arrived at his chosen candidate by making a list of what he thought were eighteen characteristics of *Shakespeare's* author — attributes inferred from his reading of the canon. Unfortunately, attempting to sketch biographical portraits of authors from their works alone is fraught with difficulty. If any of the inferred 'characteristics' are erroneous or if the list of discerned attributes is incomplete then, like a puzzle with incorrect or missing pieces, the final picture is likely to be wrong.

As an acknowledged poet, Oxford's claim to authorship has, at first sight, an element of plausibility — especially when details in some of the plays are compared with the known facts of his life; notably, his journeys through Italy and his family connections. However, a number of aristocratic candidates can make similarly impressive claims based on *their* foreign travels and family relationships — so Oxford's links to the works are not unique. Striking parallels amongst the nobility exist, precisely because they lived similar lives. Many of them were related, many received the same education and many pursued the

Short in stature and eccentric in his style of dress, the acknowledged poet Edward de Vere — 17th Earl of Oxford — was seen as a rather ridiculous figure by rivals at court.

same activities: foreign travel — especially to Italy — and sports such as tennis, hunting and falconry. Seen in this light, Oxford's apparent connections to *Shakespeare* are not particularly remarkable.

Indeed, there are very strong reasons to reject Oxford's authorship claim, not the least of which is that he died in 1604, well before events alluded to in the later plays took place. In particular, a shipwreck near Bermuda in 1609, which appears to have been in the author's mind when he wrote *The Tempest* and *Macbeth* – the latter a play closely associated with the gunpowder plot of 1605. In addition, critical analysis of Oxford's acknowledged works — the poetry — does not give the impression that his writing style is like that found in *Shakespeare*; quite simply, he did not have the same poetic 'voice' as the author. A further powerful argument against Oxford's claim is that, as a young man, he made no attempt to conceal his writing, a fact which prompts three questions:

1. Why in the mid 1590s, having previously published poems openly, did the Earl of Oxford suddenly assume a pen name (William Shakespeare) for the poems *Venus and Adonis* and *The Rape of Lucrece*?

2. Why did his literary career follow such a strange trajectory — starting in complete openness but ending in absolute secrecy?

3. Why was the later work *such* a profound secret that nobody dared whisper 'the truth' about Oxford's authorship of Shakespeare, even long after his death?

Brief chronology

1550	April 12 Born at Earl's Colne, Essex. Son of John de Vere and Margarte Golding.
1562	Father died. Edward inherited estate and title. Made ward of William Cecil, Lord Burghley. Tutored by his uncle Arthur Golding (translator of Ovid's Metamorphoses).
1564	Took a degree at St John's College, Cambridge.
1567	Entered Gray's Inn to study law. Killed a servant in the Cecil household, but Lord Burghley protected him from the law. Became a favourite of the queen.
1568	Mother died.
1571	Married Anne Cecil, daughter of William Cecil.

1574	Went abroad without leave — brought back by agents.
1575	Travelled widely in Europe — adopted Italian fashions. Eldest daughter Elizabeth born.
1576	Heard rumours Elizabeth was not his daughter. Left his wife to associate with the literati.
1579	Serious argument with Philip Sidney at a tennis match. Queen intervened to prevent a duel.
1580	Oxford's theatre company toured the provinces — including Stratford.
1581	Briefly sent to the Tower for involvement with Catholics.
1582	Wounded in a duel with Thomas Knyvet.
1583	Lost his family estates.
1586	Took part in the trial of Mary Queen of Scots.
1588	Served on board ship against the Spanish Armada. His wife, Anne Cecil, died.
1591	Married Elizabeth Trentham; thereafter faded from public life — though he continued to support and patronise a company of players.
1603	Officiated at the coronation of James I.
1604	Died of the plague in Hackney. Left no will.

Points against Oxford's authorship claim

- Both *Macbeth* and *The Tempest* were inspired by / referred to events that took place after Oxford's death in 1604.
- The acknowledged writings of Oxford (his poems) have a very different poetic 'voice' to *Shake-speares Sonnets*.
- Why would Oxford, a leading aristocrat, have been so foolish as to include the seditious deposition scene in *Richard II*?
- How did Oxford keep his authorship permanently secret? A number of friends, relatives and actors in his play troupe must have known the truth — yet there were no rumours to that effect even after his death.
- Why would Oxford call himself 'Will' — in sonnet 136 — when his name was Edward (de Vere)?
- If 'the onlie begetter' means 'the author' of *Shake-speares Sonnets* (M^r. W.H.) Edward de Vere is excluded as author simply by his initials.
- If Oxford was the author of *Richard II*, how did he manage to escape punishment at a time when Essex — 'toy-boy' of the queen — was executed?

- Why would Oxford have deliberately courted trouble by penning politically dangerous and subversive plays such as *Julius Caesar* and *Hamlet*?
- Scholars have detected significant changes in the style of the 'Shakespeare' writing after the accession of James I in 1603. How could Oxford have anticipated the changes before his death in 1604?
- There is some evidence that *Shakespeare's* author worked on the Authorised version of The Bible, all of which took place after Oxford's death from 1604 to 1610.
- Why would a leading member of the nobility, a mature earl such as Oxford, deferentially seek the patronage (for *Venus & Adonis*) of a much younger aristocrat like the Earl of Southampton?
- Why has Oxford's *acknowledged* work faded into obscurity, yet all the work that just happens to be entitled 'Shakespeare' is now famous?
- Oxford had no significant connection with the north of England. How and why did he acquire knowledge of Yorkish dialect?
- Why would Oxford, a very well known aristocrat of ancient lineage, write in sonnet 81: 'Though I (once gone) to all the world must die' and 'the earth can offer me only a common grave'?
- Contemporaries were still writing, in the present tense, about Shakespeare's author after Oxford's death.
- How did Oxford know precise details of the pageants at Kenilworth Castle (summer 1575) alluded to in *A Midsummer Nights Dream*, when he was travelling in Europe at the time?
- Oxford had enemies and rivals at court, why did none of them ever try to embarrass him by making his secret authorship public?
- Surely Oxford's descendants would have known about his secret authorship of *Shakespeare*. Why, in view of the potentially huge rewards in modern times, did they not 'go public' and provide *absolute* proof of authorship?

Collectively, these points very strongly suggest that the Earl of Oxford was not the secret author of *Shakespeare*.

William Stanley — 6th Earl of Derby (1560/61-1642)

James Greenstreet, in 1891, was the first to publicly voice support for Derby's candidature, although Abel Lefranc was the first academic to take William Stanley's authorship claim seriously. A French literary scholar, Lefranc spent thirty-five years studying the works of *Shakespeare* and came to the conclusion that the Stratford man could not have written them. In 1918 he published a book on the subject entitled *Under the mask of William Shakespeare.*

By carefully examining *Loves Labours Lost* — the first play to appear in print under the *Shakespeare* title — Lefranc reasoned that the author must have spent time living in France, that he could speak fluent French and that he understood the French character; knowledge that seems to be entirely at odds with the documented life of the Stratford man. However, the 'French connection' *is* consistent with the life of Derby. As a young man, William Stanley travelled extensively in Europe with his tutor Richard Lloyd (1582-1587). It is *possible*, though not certain, that he visited the court of Navarre whilst on the tour. The names of several characters in the play correspond very closely with real people at Navarre, which suggests either that the author visited the court himself, or else he knew someone who had.

The only evidence for Derby's writing came from one George Fenners, a Jesuit spy, who wrote in 1599 that the earl was 'busyed only in penning commodyes for the commoun players'. It is strange, however, that although Derby's play troupe would almost certainly have known that their patron had secretly written the *Shakespeare* plays, none of the actors (the commoun players) ever revealed the secret. Moreover, if the writing activity of a nobleman was such a huge 'sin' (aristocrats weren't meant to do anything so 'common' as write plays) why did Fenners not make much more of it?

Ironically, one of the chief difficulties with Derby's author-

A detail from the only known portrait of the Earl of Derby, William Stanley. Derby seems to have penned comedies, but nothing definitely known to have been written by him has survived. In view of his travels in France it is plausible he might have had a hand in writing Loves Labours Lost.

ship claim is that he died much too late. If William Stanley was *Shakespeare's* secret author it seems he wrote nothing at all after 1613, at latest, which was about thirty years before his death — a vast span of silence from a prolific dramatist. More important is the fact that in their 1623 Folio letter Heminge and Condell state that the author is dead and that is why they have performed the task of collating and editing his work. Even if Heminge & Condell lied about the author's demise — which is highly unlikely — the question remains as to why any *living* author would entrust such a demanding and important task to actors, when he could do the work himself and be sure of getting it right?

Key problems with Derby's authorship claim, as with many of the contenders, are:

a) *Why* the need for such deep, permanent secrecy about his literary activities?

b) *How* and *why* was the secret of his authorship maintained long after his death?

c) *How* did he manage to escape interrogation and punishment for writing the seditious deposition scene in *Richard II*?

d) *Why* has no descendant ever come forward with absolute proof of authorship?

Brief chronology

1560/61 Born either in London or at the family seat — Lathom House near Ormskirk in Lancashire. His father, Lord Strange, was fourth Earl of Derby; his mother was Margaret Clifford, great granddaughter of Henry VII. William spent his childhood at Meriden Manor in Warwickshire.

1572 Admitted to St John's College, Oxford.

1582 Travelled extensively throughout Europe with his tutor Richard Lloyd.

1587 Returned to Lancashire and became involved with the theatre.

1593 Appointed governor of the Isle of Man.

1594 Studied law at Lincoln's Inn. Older brother, Ferdinando Strange, fifth Earl of Derby died in very suspicious circumstances (almost certainly poisoned). On his brother's death, William became the sixth Earl of Derby.

1595 January 26 married Elizabeth de Vere, daughter of the Earl of Oxford.

1603   Became a member of the Privy Council.

1607   Made Lord Lieutenant of Lancashire and Cheshire.

1612   Kingship of Isle of Man restored to the Earl of Derby.

1617   Disbanded his company of players.

1642   September 29 died at the great age of 81 years.

Points against Derby's authorship claim

- There is no extant evidence of his writing — a suspicious absence given the volume of *Shakespeare* text and the fact that Derby lived such a long time.
- The author ceased writing around 1610-12, yet Derby lived until 1642. Whoever wrote *Shakespeare* was quite prolific, so why did Derby — if he was the true author — write nothing whatsoever in his last thirty years?
- If Thorpe's dedication means that the 'begetter' of *The Sonnets* — M^r. W.H. — is the author, then Derby (William Stanley) is ruled-out by his initials.
- If Derby was the author of *Richard II*, how did he escape punishment for writing seditious material?
- How did Derby keep his authorship completely secret? Why did nobody — friends, enemies or relatives — ever identify him as the author of *Shakespeare*?
- In view of the financial incentives, particularly in the modern era, why have none of Derby's descendants and relatives claimed that he was *Shakespeare's* author?
- Why would a wealthy, senior earl like Derby — albeit using a pseudonym — humbly seek the patronage of the twenty-year-old Earl of Southampton for the poem *Venus & Adonis*?
- Heminges and Condel indicated that the author of the plays was already dead in 1623. Derby didn't die until 1642.
- Why would Derby have allowed mistakes to occur in the first folio, when he was still alive in 1623 and able to make editorial corrections himself?
- Why would Derby write a disturbing play like *Macbeth* for James I?
- Why would a leading aristocrat have written 'though I (once gone) to all the world must die' in sonnet 81?
- Why would a well-known aristocrat, such as Derby, write in sonnet 81: 'the earth can offer me but a common grave'?
- If Derby was writing for 'the commoun players' — his own

play troupe, they must have known that he was *Shakespeare's* author since they performed his plays. Hence, the players represented a major 'security threat', yet there were never any rumours identifying Derby as the secret author of *Shakespeare*.

- Why would a wealthy aristocrat like Derby write in sonnet 37 line 9: 'So then I am not lame, poor, nor despised'?

Collectively, these points very strongly suggest that the Earl of Derby was not the secret author of *Shakespeare*.

Roger Manners — 5th Earl of Rutland (1576-1612)

The first to suggest that Roger Manners, 5th Earl of Rutland, had a part in the authorship of *Shakespeare* was Burkhard Herrman, writing under the pen name Peter Alvor in 1906. But Rutland's first true champion was a Belgian professor of French literature, Celestin Demblon. Nobody could accuse Demblon of idle speculation. In the course of his study and research he read some 5,000 books and travelled thousands of miles around Europe, in search of clues to the 'facts' contained in the plays — all the while attempting to follow in the footsteps of Roger Manners. Demblon published his first book on the subject, *Lord Rutland est Shakespeare*, in 1912.

However, a very serious problem with Rutland's authorship claim is his age. Born in 1576 he was at least ten years too young to be a credible author of *The Sonnets*. The poet implies that he is a mature man, whereas Rutland was only twenty-two when Francis Meres referred to the 'sugared' sonnets of *Shakespeare* in 1598. The timing is simply wrong. To have been the author, Rutland must have written at least a dozen of the plays (and many of the sonnets) *before* the ripe old age of twenty!

Apart from his astonishing precocity, how did such a youngster manage to keep his work totally secret from adults — especially in view of the fact that the plays were performed on the London stage and appeared in print? Moreover, Manners' forename was Roger — unlike the author of the sonnets whose name was 'Will' — and his initials were R. M. not W. H.. So, it seems that Roger Manners was not the 'onlie begetter' of *Shake-speares Sonnets*.

Finally, it's difficult to think of a convincing reason why those who knew 'the truth' about Rutland would have kept the secret long after his death, and why no descendant or relative has ever come forward with absolute proof of his authorship.

Brief chronology

1576	October 6: Born at Belvoir Castle, eldest son of John, fifth Earl of Rutland.
1587	Studied at Queen's College and Corpus Christi College, Cambridge for seven years.
1588	February 21 father died. Inherited estates in Midlands and North of England. Made a royal ward under Lord Burghley. Francis Bacon was guardian and mentor.
1595/96	Travelled extensively in Europe: Netherlands, France, Germany, Switzerland, Italy. Entered university of Padua.
1597	Sailed with Essex on the Azores expedition.
1598	Became a law student at Gray's Inn.
1599	Went to Ireland on Essex's campaign. Married the daughter of Sir Philip Sidney, Elizabeth.
1600	Travelled to the Netherlands with the Earl of Northumberland to assist the Dutch against the Spanish.
1601	Imprisoned in the Tower and threatened with execution for his part in the Essex rebellion. Fined £30,000 — an immense sum (many millions today)
1602	Allowed to return to Belvoir.
1603	King James visited Belvoir – remitted the fine and made Rutland Lord Lieutenant of Lincolnshire. Made Ambassador to Denmark. Visited Elsinore (Hamlet's castle).
1605	Entertained the King of Denmark.
1612	June 26 died Belvoir. Buried Bottesford, Leicestershire

Points against Rutland's authorship claim

- Too young to have written much of *Shakespeare's* earliest work — it seems that a mature man wrote *The Sonnets*. Rutland was only twenty by the time many of the sonnets were in circulation among the author's 'private friends'.
- How was someone so young able to get his plays performed on the London stage, without adults spilling the beans about his 'secret' authorship?
- Why did no contemporary ever claim that Rutland was the true author of *Shakespeare*?
- Rutland has the wrong forename to have been the author of *The Sonnets*.

- Initials R. M. are inconsistent with Thorpe's sonnet dedication to 'M^r. W.H.'.
- Thorpe would certainly not have referred to an earl as plain Master (Mr).
- There is no evidence that Rutland was capable of writing in the style of *Shakespeare*.
- Rutland was imprisoned for his involvement in the Essex rebellion; how did he manage to escape interrogation over 'his' authorship of *Richard II*?
- Why would the Earl of Rutland — a very wealthy aristocratic landowner — seek the patronage of the Earl of Southampton? (Dedication of *Venus & Adonis*).
- Rutland died at just thirty-six. It is difficult to believe that any author could have written the whole of *Shakespeare* by such an early age.
- How and why did Rutland acquire knowledge of Yorkish and Warwickshire dialect?
- Why would Rutland write an unsettling play like *Macbeth* for James I?
- In common with most members of the nobility, Rutland had rivals and enemies; yet none ever caused him embarrassment by revealing his secret authorship of plays and poems.
- How did Rutland — who was only five years old at the time — know details of the interrogation of Edmund Campion, alluded to in *Twelfth Night*?
- How did Rutland know details of the pageant at Kenilworth in 1575 — alluded to in *A Midsummer Nights Dream* — that took place before he was born?
- In view of the great financial incentives in the modern era, why have none of Rutland's descendants claimed that he was *Shakespeare's* secret author? (In fact, they deny it!)
- Why would a well-known aristocrat, like the Earl of Rutland, state in sonnet 81: 'Though I (once gone) to all the world must die' and 'the earth can offer me but a common grave'?

Collectively, these points very strongly suggest that the Earl of Rutland was not the secret author of *Shakespeare*.

Queen Elizabeth

A lover of drama and a poet, the most theatrical of monarchs was capable of astonishing eloquence — an attribute she probably inherited from her sharp-tongued, feisty mother Anne Boleyn. Indeed the queen's speeches, which she wrote herself, have an uncanny resemblance to speeches in the *Shakespeare* history plays. In particular, the oration that Elizabeth delivered to the troops assembled at Tilbury, before the Spanish Armada, has a very similar tenor to the address by Henry V, in the play of that name, prior to the battle of Agincourt. In fact, the queen worked through many drafts of her speeches, in order to achieve a complex, multi-layered structure that readers and listeners would have to think hard about — the more to admire and appreciate her eloquence and cleverness. So, it is the queen's distinctive literary style which has led some to the view that she secretly wrote *Shakespeare*.

Like her favourite dramatist, the Virgin Queen was a profound enigma; in fact they shared a number of characteristics including a love of music, a bawdy sense of humour and, at a more personal level, a keen sense of smell. Notwithstanding the curious similarities, however, there are compelling reasons why the queen's authorship claim cannot be taken seriously.

Points against Queen Elizabeth's authorship

- The queen could not have been the author of *Richard II* — a play that greatly angered her.
- Details in *Shake-speares Sonnets* — in particular those addressed to the 'Dark Lady' — must have been written by a man (which rules-out authorship by Mary (Sidney) Herbert, Countess of Pembroke — and any other female).
- *The Tempest* was inspired by events six years after Elizabeth's death.
- *Macbeth* was written in the aftermath of the gunpowder plot of 1605 — more than two years after the queen died.
- Thomas Thorpe states that a 'M^r. W.H.' was the 'onlie begetter' (the author) of *Shake-speares Sonnets*.
- Would Elizabeth have had the time and energy, in the autumn of her years, to write the entire *Shakespeare* canon as well as rule the country — with all the trials and tribulations *that* involved?
- The author of the sonnets (136) states his name is Will.
- Why would Elizabeth write in sonnet 125: 'Were it ought to me I bore the canopy'? The canopy carried above the queen when she was in procession.

- Why would the most famous queen in British history write: 'Though I (once gone) to all the world must die' and 'the earth can yield me but a common grave' (sonnet 81) and 'my name be buried where my body is' (sonnet 72).
- Why would the queen seek patronage for *Venus & Adonis* from the young Earl of Southampton?
- Many actors have claimed that the author understood acting with the insight of a professional. It's difficult to see how the queen, or any other female, could have gained such knowledge at a time when women were not allowed on stage.
- There are indications that *Shakespeare's* author worked on the Authorised Version of the Bible — a project that began after the queen's death.

Collectively, these points very strongly suggest that Queen Elizabeth was not the secret author of *Shakespeare*.

Group authorship

The difficulty of explaining the huge vocabulary, vast range of specialist knowledge and deep insight into the human psyche of *Shakespeare's* author has led some to conclude that no one person *could* have written the works. In despair at ever finding a convincing individual candidate they have taken the view that the entire canon was the result of collaboration — in other words, they propose group authorship.

The case for group authorship is not entirely lacking plausibility since it was certainly true that the insatiable demand of audiences for new plays meant collaboration among commercial playwrights was almost a necessity. However, in common with all the solutions examined so far, the claim that *Shakespeare* was a collaborative effort faces a number of serious objections.

Points against group authorship

- In an age of gossips, spies and informers, how did a group of writers manage to keep their literary activities totally secret?
- Why would the authors feel the need for deep secrecy about authorship? After all, they were writing for *public* performance.
- There is no evidence the *literati* ever guessed that a group of writers were penning plays and poems in secret — there were no rumours circulating to that effect at the time.
- It is almost impossible to believe that *Shake-speares Sonnets*, written in the first person throughout and

expressing very personal sentiments, were penned by a group of poets. Quite simply there were no groups of collaborating poets because, unlike plays, there was no commercial pressure to write vast quantities of verse. In any case, writing poetry is a solitary activity.

- Thomas Thorpe indicated in his 1609 sonnet dedication that the 'onlie begetter' of *Shake-speares Sonnets* was a M^r. W.H. — 'onlie' implying an individual poet. Invoking Occam's razor: if someone calling himself 'Shakespeare' wrote *Shake-speares Sonnets*, then the plays published under that title were almost certainly written by the same individual.
- Groups of collaborators — especially where there is rivalry — tend to disband quite quickly; yet 'the works' were (apparently) written over a twenty year period c 1590-1610.
- Keeping the existence of a clandestine group of writers permanently secret is far more difficult than concealing an individual writer, since the potential for leaks is so much greater.
- Sir Walter Raleigh's so-called 'School of Night' — a group of intellectuals that discussed dangerous heretical matters such as atheism and the occult — has become public knowledge, yet its existence was supposed to be top secret. It is difficult to believe that a group of writers — simply penning plays for public entertainment — would have remained completely hidden, whereas the highly secretive 'School of Night' did not.
- Like all contemporaries who wrote about 'Shakespeare', Heminges and Condell in their prefatory letter to the 1623 Folio referred to the author as an individual.

Collectively, these points very strongly suggest that the works of *Shakespeare* were not the result of collaboration.

— 6 —

The Onlie Begetter

'Shakespeare' – suspiciously above suspicion

None of the challengers considered so far presents a satisfactory alternative to the Stratford man. It is therefore necessary to seek a fresh candidate, a new contender for Shakespeare's 'crown' – an individual whose candidature must resolve one of the most perplexing mysteries at the heart of the authorship controversy: the reason for the queen's *total* inaction regarding the author of the notorious play *Richard II*.

The play's notoriety arises from a scene in which King Richard is shown being deposed, an enactment on the public stage which was regarded as sedition. The unique significance of the play is two-fold: firstly, due to the very dangerous political content, it 'should' have brought the author into direct conflict with the queen – and yet it didn't. Secondly, *Richard II* was specially performed the day before the Essex rebellion, with the aim of engendering a rebellious atmosphere in the capital. No other play, shown on the English stage, has ever been expressly used for such a purpose. Unsurprisingly, *Richard II* vexed Elizabeth greatly; her anger surfaced on two occasions:

- In summer 1601, a few months after the failed rebellion, the queen happened to be looking through archives relating to *Richard II* at the Tower of London, when she suddenly exclaimed to the Keeper: 'I am Richard II, know ye not that?' The archivist replied: 'Such a wicked imagination was determined and attempted by a most unkind gent, the most adorned creature that your majesty ever made' (referring to Essex). The queen responded: 'He that will forget God will also forget his benefactors; this tragedy was played forty times in the open streets and houses'. Elizabeth knew that the deposition of *Richard II* alluded to her, and that the play had been performed with the specific intention of inciting rebellion amongst the citizens of London.

- Two years earlier the queen had Dr John Hayward sent to the Tower (for life) simply for referring to the deposition scene in a book he dedicated to Essex.

To write seditious material (incitement to rebellion) was the most serious offence an author could commit – illegal even now. In an age of severe punishment, any dramatist guilty of such a crime would almost certainly have been executed. In view of the queen's treatment of Dr Hayward, and the fact that there was an inquiry into the play in the aftermath of the rebellion, it is *exceedingly* strange that she paid no attention whatsoever to the alleged author of the offending work. The man from Stratford was not even questioned, though two actors were. Elizabeth's total disregard of 'Shakespeare' is astonishing – indeed, it strongly suggests that there was something about the playwright which meant that she either could not, or would not, bring him to account. It seems that the author was protected not only from the law but, incredibly, that he was also shielded from the wrath of the angry monarch. The key issue is: Why would a commoner, like Shakspere, have been shown unprecedented leniency in circumstances as serious as rebellion?

The problem is equally acute for the other authorial claimants: Oxford, Bacon, Marlowe, Derby, Rutland and group authorship. It is very difficult to believe that the authorities would have deliberately disregarded, or accidentally overlooked, the author of a play that sorely angered the queen herself. Even if the dramatist was a leading aristocrat, he would certainly have been interrogated and imprisoned; after all, Elizabeth's prime favourite, the Earl of Essex, was beheaded for his part in the rebellion – yet nobody was ever questioned or punished for writing *Richard II*. It appears that whoever penned the play was either very stupid – which is *highly* unlikely – or else they knew that they could get away with it. William Shakspere could not have known that he would avoid punishment, especially for a work that was clearly seditious. The question is: who *could* have been certain beforehand that he would escape punishment for writing such inflammatory material?

A general point against any successful, well-known person writing *Shakespeare* is that talented people, no matter how 'nice' they might be, *always* have enemies. It is very difficult to believe that jealous individuals, disposed to malice and spite, would have refrained from getting the Stratford man in trouble with the authorities – yet nobody ever did. That is very strange, especially in view of the fact that the author made himself a target for anyone who wanted to snipe; indeed, he gave them plenty of ammunition – *Richard II* is just one of several very controversial plays in the canon. It is extraordinary that, unlike any other well-known person of the age, the Stratford man seems to have had no spiteful enemies.

It is remarkable that no contemporary evidence exists (not even rumour) that Bacon, Marlowe, Oxford, Derby, Rutland, a group of collaborating writers or anyone else was the secret author of *Shakespeare*. That simple fact raises a crucial question. If William Shakspere did not write the works, what kept the secret about the real author permanently secure in an age and in a profession, renowned for gossips and rumourmongers? In other words, if the Stratford man was an impostor, what was so important about the real playwright that necessitated a conspiracy of total silence, involving many of the *literati* and even people at court?

My name be buried where my body is

As indicated in Chapter 1, the name and identity of the mysterious M^r. W.H. – 'onlie begetter' of *Shake-speares sonnets* – is pivotal to the authorship question; hence, the case for the new candidate begins with the sonnets and Thomas Thorpe's prefatory dedication.

Intended as private poetry, the sonnets were almost certainly published without the author's consent and, although they do not explicitly identify the man who wrote them, except to say that his name is 'Will', they appear to contain important hints about his social status, clues that are oddly contradictory.

The sequence comprises 154 sonnets: numbers one to seventeen attempt to persuade a reluctant aristocratic 'youth' to marry; the next 109 seem to tell a vague story that links the poet and youth, while sonnets 127 to 152 concern a so-called 'Dark Lady' with whom both the poet and youth have a sexual relationship. Thematically, the last two sonnets do not belong in the sequence.

It is not known how Thomas Thorpe came to be in possession of the poetry although it is unlikely he had authorial permission to publish because in 1598, Francis Meres stated that the 'sugared sonnets' of 'Shakespeare' were meant for circulation amongst the author's private friends.

As explained in Chapter 1, the phrase 'onlie begetter' almost certainly refers to the author M^r. W.H.. With regard to his social status, it is clear that W.H. cannot have been an *acknowledged* member of the nobility, since no acknowledged aristocrat would be addressed as plain 'Master' (Mr). And yet, paradoxically, the very personal tone of the sonnets – written in a courtly style, with no trace of Warwickshire vernacular – suggests that the author was someone *of* noble birth; an inference consistent with the allusions of Thomas Edwards who implied that the author of *Shakespeare* was a *concealed* aristocrat.

More has been written about the sonnets than anything in the canon apart from *Hamlet*. Like the play, the sonnets are seemingly of an autobiographical nature, they too are enigmatic. It is unclear precisely when they

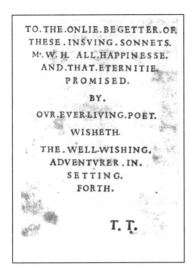

TO.THE.ONLIE.BEGETTER.OF.
THESE.INSVING.SONNETS.
Mʳ. W. H. ALL.HAPPINESSE.
AND.THAT.ETERNITIE.
PROMISED.

BY.

OVR.EVER-LIVING.POET.

WISHETH.

THE.WELL-WISHING.
ADVENTVRER.IN.
SETTING.
FORTH.

T. T.

**Thomas Thorpe's sonnet
dedication of
May 20th, 1609**

*It should be noted that: i) Thorpe did
not dedicate the sonnets to Mʳ. W.H.. ii)
Mʳ. W.H. – the 'onlie' begetter – did not
inspire the sonnets, they were inspired
by more than one person iii) Mʳ. W.H. is
not an acknowledged aristocrat iv) 'our
ever-living poet' (dead by 1609) was
not the author of the sonnets – since
that was the onlie begetter Mʳ. W.H.,
who was alive when the dedication was
written.*

were written, though most were probably composed during the late 1580s and throughout the 1590s, when sonnet-style poetry went through a brief but intense phase of popularity, especially at court. The only comparable sonnet sequence is one by Philip Sidney – *Astrophil and Stella* – which was inspired by Sidney's platonic relationship with Penelope Devereux, sister of the Earl of Essex. By contrast *Shake-speares Sonnets* mainly address a 'Fair Youth'.

In fact, the sonnets' subject matter prompts some intriguing questions. To what extent are they based on the poet's private life? Are they purely fictional, are they a sort of confessional 'diary' or are they an inseparable fusion of reality and imagination? Do they contain hidden messages? Have they been made deliberately 'enigmatic', to prevent the 'uninitiated' from uncovering their secret meaning? Even after decades of research there is no consensus about the answers.

Moreover, the sonnets present Stratfordian orthodoxy with a conundrum. If they are purely fictional the question is: having spent a great deal of time and effort writing the poetry, why didn't the money-driven Stratford businessman sell it? The most likely answer is because the sonnets concern real people. That would explain Francis Meres' statement that they were for circulation among the author's 'private friends'. But if the sonnets *are* related to real people, how did a yokel from Stratford get away with writing verse that contained very personal advice to a young nobleman, in an age when etiquette strictly forbade such familiarity?

Shakespeare's author never presents an unambiguous, authorial point of view in his plays – he never *seems* to give himself away. The same authorial reticence is also evident in the sonnets which, although apparently of a very personal nature, yield almost nothing that could be used to identify the Poet, 'Fair Youth' or 'Dark Lady'. The sonnets seem to express very private feelings and yet they are strangely anonymous. It is odd, for example, that although certain lines promise the youth eternal fame, they never actually name him! It is also rather strange that the poet wrote, in sonnet 18: 'So long as men have breath and eyes can see / so long lives this and this gives life to thee', and yet the sonnets were (apparently) meant for circulation only amongst the poet's private friends; presumably, the author thought the poetry would be published after his death.

Just as the plays lack an authorial voice, so too the poet of the sonnets is mysteriously elusive. There appears to have been an overwhelming desire on the part of the author to hide himself completely – yet it seems very odd that a player on the *public* stage, like William Shakspere, would feel such a powerful need for anonymity in all of his writings. What was it that made the Stratford man – unlike any other professional writer of the age – seek unprecedented secrecy about the *links* between himself and his literary work?

The sonnets seem to be the poet's 'personal voice', yet they do not give the impression of someone whose natural speech pattern carried any hint of the Warwickshire brogue that would be expected of the Stratford man. The 'voice' seems to be that of an urbane courtier – as if to the manor born. Indeed, with the exception of some obscene and defamatory references to the 'Dark Lady', the language is refined – a quality mirrored in the plays; all the *Shakespeare* comedies, for example, are written in a courtly style. Furthermore, certain lines in the sonnets – which appear to hint at the author's social status – have special significance in the context of the authorship controversy; some of them seem to contradict each other and, collectively, imply that the poet was neither a commoner nor an *acknowledged* aristocrat!

Consider the following:
sonnet 10, line 13: 'Make thee another self for love of me,'
In view of the rigid social structure of Elizabethan England, this highly personal request 'for love of me' supposedly by a commoner to a young aristocrat, constitutes a serious breach of formal protocol. Indeed, the tone of exceptional familiarity that runs throughout the sonnet sequence, suggests the poet was not a commoner but a member *of* the nobility.

sonnet 37, line 3: 'So I, made lame by Fortune's dearest spite,'
and **line 9:** 'So then I am not lame, poor, nor despised,'
Indications that the poet has been injured by a misfortune – an accident perhaps? There is no evidence that William Shakspere was lame.

sonnet 72, line 11: 'My name be buried where my body is,'

Not the sort of thing an *acknowledged* member of the nobility would ever write; the name of any acknowledged aristocrat would automatically appear in the historical archive – it would certainly not be buried with his body.

sonnet 81, line 6:

'Though I (once gone) to all the world must die'

Why did the poet think that his eradication from the historical record was *mandatory*? (Must Die) It is very difficult to see how a definitive assertion such as this could have come from the pen of Marlowe, Bacon, Oxford, Derby, Rutland or even Shakspere. Thanks to assiduous Elizabethan record keeping, a number of obscure facts about William Shakspere's family are known – the existence of the three sisters who died in childhood, for example. In view of the preservation of such details, why would Shakspere have thought that he, a well-known poet, playwright and actor, *must* be lost to posterity?

sonnet 81, line 7: 'The earth can yield me but a common grave,'

An assertion inconsistent with either an acknowledged member of the nobility or, indeed, any well-known personage.

sonnet 89, line 3: 'Speak of my lameness, and I straight will halt,'

Another explicit reference to the poet's lameness.

sonnet 111, lines 1, 2 3 & 4: 'O for my sake do you with Fortune chide, / The guilty goddess of my harmful deeds, / That did not better for my life provide / Than public means which public manners breeds.'

The last line: 'Than public means which public manners breeds.' seems inconsistent with a man like William Shakspere, who grew up with 'public manners' while living among raw, uncouth peasants at Stratford. However, the phrase *would* make sense for an author *of* the nobility, who had had 'public manners' foisted onto him as an actor in the public domain.

Taking stock of what the above lines imply about the poet's social status, sonnets: 10, 111 and the general attitude of the poet to the youth, suggest that the author is *not* a commoner, whereas sonnets: 37, 72 and 81 indicate that he is not an aristocrat either!

sonnet 136, line 14: 'And then thou lovest me for my name is Will.'

The poet states that his name is 'Will' – which appears to exclude the authorship of Francis Bacon, Edward de Vere, Christopher Marlowe, Roger Manners and, of course, anyone else not called William.

The 'Dark Lady' sonnets, extracts of which follow, are very uncomplimentary about the poet's mistress:

sonnet 137, line 6: '...the bay where all men ride,' and **line 10:** '...the wide world's common place'

Highly defamatory allusions, certainly not the sort of thing any woman would want to see written about her in print!

sonnet 142, line 8: 'Robbed others' beds' revenues of their rents.'

Which implies that the 'Dark Lady' 'slept around'.

> Two loves I have, of comfort and despair,
> Which like two spirits do suggest me still:
> The better angel is a man right fair;
> The worser spirit a woman coloured ill
> To win me soon to hell my female evil
> Tempteth my better angel from my side,
> And would corrupt my saint to be a devil,
> Wooing his purity with her foul pride.
> And whether that my angel be turned fiend
> Suspect I may, yet not directly tell,
> But being both from me, both to each friend,
> I guess one angel in another's hell.
> Yet this shall I ne'er know, but live in doubt,
> Till my bad angel fire my good one out

This sonnet (144) contains hints that both the poet and youth had sexual relations with the 'Dark Lady'.

Sonnet 144 makes explicit the sexual nature of the relationships between the Poet, 'Fair Youth' and 'Dark Lady' – to the extent that the poet even suggests the 'Dark Lady' might have infected the youth with venereal infection – to 'fire... out' (line 14) was to give someone a sexually transmitted disease (in those less enlightened times, it was thought women gave men VD, never visa-versa) and, in line 8, the expression '... foule pride' implies that the 'Dark Lady' was ugly.

There is a powerful sense that the poet is alluding to a real woman as opposed to the romantically idealised females that usually formed the subject of such poetry – ladies who would definitely not be ugly and who would certainly not have VD! However, it is typical of *Shakespeare's* author to 'tell it like it is'; so, against the background of these highly defamatory but apparently frank details, it's difficult to think of the 'Dark Lady' as a purely fictional character.

The foregoing analysis strongly suggests that real people, closely associated with the poet, inspired *Shake-speares Sonnets* – and that is why they were intended only for private circulation. More importantly, it appears that the poet was neither an acknowledged member of the nobility nor a commoner, but that his social status lay betwixt the two: in other words, the poet was a man *of* the aristocracy who was unacknowledged (most probably) because he was illegitimate.

Mandatory oblivion

The most remarkable feature of the sonnets is that the poet implies that he *himself* is a deep secret and that the secrecy has been imposed on him! It seems that once dead, *all* trace of his existence *must* vanish – even his name will be buried with his body. However, it is very hard to see why William Shakspere, a man at the centre of the London theatre world: a playwright, play-manager and actor – a writer who Ben Jonson called the 'soul of the age', 'wonder of our stage' and 'starre of poets' – would write that, after death, all trace of his existence *must* be lost to posterity!

The most likely explanation for the *mandatory* secrecy enshrouding the author of the sonnets is that a cover-up was instigated by those with vested interests at the very zenith of Elizabethan society – only they had the power to ensure that the greatest secrets would remain permanently secure in an age when secrets, generally, were very difficult to keep. Underpinning the thesis in this book is the claim that a conspiracy of silence protected the highest in the land from deeply embarrassing and potentially very dangerous revelations.

The situation was not unlike the case of Henry Fitzroy, the illegitimate son of Henry VIII and his mistress Bessie Blount. The king did not disown the boy but, when Fitzroy died in his teens, there was a concerted effort to remove all trace of his existence – he was even buried in secret at night. It seems that the author of the sonnets is aware that something similar will happen to him, viz: sonnet 81: 'Though I (once gone) to all the world must die' and sonnet 72: 'My name be buried where my body is.'

The carefully constructed 'Shakespeare ruse', known only to a few people at court and in the literary world, hid a very special secret whose disclosure four centuries ago would almost certainly have changed the course of history. That is why the truth about 'Shakespeare' was meant to remain hidden forever, why even the angry queen could not punish the man who wrote the notorious play *Richard II*, and why the dark veil of secrecy enfolding the real author has, until now, proven so difficult to penetrate.

Indeed, the man who actually wrote 'the works' did not *officially* exist; he was forced to spend his entire adult life hiding behind various false names and identities. The profound secrecy surrounding the author means that no documents, explicitly referring to him, will ever be found in the public records – so, the usual methods of historical research play only a small part in establishing his biography.

Due to the unique circumstances it has been necessary to investigate the authorship issue using unorthodox techniques. By adopting a completely fresh perspective and employing radically new thinking, many astonishing discoveries have been made. Through breaking the 'Shakespeare Codes' – special anagrams hidden in Shakespeare-related texts by the author and at least thirty of his contemporaries – it is now possible to answer not only previously unanswerable questions, but to answer many new questions previously unasked. As a result the biographical portrait of the real author that has emerged from the analysis, bears no resemblance whatsoever to the image of the traditional author – the yokel from Stratford-upon-Avon.

Appearance and Reality

In the beginning...

At the time of Elizabeth's coronation in 1559, England was close to bank-ruptcy; in fact, the coinage was so badly debased that many foreign traders no longer accepted it. Rags to rags in just two generations, that's how it might have seemed when the Protestant Elizabeth Tudor – questionably legitimate, unwanted daughter of Henry VIII and his despised second wife Anne Boleyn – was crowned Queen of England and Ireland at Westminster Abbey on Saturday, January 15th (a date determined as particularly auspicious by the royal astrologer, Dr John Dee).

Elizabeth was proud to be thought of as Henry VIII's daughter, though in stark contrast she never mentioned her mother, Anne Boleyn. The silence was perhaps understandable since Anne was reviled and hated by the people – they even called her the 'whore-witch'. It was she, they said, who had cast a spell over Henry to lure him into an unholy marriage; as the offspring of such an accursed union, the omens for Elizabeth were not the best. But those who thronged the snowy streets of London that wintry afternoon, and witnessed the coronation procession, saw a twenty-five year-old princess with golden-reddish hair, long and flowing as befitted a virgin, dressed in a purple velvet gown – chosen to contrast with her colouring. And so it was that the tyrant king's brilliant daughter got off to a rapturous start in the most important of all relationships – with the people.

Flame-haired Elizabeth was the embodiment of a fairy-tale princess. Like a solitary guiding star, shining in an ominously dark firmament, she appeared as a beacon of hope in time of need and gave cause for many to rejoice. Indeed, it was Elizabeth's proudest claim, at the end of her life, that she had reigned 'with the loves of her people' and her proudest boast that she was 'mere' (pure) English. But what the crowds saw on that chill winter's day was only the first glimmer of an historic phenomenon that was to reach incandescent brilliance, many years later, in 'the cult' of the Virgin Queen; an astute bit of propaganda which presented the mature Elizabeth as a woman 'mystically wedded' to the state. However, marriage to the state would do nothing to resolve the great perennial question of her reign: who would follow the last Tudor monarch on the English throne?

In an overwhelmingly male-dominated world the married Elizabeth would inevitably have found herself in her husband's shadow, a position that would have seriously weakened her power and influence – a role that the autocratic daughter of Henry VIII would have found intolerable. Quite simply, Elizabeth had no intention of sharing power with anyone – still less of playing second fiddle. She said as much herself. In the queen's private thoughts marriage was almost certainly never a realistic option except, perhaps, in the earliest years of her reign when all she could think about was the dashing young Robert Dudley, Master of the Horse.

The Virgin Queen – a woman in denial

Serendipitous discovery – Left, a lost portrait of Elizabeth I?
Right is the Armada portrait.

As indicated at the start of Chapter 1, the inspiration for this book came from the chance discovery of an Old Master portrait in 2001. The artist is unknown (possibly Gheeraedts II) but the date – judging by the ruff design – seems to be around the mid 1590s. Various elements in the picture, including the large number of pearls, dark reddish wig, colour scheme and similarity of the face to acknowledged images of the queen – e.g. the 'Armada' portrait – strongly suggest that this is a 'lost' portrait of Elizabeth I. However, the thesis in this book does not depend on whether the image really depicts the Virgin Queen, the portrait simply acted as the stimulus for a new line of research into the authorship controversy.

Several hundred portraits of Elizabeth I were made during her lifetime (1533-1603) of which about 135 are known to have survived. Many were originally displayed in manor houses around the country, so that the locals could go and see a recognisable if highly contrived image of their sovereign. Although so many portraits of Elizabeth still exist, it's difficult to be sure what she really looked like – partly because there were few good portrait painters in England at the time, partly because her appearance changed and partly because there was a deliberate attempt, in the 1590s especially, to make the queen look much younger than her true appearance (the so-called mask of youth). In addition, Elizabeth did not like sitting for portraits, so a number of formulaic images were used to represent her. As a result none of the portraits can be regarded as a definitive likeness.

Masking reality

Behind the elaborate appearance of the iconic portraits, however, and beneath the time-hardened inch-thick mask of the 'Virgin Queen', reality was rather different. The myth of virginity was probably as much an emotional shield for Elizabeth herself – a woman in denial – as it was an attempt to try and deceive her more gullible subjects about the true state of her moral and physical purity.

For the queen personally, the charade of virginity and the mask of eternal youth probably served an equivalent purpose – as a psychological defence against the corrosive effects of time. The impossibly vain monarch was afraid of growing old, so she kept a rack of false faces hanging in her mental wardrobe, each one an attempt to deny, or at least conceal, reality. The queen had a fanciful name for each mask – Gloriana, Belphoebe, Diana, Cynthia, The Sun, Pallas Athena – and expected to be treated as a sort of living goddess by her sycophantic courtiers. Elizabeth knew that in public life it isn't what you really are that matters, only what people think you are – and in that sense, the mask is everything. So the mightily proud Tudor monarch hid behind an array of elaborate guises in public whilst keeping the private reality a closely guarded secret.

But as the queen aged the gap between public appearance and private reality grew steadily wider and she became a grotesque parody of her younger self. The image of Old Gloriana with ill-fitting red wigs, blackened teeth and ghastly-white makeup is eccentric, disturbing and sad. However, it says a lot about the most remarkable sovereign in British history that she insisted fawning courtiers pay the most exaggerated compliments to a beauty that was, as she eventually admitted herself, a myth.

The inscrutable queen

Elizabeth Tudor shared with her parents a very volatile temper and so her personal motto which was also her mother's – *semper eadem* (always the same) – was somewhat ironic. The queen was indeed always the same, predictably unpredictable. Like the fickle English weather she could be glorious sunshine one minute, thunder and lightening the next. In fact, her behaviour and language was, on occasion, very far from lady-like; the royal temper tantrums could be so fierce that it was not unknown for the queen to faint in an apoplectic fit! Once, she boxed the ears of her special favourite Robert Devereux, the Earl of Essex, for insolently turning his back on her and, in another paroxysm of anger, broke the finger of one young lady of the court who had the temerity to marry without first seeking royal permission.

Although barred from becoming sovereign by Act of Parliament, in 1536, (later rescinded) and by the will of her half-brother Edward VI, Elizabeth defied all the odds and went on to hold ultimate power for nearly forty-five years. It would have been a staggering achievement for anyone, but it was all the more remarkable for a 'weak and feeble woman' who had never been expected to rule. But then Elizabeth learned at an early age, in the school of hard knocks, that one must do or say whatever is necessary to ensure personal survival – after all, her father had had her mother's head cut off – and she realised that nobody, not even her closest advisers, warranted absolute trust. As a result, Elizabeth became an accomplished actress and dissembler – a necessity, perhaps, in the face of the deceptiveness she found in many of those with whom she had dealings. So, the Virgin Queen was capable of telling the 'Big Lie', if it meant it would save her face, save her money or save her skin.

Although Elizabeth was tough, the woman concealed behind the inscrutable royal façade, felt the loneliness and vulnerability of life at the very pinnacle of a world, where ultimate power usually lay in the hands of men. The feeling was probably amplified by the difficulty many men had in accepting a female, as the most powerful person in the land. Part of her strategy for dealing with this problem was to assume the role of honorary man – she often referred to herself as a 'prince' – and, at times, even cultivated a sort of androgynous image.

The fiery Tudor Queen was the most intellectually gifted of monarchs; it goes without saying she was rather cleverer than most of her courtiers and ministers. An outstanding linguist – she spoke eight foreign languages; a polymath – said to know more than a professor at the university; a woman with an uncanny insight into human nature and a sovereign who possessed an especially keen instinct for survival. All capabilities that were to prove vital during the many trials and tribulations of her long reign. However, Elizabeth did not face the problems entirely alone; through many of the most difficult times there was one man who provided the kind of personal support that only someone on the closest terms could give...

Robert Dudley (1532? – 1588) Earl of Leicester

Born at Sheen, near Richmond, Robert Dudley was the fifth son of John Dudley and Jane Guildford. He was tall, athletic and handsome – unsurprisingly, a man with a reputation for the ladies. As the portrait suggests, he had a rather prominent nose that gave his face a kind of hawk-like appearance although jealous enemies, prompted by his dark good-looks, called him 'The Gypsy'. Without doubt Robert was the star of his family and the most dashing courtier of his generation. He was also, without question, the greatest love of Elizabeth I and for much of his adult life, even when married, Robert Dudley – Earl of Leicester as he was titled in 1565 – was the queen's unofficial consort.

A graduate of Trinity College Cambridge and a reforming Chancellor of Oxford University, Dudley held academics and the world of learning in high esteem. He made his respect for intellectual and cultural achievement manifest as the most generous patron of scholars and the *literati*. By 1560 he had established a troupe of touring players – later called 'Lord Leicester's Men' – the first itinerant play troupe in England.

Robert Dudley, Earl of Leicester, greatest love of Elizabeth I – as she admitted herself.

But it was Robert Dudley's superb horsemanship and expert knowledge of horses, that first brought him into regular contact with the queen. Soon after her accession in November 1558, Elizabeth made him 'Master of the Horse' – a relatively minor role in the scheme of things, but a crafty appointment because it meant she had a legitimate reason to see 'sweet Robin' every day. So, during the early years of the reign especially, the two of them were hardly ever apart and there was much gossip among the ladies at court, about when their mistress would marry Lord Robert.

However, Robert Dudley was arrogant, conceited and almost universally hated by rivals. The hatred was born of envy, as the queen bestowed upon 'The Gypsy' her special favours – above all, contact with the royal person *in private*. Regarded with deep suspicion by almost everyone, Dudley was viewed as a man of dark Machiavellian character: highly ambitious, calculating and manipulative. According to the not entirely unbiased opinion of contemporaries, he was a ruthless schemer who would stop at nothing to advance his cause even if it meant killing in order to do so.

Indeed, there were many who believed that Robert Dudley was a murderer and that in 1560 he had killed his first wife, Amy Robsart, to clear the way for marriage to the queen; but at the inquest into Amy's death Dudley was exonerated of any involvement. However, in sensational cases some of the mud sticks and, as a result, the prospect of marriage to the queen suffered a very serious setback. It is worthy of note, in that regard, that the only person to benefit from the tragedy of Amy's untimely demise was the man who, out of fear for his own position, was the most strenuous in opposing marriage between Elizabeth and her special favourite. That man was Sir William Cecil – Lord Burghley – the queen's omni-competent chief minister for thirty-seven years and the mastermind of much government policy.

William Cecil (1520-1598) was created Lord Burghley in 1571. Like many who found themselves in high office under the Tudors, Cecil was not of the aristocracy. Both Henry VIII and Elizabeth I tended to bestow power by reason of ability and merit rather than accident of birth. A workaholic, combining the roles of Prime Minister and

William Cecil (1520-1598), Chief Minister for thirty-seven years.

Foreign Secretary, he regularly put in a sixteen hour day. Probably satirised in *Hamlet* as the sententious old courtier Polonius, his recreation included riding round the gardens of his extensive estates on a mule. Troubled with gout for many years – it was thought through eating too much of his favourite food, cow brains – he eventually lost the use of his legs and had to be carried everywhere.

Two great houses

The Dudley family could not boast an ancient pedigree, they were not 'true' aristocrats; in fact, the original name was Sutton – 'Dudley' was taken from a castle in Staffordshire. The family first came to prominence during the reign of Henry VII (1485-1509) – founder of the Tudor dynasty – when Edmund Dudley (1462-1510), Robert's grandfather, was appointed finance minister. As the king's ruthless collector of taxes, Edmund was very unpopular with the people and, after the death of Henry VII, he was made a political scapegoat by the new king, Henry VIII (1509-1547), and executed as a traitor.

Phoenix-like, the Dudley family began to rise from the ashes of ignominy with the leading Protestant John Dudley (1504-1553), son of Edmund and father of Robert. In 1542 John was made Lord High Admiral and, in that capacity, he helped to build the first English navy. After Henry VIII's death in 1547, during the reign of the Protestant boy-king Edward VI, John Dudley effectively ruled the country. But like his father before him, he too was executed as a traitor – by the Catholic queen, Mary Tudor – for a leading role in an attempt to install on the throne his relative, the teenage Protestant Lady Jane Gray, following the early death of Edward VI.

Although the Dudleys were not true blue-bloods, Robert had always been close to the innermost royal circle. As a boy he was classmate and playmate of Prince Edward (later Edward VI) Elizabeth's half-brother and the legitimate son of Henry VIII by Jane Seymour. In 1554, a young man in his early twenties, Robert Dudley found himself, on charges of treason, imprisoned in the Tower of London at the same time that the Princess Elizabeth was being held there. The Catholic queen – Mary Tudor, 'Bloody Mary' as she became known – incarcerated both of them because of their very strong Protestant associations. It was possibly the shared experience of uncertainty and terror in the Tower – a genuine fear for their lives – that helped bring the two of them together. Indeed, it is noteworthy that after his release on the intervention of Mary's husband, Philip II of Spain, Dudley sold some of his properties and gave the proceeds to Elizabeth when she found herself in financial difficulties. It seems she never forgot his kindness and generosity, though the cynical would probably have argued that the 'Gypsy' was, as usual, motivated by self-interest.

Against the background of their very closely entwined family and personal histories it is unsurprising that many of the queen's subjects believed not only that Elizabeth Tudor and Robert Dudley were lovers, but that she had a secret child by him. The fundamental assertion underpinning this book goes one step further by claiming that the child – a boy – eventually became famous as William Shakespeare, the pseudonym under which he wrote.

That the Tudors and the Dudleys – the most talented and influential dynasties in sixteenth century England – should produce one of the greatest Englishmen is hardly surprising. Moreover, the claim that Elizabeth I had a secret child is very strongly supported, not only by much circumstantial evidence, but also by the recent discovery of a wealth of hidden information – presented here for the first time.

− 8 −

Fire in
the Blood

A right royal secret

Racing on horseback at breakneck speed through the open countryside, well away from the spies and sycophants at court, Elizabeth got some respite from the constant clamour for her attention. More to the point, with the freedom that the great outdoors engendered, there was a wonderful opportunity for her personal relationship with Lord Robert to fully develop. Of course, having made Dudley Master of the Horse, the circumstances were entirely a creation of the queen herself.

Elizabeth soon found a plausible excuse – the dampness of his rooms – for Dudley to move into apartments adjacent to hers and a rumour began to circulate that they had been secretly married, in June 1562, at Baynards Castle, the London residence of the Earl of Pembroke. In fact, throughout the 1560s many commoners were brought before magistrates claiming that Dudley and the queen had a sexual relationship; one witness asserting, in open court, that Robert Dudley had 'swived' her. Even foreign emissaries, during the early years of the reign, noted Elizabeth's outrageously familiar behaviour with the Master of the Horse – openly flaunting her affection by fondling Dudley in full view of the dignitaries, much to their surprise and embarrassment. It was plain to all that the two of them were far more than just good friends; indeed, they seemed to be living as man and wife.

In fact, when Dudley died in 1588, Elizabeth locked herself in a room for several days – the door had to be broken down – and when the queen died in 1603, a pearl encrusted casket was found in a drawer next to her bed, inside was a letter written to her by Dudley shortly before his death. On the outside the queen had inscribed 'His last letter'. Two indications of just how important the relationship had been.

There is no question that, at the beginning of her reign especially, Elizabeth was utterly infatuated with 'sweet Robin' – her 'eyes' as she called him, a pet name that hints at the very special relationship Dudley enjoyed with the sovereign. In fact, she said herself there was only one man in

The garden at Hampton Court, originally designed by Henry VIII. It was possibly here, in October 1562, that the queen went for a stroll just before being taken seriously ill.

England she would marry – and that was Lord Robert. But, so early in the reign (1560-1563) the queen's position was insecure, she certainly could not afford to get embroiled in personal scandal. Her enemies – such as the Catholic Mary, Queen of Scots and Philip II of Spain, former husband of Mary Tudor – would have made unfavourable comparisons with Elizabeth's hated parent, the whore-witch Anne Boleyn, mother of English Protestantism.

Moreover, after the ruinous reigns of her profligate father, zealous Protestant half-brother and intolerant Catholic half-sister, the Tudor dynasty could ill-afford further turmoil. Stability was a key to national security. So, right from the start, the pressure on the queen to find a suitable husband and have children was intense. Unfortunately for Elizabeth, as far as those with political influence were concerned, the 'wife-murdering' Gypsy simply would not do. But then, like her reviled mother, Elizabeth had a mind very much of her own – nobody was going to tell the queen how to conduct her private life.

On the morning of Sunday 10th of October 1562, at Hampton Court Palace, there was growing concern among the ladies of the bedchamber that things were a few days overdue. They knew their royal mistress was pregnant and that she was, perhaps, a little beyond full term – so, a hot bath and brisk walk were recommended to hasten nature's course. Having duly taken the advice, the queen returned from the autumnal palace gardens unwell. During the next few hours an event took place that was meant to remain hidden forever – a shameful Royal secret that would have cost a man's life to reveal – Elizabeth Tudor, unmarried Queen of England, gave birth to a son.

The sickness that almost killed the queen was not, as the history books claim, due to an attack of smallpox. The progress of the illness, its symptoms and after-effects – or notable lack of them – were totally inconsistent with smallpox. Indeed, Elizabeth insisted herself, whilst she remained lucid and in possession of her faculties, that she did not have 'poxe' – an assertion with which her ladies-in-waiting agreed. What really ailed the queen, as both she and they knew, was an infection contracted during childbirth – a common cause of death amongst child-bearing women in those days.

On the following Wednesday, with the fever worsening, Lord Hunsdon (Henry Carey, the queen's cousin) decided to call in Dr Burcot, his German physician. Burcot knew there was an outbreak of smallpox at the time and, seeing Elizabeth's condition, assumed that she had contracted the infection. It is certain, however, that Burcot had not been told the crucial fact about his royal patient – that a few days earlier she had given birth. Of course, even if he had been astute enough to guess what was wrong, Burcot could not possibly have voiced the truth.

The doctor had been taken to the queen not simply to offer a diagnosis, but to perform the much more difficult and onerous task of restoring her to full health, as quickly as possible. However, Elizabeth knew for certain that the smallpox diagnosis was wrong and, as a result, became very angry with the German physician – perhaps reasoning that since his diagnosis was incorrect, he was bound to provide inappropriate treatment. Burcot probably never asked himself *why* the queen was so sure he was mistaken; after all, she was seriously ill and could not have been at her most assertive and combative – yet Elizabeth not only contradicted the doctor's judgement but roundly berated him as well! Naturally, Burcot was deeply insulted and, like many an unfortunate minion at court, felt the pride-wounding sting of the queen's sharp tongue.

In those days, the standard (Arabian) treatment for smallpox was to place the infected person in front of a large fire, wrapped in a red sheet with red drapes across the windows. Despite having taken these measures, the queen's fever worsened and on the Saturday, she fell into a coma – it seemed she was close to death. Burcot was sent for again but, with Elizabeth's harsh words ringing in his ears, it almost literally took wild horses to drag him back.

Still of the opinion that the queen had succumbed to smallpox – even though nearly a week after the illness started a rash had yet to appear – Burcot left a potion, the sort of thing that passed for medicine in those days, in the hope it might effect a cure. When the queen regained consciousness, she consumed much of the concoction and within twenty-four hours a rash duly appeared – on the back of a hand. However, the first external sign of smallpox is always a facial rash. So, it seems that whatever caused the queen's skin irritation was *not* smallpox – indeed, it is virtually certain that she experienced an allergic reaction to Burcot's medication. Moreover, if the queen had suffered an attack of 'poxe' she would probably have been disfigured for life; in fact, she survived the illness without blemish.

Small chance of smallpox:

There are several reasons to seriously doubt that Queen Elizabeth's illness at Hampton Court in October 1562 was due to smallpox, viz:

1. The time taken for a rash to appear, about a week, was much too long.
2. The *first* sign of a rash, on the back of a hand, was in the wrong location.
3. The queen insisted herself that she did not have 'pox' – why was she so sure?
4. Elizabeth berated Dr Burcot for his diagnosis – even though very ill, she contradicted his assessment.
5. The ladies-in-waiting did not think the illness was smallpox either. In an age when the disease was common, it would have been quite easy for them to identify the symptoms.
6. The queen was left unmarked by the illness – yet serious disfigurement is usual with smallpox.
7. In the years that followed, Elizabeth never referred to her sickness of October 1562 as 'pox' – it was always just her 'illness'.

'For *your* sake I have passed the pikes'

It had been a very fraught time. For several days the queen's life hung by the slenderest of threads, as though she and her realm were being weighed in the balance by the invisible hand of Fate. Cliques of nervous courtiers and government officials held meetings to try and decide whom they would support as claimant to the throne in the event of her death. It was, in the circumstances, an ironic problem.

About a month after the illness, when the recuperating queen and her entourage of ladies were walking in the park, they encountered Robert Dudley and a group of his friends practising archery. Whereupon, in front of several witnesses, Elizabeth said to him: 'you are beholden to me, because for your sake I have passed the pikes'. To *pass the pikes* – an archaic phrase – is to experience dangers and difficulties but to come through unscathed. Of course the question is: why was Dudley beholden to the queen for the great danger – the illness – that had recently befallen her? It made no sense for

Elizabeth to imply that she had been made to suffer for the sake of Dudley – unless *he*, in some way, helped to cause the sickness. But whatever illness the queen had been subject to, on Lord Robert's account, it could *not* have been smallpox – a disease he never contracted.

In Elizabethan times it was considered a most shameful thing for *any* aristocratic lady to have an illegitimate child. So, when 'natural' children were born – and every year saw at least one such happening among the ladies at court – the infants were raised in secret, out in the country. If the queen found out that one of her maids of honour had 'fallen', the unfortunate woman could expect to be banished from court – or even sent to prison!

It was imperative that the masses never had their strong suspicion confirmed – that the queen had a secret child. Firstly, public knowledge of the royal bastard's existence would have created the potential for conflict – perhaps an uprising at, or even before, the time of the succession. Elizabeth knew from personal experience gleaned during the reign of her half-sister 'Bloody Mary', that an heir presumptive can give rise to factions – and factions, in turn, can foster rebellion. Thus, for the most important of political reasons, it was vital that the child's existence was kept secret. Secondly, the haughtily proud Elizabeth Tudor would have felt profound shame at having to admit publicly that she was, in fact, an unmarried mother!

So, from the day he was born, it was inevitable that the queen's illegitimate son would always be a non-person. Officially he did not exist; if stories about a secret royal child were to escape – and they certainly did – there must be no material evidence to substantiate them. Of course it was clear that the queen could not bring up the child – the boy was definitely Lord Robert's responsibility. However, in view of Dudley's alleged murderous proclivities, infanticide might have been tempting – although it would not have been a realistic option. Killing the infant would have destroyed royal flesh and blood and extinguished the (potential) heir to the throne – an act of high treason, even if the child was a severe embarrassment, whose existence threatened Elizabeth's personal reputation and the long-term stability of the realm.

Dudley knew that the infant could not be brought up in his own family because, having no wife at the time, the arrival of a new-born child on the scene would have been a little difficult to explain. Furthermore, the boy's presence in his household would have aroused a great deal of suspicion, especially with rumours about a secret royal child starting to circulate. Moreover, for the purpose of concealment, the boy had to be given a surname other than Dudley – and yet, the changeling would have to be hidden within the tight-knit confines of Robert's closest relatives. Whoever was chosen as foster parents had to be utterly reliable and discreet; they had to be of the right social class, the right age, the right religion and, to avoid potential conflict with siblings later in life, they must not have children of their own.

The stringent requirements narrowed the range of possibilities considerably; indeed, the solution was all but inevitable. Only one couple satisfied the conditions perfectly: Catherine and Henry Hastings – Dudley's trusted sister and brother-in-law. In fact, Catherine was probably the closest relative in the family to Robert; an indication of their intimacy is suggested by a letter she wrote in 1561, informing him of Henry's embarrassing circumstances – it seems they had 'only' £40 with which to attend court. In light of that knowledge, Robert Dudley almost certainly offered to alleviate the Hastings' financial difficulties, in exchange for taking his secret son into the bosom of their family.

A tick list helps to show why Catherine and Henry Hastings were chosen as the adoptive parents:

Age – almost exactly the same as Elizabeth & Dudley.
Social status – Henry had a royal pedigree, doubly descended from Edward III.
Religion – Puritan Protestant, like Dudley.
Family – childless.
Family connections – the boy's paternal aunt and uncle.
Location of home – Stoke Park Manor House, near Windsor.
Ancestral seat – Ashby-de-la- Zouch, Leicestershire.
Financial status – by aristocratic standards, impoverished
Reliability and discretion – completely trustworthy.

Henry Hastings (1535-1595) – 'the Puritan Earl'

The eldest son of Francis Hastings and Catherine Pole, Henry Hastings was born at the family seat of Ashby de la Zouch. His father was a descendant of the Duke of Buckingham and his mother was a descendant of the Duke of Clarence, brother of Edward IV and Richard III. Being doubly descended from Edward III, Henry Hastings had a strong claim to the throne.

Like his brother-in-law Robert Dudley, Henry had been a classmate of Prince Edward and so, from childhood, was a member of the inner royal circle. On the death of his father, Francis, in 1569, Henry became 3rd Earl of Huntingdon. Known as the 'Puritan Earl' for his ardently Calvinist beliefs, he was made Garter Knight and in 1569 briefly guarded Mary, Queen of Scots at the start of her long exile in England. In 1572, three years after an uprising by the Catholic northern earls, trusty Henry was made President of the Council in the North – a position he held for the next twenty-three years until his death.

It was an important post, though somewhat isolated from goings-on at court; nevertheless it meant that Henry Hastings was viceroy over all of England north of the Trent, except Lancashire. The fact that he was given a key appointment based at York – at least a one-week ride from London – is a measure of just how much Elizabeth trusted him, since enemies were usually kept close to court, the better to keep an eye on them. Thus, Henry spent much of his time at the King's Manor in York, maintaining a watch on the potentially rebellious northerners. Having paid all the expenses of the presidency himself, he left huge debts when he died in 1595. As usual, the queen gave no financial help.

Henry Hastings was considered one of the strongest claimants to the throne after Elizabeth. Indeed, Dudley even pledged men-at-arms to assist him in the event of the queen's death, in October 1562. Elizabeth was herself very conscious of Henry's claim to the throne – a fact that irritated her somewhat because, like her tyrant father, she could not stand rivals. But the queen knew that, if she were to die, Hastings – the Earl of Huntingdon – would stand a good chance, with Dudley's help, of becoming her successor.

An honourable man of integrity, and hugely indebted to Robert Dudley, 'King Henry' would have felt duty-bound to ensure that the boy in his care received all the necessary protection – an arrangement which would almost certainly *not* be the case with any other monarch, since the child would be perceived by anyone else as a potential threat. And so, as insurance against Elizabeth's early demise, it was a sensible precaution to make the Earl of Huntingdon the foster father of her secret child.

Trusty Tamworth

The Hastings family owned a newly built home, Stoke Park Manor House, at Stoke Poges – a small village about four miles north of Windsor; out of sight of the gossips at court, although conveniently close to the castle. The question is, how did the newborn infant make the journey from Hampton Court to his foster home? Was it trusty Tamworth, Robert Dudley's personal body groom, under cover of darkness on a chill autumn evening, who spirited the infant away up the Thames to his adoptive family? Of all Dudley's servants, Tamworth was the one most likely to have known the 'Big Secret' – not only that the queen and Lord Robert had a child but exactly what became of it. Circumstantial evidence very strongly supports that view: Tamworth slept in

Henry Hastings – 3rd Earl of Huntingdon – had a strong claim to the throne.

the same room as his master, and stood guard outside the door whenever the queen and Dudley were alone together. If *anyone* knew the true state of their relationship Tamworth did.

Of crucial significance is the fact that when Elizabeth was at the height of her illness, but still in possession of her faculties, she made provision that in the event of her death Robert Dudley was to be made Lord Protector of England, with an annual allowance of £20,000 and, quite separately, that Tamworth was to be paid £500 per annum – a very considerable sum every year. The key question is: why was Dudley's body groom – a mere servant – in the queen's mind at that very difficult time; what had *he* done for Elizabeth to warrant unprecedented generosity? Such munificence on the part of the notoriously tight-fisted queen, especially in respect of a minion who was not even her employee, is *exceedingly* strange and certainly looks like hush money – but was it?

Elizabeth had not yet assumed the title 'Virgin Queen'– with no special 'reputation' to protect – so it is unlikely she was thinking of paying Tamworth a huge sum (every year!) just to keep his mouth shut about her liaison with Lord Robert. In any case, 'hush money' would have been paid by Tamworth's employer – Dudley himself. Once dead, Elizabeth's sexual peccadilloes would have been passé – people would have been too concerned with the new monarch, to gossip much about the shenanigans of Anne Boleyn's daughter. But if progeny resulted from the relationship with Robert Dudley, that would be a very different matter! The size of the intended payment and the crucial fact that it was annual – a pension – suggests it was meant to conceal a very important on-going secret. It seems that the dead queen's indebtedness to Tamworth would have been very deep and perpetual! At £500 per year, over a twenty year period, the total payment would have been £10,000 – the equivalent of ten million pounds today – and all of it to a nobody like Dudley's body groom. Why? The most logical explanation is that Elizabeth wanted to buy the services of Tamworth so that, when she was dead and no longer in power, he would be her extremely well-paid ultra-loyal servant – who would guarantee protection for her secret child.

Although great care was taken in hiding the changeling, rumours about a secret royal child were beginning to spread. In fact, the government was so alarmed by the stories that a law was passed, making it treason to state that the queen had a child. Indeed, several unfortunates were executed at Norwich in 1570 for making just such an assertion. What did those people *know*? Had they seen the queen's 'condition' with their own eyes in August 1562 when, due to a 'mystery illness', she suddenly cut short her annual summer progress and returned to London? The very fact of the executions strongly suggests that the people at Norwich *knew* something of great import – that they were not simply gossips passing on a second-hand story, but eye-witnesses to a huge secret. Little did they think, in telling the honest truth, that it would cost them their lives.

However, the unfortunate townsfolk of Norwich were not the only ones to be punished; many people, around the country, were given long jail sentences, fined very heavily or had their tongues cut out and ears cut off, just for spreading stories about a secret child of the queen. It is astonishing that, even with the most severe punitive measures in force, the rumours continued to reverberate long after the executions at Norwich. Indeed, stories about a royal child were still circulating in England as late as the 1580s and by then had spread throughout the courts of Europe. The persistence of the rumour, especially in such a dangerous climate, powerfully attests to its credibility.

No smoke without fire

So there is very good circumstantial evidence that Elizabeth I and Robert Dudley had a secret child. The main historical points leading to that conclusion are:

1. The incorrect diagnosis of Elizabeth's near-fatal illness in October 1562. Serious illness resulting from child-birth was very common at the time.

2. Elizabeth's pointed comment to Dudley, the following month, in front of witnesses.

3. Elizabeth's uncharacteristically generous (proposed) remuneration for Tamworth, Dudley's personal groom, in the event of her death in October 1562 – ongoing payments of £500 per annum.

4. The execution of several people at Norwich in 1570, for claiming the queen had a child – yet others who made the same assertion were not executed.

5. Even in the face of the most severe punishments, rumours persisted – over a period of at least twenty years – about the existence of a secret child of the queen.

6. Elizabeth's comment in a letter to the Speaker of the House of Commons, in February 1563, that her recent serious illness had been 'God's chastisement'.

9

W.H.

Although a changeling, the illegitimate infant had to be given an official christening; it was imperative that he was named in accordance with convention. The service would have taken place amidst great secrecy at St Giles Church, Stoke Poges – adjacent to Stoke Park Manor House, London home of the Hastings family.

Mysteries at St Giles*

St Giles Church and the Hastings Chapel are located about 200 yards from the Manor House. The royal bastard would have been christened here within a week of birth. He was probably named 'William' either after a child of the Hastings family who had died some years earlier (a tradition at the time) or after William, Lord Hastings who was executed by Richard III in 1483, and whose body had recently been reburied at the Hastings Chapel.

The christening would have been performed by the incumbent vicar, one Richard Pennington*. According to records at St Giles, Pennington rose from obscurity and sank back into oblivion within a year (1562-1563), one of only four vicars in 800 years of recorded history to leave within twelve months of appointment. In view of the highly unusual circumstances, it is very likely that 'Richard Pennington' was the pseudonym of someone brought in specially to carry out the clandestine christening. Compounding the mystery is the curious fact that the register at St Giles began in March 1563, whereas the registers of two adjacent parishes commenced *before* 1562. It seems probable that the earliest records at St Giles, covering the crucial period in question, were deliberately removed.

Son of the royal virgin

William Hastings grew up in a Puritan Protestant home, in the care of aunt Catherine – a woman who became well known for the promotion of Protestant education; however, it is unclear if William was an adherent of

* Church of England archivists know nothing of Richard Pennington – a vicar with no CV!

Puritan Protestantism in adulthood. His religious convictions are uncertain and remain a matter for speculation, although it seems he was ordained as a 'divine' at Petworth and that he spent time as a preacher. Indeed, there is much in *Shakespeare* which suggests the author knew a great deal about the scriptures – no less than 42 books of the Bible are alluded to in the canon, but without once referring directly to Jesus Christ – and a cleric, of one sort or another, appears in many of the plays.

On discovering his true identity, young William would probably have been quick to recognise the special significance of his *almost* unique status as 'the son of a virgin'. So, there is a distinct possibility that he saw himself as a messianic, Christ-like figure – an aspect of *Shakespeare's* author discerned by Caroline Spurgeon. Whatever his religious persuasion, the royal changeling would certainly have received a first-rate humanist education, since both the Tudor and Dudley families ensured that all their offspring, girls as well as boys, were given the best schooling. It is possible that William was taught using the rigorous scheme devised for young aristocrats by Lord Burghley, a didactic method whose most illustrious products were Francis Bacon and Robert Cecil. Moreover, just as Henry VIII gave his daughter an education fit for a king – even though he never imagined she would become the monarch – Elizabeth likewise wanted to contribute to the upbringing of her son and, since she was an expert linguist, taught him how to learn languages herself. In addition, it is likely that as part of a wide-ranging education, young William learned to act with the Children of the Chapel at Windsor – so drama would have been part of his world from an early age.

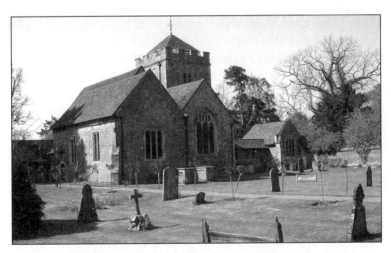

St Giles Church and the Hastings Chapel (left), Stoke Poges.

Naturally, one wonders what sort of childhood the boy experienced living out in the country at Stoke Park, with Windsor Castle and his mother so near and yet so far? Did he have any friends? Did he make his own entertainment? Was he precociously clever? Did he absorb himself in study as a way of escaping loneliness? When was he told of his true identity? How did he react on learning that he was the 'royal bastard'? In light of the deception, how did he come to he regard his real parents? Did he grow up mistrusting people? Was he secretive or open? Did he have tantrums, or was he placid? Was he sociable or aloof? One can only guess at the answers although the schoolboy William Page in *The Merry Wives of Windsor* (which might represent the author as a boy) is depicted as a bright but shy child.

Genius in the genes

The abundance of literary and linguistic talent, on both sides of William Hastings' family, suggests his abilities were largely inherited. His intellectual pedigree could hardly have been better: mother was a polymath and polyglot, a brilliant Latin scholar who spoke French and Italian to translator standard. Grandfather Henry VIII spoke five languages, grandmother Anne Boleyn spoke three while great-grandfather Thomas Boleyn – a diplomat said to speak the best French at Henry's court – was descended from the Earl of Ormond, a famous translator.

As a child, William's uncle, the precocious boy-king Edward VI, corrected the spoken Italian of adults; cousin Sir Philip Sidney, son of Robert Dudley's sister Mary, was a famous poet. Mary (Sidney) Herbert – Countess of Pembroke – Philip Sidney's sister, a scholar and poet herself, was the most highly educated woman in England after the queen. In addition, the paternal grandmother, Jane Guildford, was renowned for her eloquence and wisdom as were her daughters Catherine Hastings and Mary Sidney – the boy's aunts.

William Hastings' biological father, Robert Dudley, was reckoned a good conversationalist and a good administrator, although his academic talents were of a mathematical rather than linguistic kind. And the remarkable Sir Robert Dudley – Dudley's son by Lady Douglas Sheffield, William's younger half-brother – was a gifted mathematician, engineer, architect, explorer, ship-designer, navigator and cartographer. The most brilliant member of the Dudley family after William Hastings himself.

In stark contrast it seems that all of Shakspere's blood relatives were illiterate.

To the manor born

Built in the 1550s, the west wing of Stoke Park Manor House – about a quarter of the original building – is all that remains of the childhood home of

The west wing of Stoke Park Manor House, Stoke Poges.

William Hastings. As well as living at Stoke Park as a boy it is possible that, in his youth, William also spent time at Ashby-de-la-Zouch, the ancestral home of the Hastings family. Moreover, it seems that the Shake-Speare name – the poet's mask – was extracted from the manor title (Stoake Parke Manor House, old spelling) using a special anagram technique devised by Hastings himself.

In 1576, on the death of her father, Stoke Park became home to the beautiful Penelope Devereux who, at the age of thirteen, was adopted by the Hastings family. Penelope was the older sister of Dorothy and Robert Devereux (2nd Earl of Essex). In 1578 Robert Dudley married Walter Devereux's widow, Lettice Knollys. As a result, Robert Devereux and William Hastings became stepbrothers.

Initial impressions
This very old graffiti – the style of 'W' went out of fashion in the eighteenth century – is carved by the door at St Giles. Why, long ago and with plenty of

space to write initials, was W+P partly superposed on WH? It seems likely that the initials were deliberately linked to show that, as teenagers, William Hastings and Penelope Devereux were on close terms; they would certainly have had ample opportunity to get to know each other well in the Hastings' family at the same time. Hence, the initials were probably inscribed during the 1570s by the adolescent William Hastings.

Lord Leicester's Men

Sometime around 1560, Robert Dudley became the first Englishman to patronise a troupe of travelling players. After his ennoblement in 1565, the play troupe was titled Lord Leicester's Men. The innovation appears to have set a trend as a status symbol for the very rich and several leading aristocrats followed suit, patronising their own itinerant players.

It was probably through Lord Leicester's Men that young William Hastings was introduced to the professional theatre and how he got to know Richard Tarleton, the most famous clown in England. Tarleton worked with Leicester's Men during the 1560s and 1570s when William was growing up. So, it's plausible that as *Shakespeare's* author, Hastings was alluding to Tarleton – the dead jester – when Hamlet addresses Yorick's skull in the graveyard scene, and tells Horatio that he knew the clown as a boy: 'Alas poor Yorick, I knew him Horatio, a fellow of infinite jest...'

In summer 1575 Leicester organised, in honour of the queen, a series of spectacular pageants and displays at his splendid country home – Kenilworth Castle. It is very likely that, as a youth, William Hastings paid occasional visits to his father's Warwickshire residence and thereby acquired a smattering of the local dialect that appears in the works. Indeed, it is worthy of note that a detail featured in one of the displays – a mermaid on a dolphin's back – is alluded to in *A Midsummer Nights Dream*.

Uncle father, aunt mother

After Uncle Henry moved to York in 1572, Aunt Catherine – who probably spent much of her time in the south – would have taken the boy along whenever she went to visit her husband. It was almost certainly during those years, on sojourns in the north, that William acquired his knowledge of Yorkish vocabulary – which comprises about 85% of all the dialect in *Shakespeare*. William's later formative years, from mid-teens to early twenties, were probably spent in an environment where Leicester had a significant influence on his activities. The question was what to do with a very bright young man who *must* remain hidden from the public? It seems the answer was to turn him into a spy, making use of his natural talent as an acute observer of people, with an excellent memory, and an ability to act. As a 'reporter' of over-heard private conversations, young William would have acquired a very good background for his future writing career. And his knowledge of north-country dialect would have been invaluable if, as a spy in his late teens and early twenties, he helped Uncle Henry keep an eye on Catholics in the north of England.

Edmund Campion – alias – 'Hastings'

In summer 1580 two Jesuit spies, Robert Parsons (Persons) and Edmund Campion, were sent incognito to England from Douai in northern France. The purpose of their mission seems to have been to make contact with followers of the Old Religion, notably in the Catholic strongholds of the West Midlands and the North, and to lend support to their beleaguered brethren. In response someone – almost certainly Leicester – organised a nationwide manhunt to track down the disguised priests who had taken the precaution of following separate paths.

It seems that when William Hastings was just eighteen years old he became involved, through his father, with the search for Edmund Campion. As a result, he probably travelled extensively throughout north-west England, during winter/spring 1581 – possibly in the guise of an actor or tutor – all the while on the trail of the Jesuit priest.

When Campion was travelling incognito through the north-west it so happened that Leicester's former personal chaplain, a man by the name of Chadderton, was Bishop of Chester. It would have been Chadderton's responsibility as bishop to oversee the pursuit of Campion in his diocese and send intelligence to Leicester. It is therefore plausible that William Hastings,

Pictured with fife and tabor, the famous clown Richard Tarleton joined Lord Leicester's Men in the 1560s. It was possibly Tarleton – perhaps a sort of father figure to young William Hastings – who introduced the boy to comedy and clowning. The Hastings-Tarleton relationship in real life was probably reflected in the Hamlet-Yorick association in the play.

working for his father, reported to the bishop with information gathered on his travels. So, the question arises as to whether graffiti in Chester Cathedral was left by the eighteen year-old spy, when reporting to Chadderton under the code name William Shakespeare.

Originally bounded on three sides by an artificial lake, the stark shell of Kenilworth Castle is all that remains of Leicester's palatial abode, after it was laid waste during the civil war.

An additional link between *Shakespeare's* author and Chester appears in *Loves Labours Lost* in the guise of the Nine Worthies – characters that were not creations of the playwright, but originally appeared in the Chester summer plays. The implication is that Hastings saw the summer plays himself when he visited the city. Although the evidence is circumstantial, it is certainly plausible that he spent time working as a spy in north-west England, in 1581, tracking Edmund Campion. Against that background, it is not beyond the bounds of possibility that Hastings was the William Shakeshaft mentioned in Alexander Houghton's will of August 1581. The inference is that, disguised as 'William Shakeshaft' (or Shake-speare) the young but well educated spy was employed as a tutor at Houghton Tower, at the same time that Campion was hiding there writing a secret tract.

The wily Robert Parsons managed to evade capture and returned safely to the continent. His confederate, however, was not so fortunate. Campion was eventually captured and ignominiously dragged back to London where he was brought before the queen and the Earl of Leicester. The Jesuit priest was offered a pardon if only he would acknowledge Elizabeth as Governor of the Church of England; but, despite the best attempts at persuasion, he refused. So, he was interrogated and put on trial. Remarkably, details of the interrogation seem to be alluded to in *Twelfth Night*, when the imprisoned killjoy Malvolio is subjected to a humiliating inquisition.

It is especially noteworthy that at his trial, Campion was specifically asked by the prosecution why he travelled in disguise under a false identity and, in particular, why he called himself 'Hastings'. Curiously, he failed to offer an explanation for the choice of name – which raises the question as to whether he knew that Leicester's son was on his trail. Leicester had been Campion's patron some years earlier, so it is possible that the Jesuit priest either knew the young William Hastings personally, or else knew of his existence.

The trial was a sham, the result was never in doubt, and Campion was found guilty of treason. He knew from the moment of capture that he would have to face the full horror of a traitor's execution: hanging, castration, disembowelment, decapitation and quartering. He also knew that, in order to prolong the agony, achieve maximum punitive effect and entertain the baying crowd, every effort would be made to keep him conscious throughout the appalling process. Indeed, it was said that an expert executioner could show the still-beating heart to the unfortunate wretch, before the eyes closed forever.

But in Campion's case the bloodthirsty mob, eagerly awaiting an exhibition of extreme violence, was to be disappointed. On the queen's (or Leicester's) orders, the Jesuit priest was spared the worst torments of the scaffold and allowed to die by hanging before the lifeless body was cut down, castrated, disembowelled, decapitated and – the gory remains still steaming – hacked into quarters. The butchered parts were dispatched to the four corners of the realm, while the severed head was skewered on a pike and stuck atop the gatehouse of London Bridge. Campion's dismembered body was a ghastly warning to would-be traitors and a grisly feast for the crows. That is probably what he wanted all along – a martyr's death and posthumous reward: the immortality of sainthood, which was duly conferred.

This graffiti is inscribed on a wall in Chester Cathedral. Although the figures are badly eroded, the remains of an old-fashioned 'W' can still be seen and, immediately to the right, a symbol that seems to represent a shaking spear – much as a cartoonist might draw it. Was 'Shakespeare' depicted here as an icon because it was being used as a symbolic name?

Hastivibrans = Shakespeare

The epithet of Pallas Athena, goddess of knowledge, wisdom and truth is hastivibrans – the spear shaker, Latin equivalent of Shakespeare. It is noteworthy that **hasti**vibra**ns** contains 'hastins' in sequence. It is also worthy of note that Pallas Athena was a virgin soldier, defender of the realm and symbolically associated with Queen Elizabeth herself. Thus, Pallas Athena simultaneously links the Virgin Queen, Shakespeare and Hastings.

For security purposes, but also perhaps for psychological reasons too, William Hastings used a number of false names. As well as the *Shake-speare* title, under which he wrote plays and poems, he also used the pseudonyms: Phaeton, Martin Marprelate, Labeo, Aetion and Sir Arundel Talbot. Indeed, the first of Jonson's anagrams – that refers to Hastings in his 1623 Folio verse – warns 'the future' that the author 'used many false name titles', so it's possible that several more code names exist beside the ones here.

The nameless 'Right Honourable'

Three generations of the Dudley family were associated, in one way or another, with seafaring. The first was John Dudley – Robert's father – who was appointed Lord High Admiral of England, by Henry VIII, and helped to build the first English fleet. The second was Robert Dudley himself, who took a very keen interest in all aspects of exploration, even sponsoring expeditions by some of the leading adventurers of the day, including Francis Drake and

Public executions, an explicit demonstration of the absolute power of the state, had a significant deterrent effect and provided the most horrendous entertainment imaginable for the jeering crowds. Few would be willing to experience such a death just to 'prove' that the queen had a secret son; fear of execution kept the Shakespeare ruse permanently secure.

Martin Frobisher. The third was Sir Robert Dudley – swashbuckling son of Robert Dudley and Lady Douglas Sheffield – an accomplished seafarer who wrote a celebrated book on cartography. With such strong maritime associations in his family, it is unsurprising that 'the sea' was never far from the mind of *Shakespeare's* author.

In 1594, at just twenty years of age, the adventurous Sir Robert Dudley joined Raleigh's expedition to West Africa and the New World. Sir Robert's captain on the voyage, Tom Wyatt, was noted for his ability to write excellent travel logs. On the expedition in question, Wyatt's reports were sent to an anonymous recipient who was only ever addressed as 'Right Honourable'. The significance of the mysterious nobleman lies in the fact that William Hastings and Sir Robert Dudley were half-brothers. Thus, it is likely that the eloquent Captain Wyatt was writing detailed accounts so that Hastings – the unnamed 'Right Honourable' – could use them as reference material.

New World adventures (1584 & 1609)

According to anagrams by the seventeenth century writer William D'Avenant, Hastings suffered a serious accident at sea – a 'costly' fall – possibly whilst on an expedition to establish the Virginia colonies with Sir Walter Raleigh in 1584. The accident might have left him permanently disabled – the poet's 'lameness' is referred to three times in *The Sonnets* – and it seems he might have suffered brain damage also. Indeed, another of D'Avenant's anagrams says: 'Hastings thought that the brain had been shattered'. Serious head injuries can cause significant changes to personality and, in some rare cases, have been known to significantly enhance an individual's creative abilities – moreover D'Avenant indicates in one anagram that Hastings wrote The Works after the accident.

It is likely that William Hastings was restricted by his injuries, especially if he was lame, and that he probably experienced extended bouts of pain. In an age when medical care was very primitive, little could be done to repair serious injury. He might have found some relief by writing and, possibly, through the use of opiates as well. Always in hiding, and perhaps partly incapacitated, he probably passed some of his time reading and writing in one or other of the large, well-stocked libraries of relatives and friends – in particular those at Petworth, Wilton, Penshurst and Essex House in the Strand, London residence of his step-brother the Earl of Essex.

The dedication in *Shake-speares Sonnets* is a personal tribute from Thomas Thorpe, the publisher, to M^r. W.H.. In fact, Thorpe calls W.H. a 'well-wishing adventurer' – someone who seems to be setting forth on a venture. The venture alluded to was probably the one which, at the time the sonnets were registered on May 20th 1609, left London on May 15th and

Falmouth on June 2nd – it was the very same voyage that provided material for *The Tempest*. Thus, Thorpe's dedication links M^r. W.H. to *Shake-speares Sonnets* and the sea voyage alluded to in the last play. That connection is a further reason why the initial 'H' is very unlikely to have been a typographical error (which should read 'S') since M^r. W.S. – the Stratford man – was certainly not an 'adventurer' setting forth on a voyage to the New World in May 1609. Indeed, Shakspere was at Stratford in June settling a long-standing dispute with John Addenbroke.

It is possible – even probable – that Hastings embarked on the expedition to the New World with the intention of starting a new life there. He must have known that with King James on the throne he was very much persona non grata and his days in the land of his birth were numbered. However, it seems that things in the New World didn't work out and he returned to England to find that, in his absence and without his consent, *Shake-speares Sonnets* had been published – including, crucially, the defamatory verses about the 'Dark Lady'. As a result, Hastings found himself ensnared in a duel – a trap set by Ben Jonson, probably on the king's orders – that was intended to bring about his demise. So, after William Hastings died in the duel in 1610, Shakspere had no pressing reason to remain in London and promptly returned to his friends, family and business interests in Stratford. In fact, Thomas Greene, Shakspere's cousin, was told to vacate New Place that year.

The mysterious Martin Marprelate

Following the defeat of the Spanish Armada, Leicester suddenly died on September 4th 1588 amid rumours of poisoning by his wife, Lettice Knollys. The death proved a watershed in William Hastings' life and was the event that inspired an early play by him, now lost, but known to scholars as *Ur-Hamlet* (1588/89) – probably the first version of the play which appeared in the 1623 folio as *Hamlet, Prince of Denmark*.

In October 1588, the month following Leicester's death, the first of a series of scurrilous satirical tracts appeared in print under the pen name 'Martin Marprelate'. The pseudonymous author, *apparently* writing as a raving Puritan, singled out the bishops for special attention, even revealing salacious details of their private lives. In all seven tracts were published – six by an illegal mobile press – and they sold well, much to the ire of the Archbishop of Canterbury William Whitgift. However, it is most strange that although an intensive nation-wide search eventually cornered Marprelate's printers and found the mobile press hidden near Manchester, the author himself was never captured or identified, even though the printers had been tortured at the queen's behest.

Anagrams indicate that Martin Marprelate was a code name of William

Hastings; this explains why the author of the notorious work – the first satirical writing in English – was never publicly identified or brought to account. As the unacknowledged, secret son of the queen, it would seem that Hastings was beyond reach of both the authorities and his mother. In other words, he was a law unto himself and knew that he could get away with anything.

Man and boy

The following are biographical 'points of contact' between William Hastings and his natural father Robert Dudley, the Earl of Leicester.

- The adopted name 'Hastings' – from Leicester's sister Catherine Hastings.
- Hastings' knowledge of Warwickshire dialect – Leicester's main residence outside London was Kenilworth Castle, in Warwickshire.
- Hastings' knowledge of details of the displays, staged by Leicester, at Kenilworth in summer 1575.
- Hastings' involvement in the pursuit and capture of Edmund Campion in 1581 – almost certainly organised by Leicester.
- Hastings' professional knowledge of acting – Leicester had his own play troupe.
- Hastings' fascination with Italy – Leicester admired all things Italian.
- Hastings' knowledge of seafaring – Leicester was very interested in maritime matters, especially exploration and the theory of navigation.
- Hastings' detailed knowledge of battlefield conditions (eg *Henry V*) – spent time with Lord Leicester's play troupe in the Low Countries (1585-87).
- Hastings' involvement with espionage – Leicester ran his own spy network.*
- Hastings' knowledge of Elsinore (Hamlet's castle) – Leicester's Men visited Elsinore in 1586.
- Hastings' likely association with Richard Tarleton, the famous clown with Leicester's Men.
- Hastings' first meeting with Shakspere – Leicester's Men performed at Stratford in 1587.

* All the documentation concerning Leicester's spy network has been destroyed.

Elizabeth's second favourite

Soon after Leicester's death in September 1588, the fifty-five year-old queen began her turbulent relationship with Robert Devereux, Earl of Essex – a 'boy' thirty-four years her junior. The relationship was certainly strange; a symbiotic affair with Essex eagerly accepting Elizabeth's patronage while she fed, vampire-like, on the vitality of his youth. The existence of that rather odd 'friendship' provides a plausible explanation for Hastings' motivation in writing some of the sonnets. As the queen's son, he might have found the relationship with his step-brother repellent – it's also possible he was jealous of the time and attention his mother bestowed upon the handsome young earl. Hastings, by contrast, was not exactly handsome – it seems he had a large nose and looked like his mother.

In a malicious attempt to wreck the relationship, the first seventeen sonnets urge the 'Fair Youth'* to marry and have children. Hastings knew that once married, Elizabeth would lose interest in Essex and, indeed, the 'affair' did cool for a while after his marriage to Philip Sidney's widow, Frances Walsingham, in 1590. But the 'star of England' – as Essex was known – soon found himself back in royal favour, playing cards with the insomniac old queen until sunrise.

It appears that Hastings' first poetic attempt to scupper the peculiar affair between his mother and step-brother failed – so what was he trying to do in the remaining (109) sonnets addressed to the youth? There is little doubt that the poet 'loves' the youth – but in what sense is not clear. Did Elizabeth have sight of her son's poems, was Hastings trying to 'queer the pitch' for his mother – hinting at some sort of perverse ménage a trios – in an attempt to disrupt the affair with her 'toy-boy'?

Whatever the answer, it would probably have seemed strange to the general reader that, unlike any other sonnets of the age, the majority of *Shakespeare's* were written in very personal terms from one man to another!

Fair is foul and foul is fair

William Hastings never married although it appears that he had at least two mistresses: Jane Daniel, wife of John Daniel – by whom it seems he probably had a son, William, who died in childhood – and the unmarried Margaret Radcliff, Elizabeth's chief maid of honour, by whom it seems he had at least one daughter who survived into adulthood.

The so-called 'Dark Lady' of the sonnets was almost certainly Jane Daniel, nee Jeanne de Ketulle, daughter of Robert de la Kethulle, Lord of Rehoven. It

---

* 'Youth' is a relative term. Essex was only four years younger than Hastings – but life expectancy was only half what it is today, so the age difference now would correspond to about eight years.

is thought that Jane came to England from Flanders in about 1588 and found employment with Frances Walsingham, widow of Sir Philip Sidney and (from 1590) wife of the Earl of Essex. It is likely that Jane met Essex and/or Hastings when they were with Leicester's entourage in the Low Countries (1585-87) – that would explain how she managed to get a job working for Essex's wife in England.

A French-speaking Huguenot and tire-maker (headdress-maker) by trade, Jane Daniel almost certainly knew Christopher Mountjoy, since he too was a French-speaking Huguenot tire-maker – the world of Huguenot tire-makers in London was not exactly vast. Furthermore, Jane Daniel was a woman who 'got about' a bit and Christopher Mountjoy had a reputation as a libertine. In addition, William Shakspere lodged for a time with the Mountjoy family, in Silver Street; hence, a link exists through Jane Daniel and Christopher Mountjoy that connects Shakspere with Hastings.

Jane had three sons; the first (John) survived, although the other two died in childhood. The second son was called 'Devereux' and the third was named 'William'. According to the sonnets, the 'Dark Lady' seduced the 'Fair Youth', so it seems a distinct possibility that the boys were named after their respective fathers. It is worthy of note, in this context, that the records of Hackney Church in late May 1601, show that the infant William was christened in a very expensive crimson gown – consistent with a child of aristocratic status – and the Daniels were living at Hackney parsonage at the time.

A ward of the queen, a spy, a good-for-nothing and a scrounger, John Daniel (*aka* Lord Daresbury) was always pleading poverty and wrote many begging letters to Essex and Robert Cecil. In fact, he had long been living beyond his means in London – as though a wealthy aristocrat – and was prepared to do anything for money. So it's perhaps unsurprising, especially in view of Jane's 'reputation' (the sonnets refer to the 'Dark Lady' as 'the wide world's common place' and 'the bay in which all men ride') that John Daniel, who was much older than Jane, used her as a 'whore-wife' – as one of Jonson's anagrams boldly states. Another anagram by Jonson, in the last line of his 1623 Folio commendatory verse, indicates that Lady Daresbury – Jane Daniel, the defamed 'Dark Lady' of the sonnets – was used as a trap to ensnare Hastings in the duel that cost him his life.

The 'other' mistress of William Hastings, Margaret Radcliff, could not have been more different. The Radcliffs were the leading Catholic family in the Manchester area. Margaret was eleven years younger than William. They probably met when he was touring England with his father's play troupe in 1587 – she was only fourteen, the same age as Juliet (much is made of Juliet's age in the play). It seems she became pregnant by Hastings and gave birth to an illegitimate daughter. Margaret Radcliff was the most highly favoured of all Elizabeth's maids of honour; but sadly, in November 1599 at just twenty-six years of age, she committed suicide (shades of Ophelia?) by starvation, after her brother died in the August of that year, during Essex's campaign in Ireland. Like Sebastian and Viola in *Twelfth Night*, brother and sister were very close.

A writer in hiding

Another of Jonson's anagrams, in his commendatory folio verse, states that: 'Hastings, honed our fires, for heat at Petworth' which seems to imply that Hastings used the ideas of his contemporaries for inspiration, whilst writing (in secret) at Petworth House. The 'ideas' were probably acquired at clandestine meetings of intellectuals and writers, such as the famous 'wit matches' that took place on the first Friday of each month, at the Mermaid Tavern in Bread Street.

Presumably, Hastings was a very acute listener with an excellent memory, like his mother. One of the anagrams indicates that he originally wrote play parts for 'friends at Petworth House', not the professional London stage. Since Petworth (and Wilton) was a long way from the capital and the scrutiny of the official censor, the Master of Revels, it is possible that some of the female parts in *Shakespeare* were originally written for female actors – rather than the specially trained boys of the professional theatre, who would have been a bit thin on the ground in places like Petworth and Wilton.

It seems that after the plagues of 1592-1594 – an outbreak which closed the London theatres for two years – William Hastings took up lodgings with Henry Percy and his wife Dorothy Devereux, younger sister of Penelope and Robert Devereux (Essex), at Petworth House on the West Sussex Downs. The 9th Earl of Northumberland, Henry Percy (1564-1632) became known as the Wizard Earl because of his scientific interests. In fact, Henry set himself the immense task of accumulating all worthwhile knowledge – which, for a super-polymath, was still possible at that time. In that hugely ambitious exercise, Henry was helped by three scholars: Thomas Harriot (1560-1621) – a traveller to the New World and an expert in mathematics and astronomy; Walter Warner (1550-1636) – an expert in algebra who acted as Henry's librarian; and Robert Hues (1553-1632) – a scientific geographer who had undertaken a world voyage in 1586-88. Unsurprisingly, they were known as The Three Magi.

Although Henry Percy was brought up in the Protestant tradition the family, with its ancient northern roots, was one of the most powerful Catholic dynasties in the land. Like many of his class and generation, Henry had been a wastrel in his youth. But in later life he underwent a sea-change and became a somewhat irascible, scholarly recluse and retreated into a rather gloomy private world – probably due in part to his increasing deafness.

William Hastings was hidden in death as well as in life – 'sad true lover never find my grave, / to weep there.'. The name 'Petworth' – the location of his grave – is buried in the last words of Feste's beautiful elegiac song in *Twelfth Night* (Act II Sc IV) – '... to weep there.' Anagrams indicate that William Hastings is buried in a deep vault at Petworth Church and that the 'Shakespeare diaries' are interred with him.

Perched on the southern edge of a low plateau, overlooking the rolling Sussex Downs, the village of Petworth is relatively isolated, even today. People living there in the sixteenth century had no choice but to make their own entertainment – London, with its panoply of enticing diversions, was at least two days' ride away. So, as the 'resident genius' at the big house, the

According to evidence in anagrams, William Hastings often hid-out at Wilton House, home of his cousin, the brilliant Mary (Sidney) Herbert. It was here that Mary created the first literary salon – a group of writers and intellectuals now regarded as the foundation of the English renaissance.

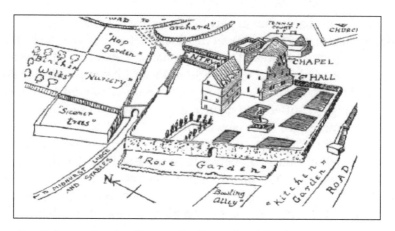

Detail from a sketch of Petworth village, dated 1610, gives an impression of the old house and gardens about the time Hastings lodged here.

amateur dramatist wrote plays as a pastime to amuse himself and to entertain the locals – a rag-bag of individuals, representing a diverse sample of Elizabethan England's inhabitants: aristocrats – the Percy family, intellectuals and scholars (the men who worked for Henry on his great project) as well as local tradesmen, farmers and peasants. Consequently, there is something in *Shakespeare* for everyone: bawdy jokes, tragedy, farce, satire – the lot, all mixed together in a highly unorthodox format.

For much of his life, William Hastings seems to have been a rootless individual, perhaps not unlike the melancholic wanderer Jacques who appears in *As You Like It* and offers his world-weary view of life in the 'seven ages of man' speech. Notwithstanding his lameness, Hastings (like his parents) probably enjoyed being 'on the move' – a traveller never staying in one place very long, he probably spent much of his life either in hiding or in transit. However, Petworth (like Wilton) was a place of lodging which offered Hastings sanctuary and an opportunity to study and write in the peace and quiet of a well-stocked library, with a few intellectual friends for company.

10

'Persona Non Grata'

Three critical questions

1. How did Hastings become *Shakespeare's* author?

- Natural linguistic talents and an ability to 'read' people: attributes inherited from a mother who was herself highly articulate and an uncanny judge of character – like her father, Henry VIII.
- Almost certainly given a humanist education, perhaps through the rigorous system devised by Burghley. Taught to learn languages by his mother.
- Angry – as one of his own anagrams in the sonnets indicates – though it seems he probably channelled some of the anger into his writing.
- Access to the best libraries and tutors – some of the finest minds in England and Europe frequented Elizabeth's court.
- Detailed knowledge of the aristocracy through family connections.
- Lived in an age of adventure and discovery, when the old world-view was being revolutionised in the aftermath of the Renaissance and the Reformation.
- Widely travelled in England as a young actor/spy with Lord Leicester's Men; also visited the Low Countries, Denmark, probably France, Italy and the New World.
- Worked for his mother as the 'royal spy' – an occupation that significantly enhanced his ability to write about people from an 'insiders' view.
- Raised with theatre in the family – in particular, his father's play-troupe and theatre-loving mother. Probably learned to act, as a boy, with the Children of the Chapel at Windsor.
- Taught to write sonnet-style verse by the acknowledged poet Edward de Vere, 17th Earl of Oxford.

These points show how the phenomenon of *Shakespeare* involved much more than the author's innate abilities – his mysterious 'genius'. The extraordinary circumstances of Hastings' life were very important factors in his development. Those conditions will never be repeated, which is one of the reasons why the works will remain uniquely special.

2. Why did Hastings not step out of the shadows and stake his claim to the throne?

Two possible answers are:

- Hastings *did* make an attempt to claim the throne – albeit concealed. Essex's botched rebellion in 1601 might have had a hidden agenda, namely to replace Elizabeth with her unacknowledged son. If that was the case, Essex would have been to William Hastings what Robert Cecil actually was to James VI of Scotland – the kingmaker. Essex and Cecil were bitter enemies; it is therefore highly unlikely that Essex would have taken the considerable risk of staging a rebellion, only to place on the throne the very man that Cecil wanted to see there. Moreover, the Scottish king was not stupid; it is very unlikely he would have accepted the throne in such questionable circumstances. If James was to succeed Elizabeth, the critical transition of dynasties from Tudor to Stuart *had* to appear legitimate.

- Anagrams suggest that Hastings was 'timid' and 'docile'. Unlike his half-brother Sir Robert Dudley it seems he was not a swashbuckling extrovert but a scholar and notebook keeper. Like Hamlet and Prospero, he was a man of thought rather than action – and perhaps unable to make up his mind, like his notoriously indecisive mother. It is possible that with those traits, he lacked the courage to openly claim the throne – at least, not without the official acknowledgement of the queen. By the time James was crowned in 1603, it was too late – William Hastings himself had no absolute proof of identity and, in any case, he was illegitimate. Moreover, the atmosphere brightened on the death of the old queen – in expectation of better times, and James was greeted enthusiastically by most of his English subjects. So there was no mood for rebellion amongst the general populace, at the start of the new reign.

3. Why did the queen not name William Hastings as son and heir on her deathbed?

Even at the end of her life, Elizabeth could not publicly acknowledge her illegitimate son. The factors preventing a deathbed disclosure were a combination of personal, political and practical:

Personal: Elizabeth was impossibly vain; she had always been determined to go down in history as that mythical being the unsullied, 'Virgin Queen' married to England – she had said as much herself. It was therefore impossible for such a headstrong woman to publicly admit that she had lived a lie all those years, since the beguiling image she had worked so hard to build and maintain would have been shattered – along with her reputation.

Political: If Elizabeth *had* swallowed her pride and acknowledged William Hastings, it would have created a very serious difficulty: her son was illegitimate, therefore, he could not become king. However, naming Hastings would have put him squarely in the public domain, and so the succession would probably not have taken place uncontested.

For several years before Elizabeth's death Robert Cecil, the chief minister, had been making arrangements in secret for King James of Scotland to succeed her. It was vital for Cecil personally, as the 'kingmaker', that his plan should run smoothly without the dangerous complication of a contest, which might provoke civil unrest and create the real possibility that he might get the chop if it went wrong. To safeguard his own future, Robert Cecil had to be sure his candidate would get the top job; therefore, there must be no contest. Hence, William Hastings must not appear on the scene.

Practical: How would astounding and potentially destabilising disclosures made by the queen, on her deathbed, reach the public domain? Anything of a astonishing nature that Elizabeth might have uttered, as she lay dying, would have been censored; nothing she might have said about an unacknowledged son would have left the room. A revelation of that magnitude would definitely not have been in the interests of Robert Cecil; indeed, he would have made certain that nothing of such a sensational nature reached the outside world.

Relatives, friends and powerful enemies
Sir Philip Sidney (1554-1586) – paragon of the age

Although not much cared for by the queen herself, Philip Sidney was seen by many contemporaries as a sort of paragon – the epitome of 'Renaissance Man'. Like his brilliant sister Mary (Sidney) Herbert, he was a shining example of the calibre of literary talent amongst William Hastings' closest relatives – the posthumously published sonnet sequence *Astrophil and Stella* and *Arcadia* being his most famous works.

In 1586 Sidney found himself in the Low Countries with his uncle, the Earl of Leicester, and a number of other English nobles, helping the Dutch fight the Spanish. In the March, Sidney wrote a letter from Utrecht to his father-in-law, the spy master Sir Francis Walsingham, complaining that a letter he had sent to his wife – Walsingham's daughter, Frances – had been given instead to Lettice Knollys, Leicester's wife, by a messenger who Sidney called: 'William, my Lord of Leicester's jesting player'. Sidney was very angry about the mix-up because it seems that, due to the sensitive nature of its contents, the letter could not have been delivered to a more 'inappropriate' recipient – a mistake that seems to have been calculated to cause upset, by the messenger himself.

The question is: who was the 'William' to whom Sidney was referring? Will Kemp, a famous comic actor, was with Leicester's men at the time – but he was always referred to either as 'Will' or 'Kemp', *not* William. In any case, it's very unlikely that such a key player would have been sent on a journey to England, lasting several weeks, just to deliver a letter – especially at a time when his professional services were needed by the play troupe. It looks as though the 'William' of Sidney's letter was someone other than Kemp. However, it is unlikely that the individual in question was an 'ordinary' actor, because Sidney was known for his harsh temper – especially with underlings. In light of that knowledge, what 'ordinary' messenger would have dared to inflame Sir Philip Sidney by deliberately misdirecting his letter – to the worst possible recipient?

It seems the messenger knew precisely

Soldier, scholar, poet and courtier, Sir Philip Sidney – the famous 'Renaissance Man' – was the eldest son of Mary Sidney, Robert Dudley's sister, brother of Mary (Sidney) Herbert and cousin of William Hastings.

what he was doing and that he deliberately bungled the delivery with the intention of causing trouble, perhaps because he was put-out at being used as a mere courier – work fit for a 'slight, unmeritable man' as it says of messengers in *Shakespeare*. The episode has the hallmarks of malicious intent – which suggests the letter-bearer might have been William Hastings who was probably touring with Leicester's Men in northern Europe, between 1585 and 1587. It is notable that Sidney called William a 'jesting player' – perhaps comedy was Hastings' preferred medium; afterall, many of the early *Shakespeare* plays are comedies and the dramatist was almost certainly influenced in boyhood by the famous clown Richard Tarleton.

Furthemore, though perhaps a coincidence, the word 'jesting' – given a Spanish pronunciation – sounds like 'hasting', a pun perhaps on Hastings name – maybe an 'in joke' known to Sidney and Walsingham. The possibility is made more likely by the fact that the Spanish were in conflict with the English at the time. Indeed, it would have been in the Low Countries that Hastings witnessed the sort of battlefield conditions portrayed in *Henry V* – there were no battles in Elizabethan England that the author could have seen himself.

Philip Sidney died in October 1586, several days after receiving a leg wound at the battle of Zutphen. A well-known story recounts that, after receiving the seemingly non-life threatening injury, Sidney gave his water bottle to a dying soldier, not realising that his own wound would prove fatal.

Robert Devereux, 2nd Earl of Essex (1566-1601)

Robert Devereux, Earl of Essex, was the son of Walter Devereux and the beautiful Lettice Knollys. The second great favourite of Elizabeth I, after Robert Dudley himself, he was stepbrother to William Hastings. Brilliant, but rash and unstable, Essex had a strange habit of retiring to bed for several days on end in a fit of pique when things were not going his way – an eccentric pattern of behaviour also exhibited by Mary, Queen of Scots.

There is a possibility that Robert Devereux was, in fact, the illegitimate son of Leicester – which might explain why Elizabeth was so taken with him. Rumours circulated to that effect at the time and it seems to be the case that Leiceseter and Lettice Knollys had a very close relationship in late 1565. It is therefore perhaps significant that Devereux, the Earl of Essex, was born in November 1566. If the story is true, Leicester fathered three brilliant half-brothers – all bastards: William Hastings (by the queen) Robert Devereux (by Lettice Knollys) and Sir Robert Dudley (by Douglas Sheffield). Leicester had a legitimate son by Lettice, also called Robert, nicknamed 'the imp' – a deformed child who died young. The beautiful Lettice (1540-1634) was the daughter of Sir Francis Knollys (treasurer of the queen's household) and

Catherine Carey, daughter of Mary Boleyn, Anne's older sister. Thus, as the granddaughter of Mary Boleyn, Lettice was a relative of Elizabeth and so Robert Devereux, the Earl of Essex – the aging queen's 'toy boy' – was her blood relative too. In 1578, after Walter Devereux's death, Leicester married Lettice amid rumours that he had poisoned her husband. Understandably, in view of her strong feelings towards him, the marriage caused the queen considerable anguish and Leicester was banished from court – even though he had done nothing technically wrong in marrying. Elizabeth eventually forgave the transgression and Leicester was reinstated at court although, in marked contrast, the queen never forgave the beautiful Lettice for stealing

Robert Devereux, Earl of Essex, second great favourite of Queen Elizabeth.

'her' man. It is noteworthy, in this context, that the sonnets praise the beauty of the 'Fair Youth's mother in 'the April of her prime' – a particularly apt allusion if the 'Fair Youth' was Essex.

James I of England – James VI of Scotland (1566-1625)

James Stuart had a technically flawed claim to the English throne; according to Henry VIII's Act of Supremacy of 1544, the Stuarts were explicitly excluded from the line of succession.

The bisexual son of Mary, Queen of Scots and Lord Darnley (her cousin), James Stuart was the Protestant grandson of James IV of Scotland and Henry VIII's older sister, Margaret. In March 1603, on the death of Elizabeth I, his title changed from James VI of Scotland to James I of England and Ireland. He was initially welcomed by his new subjects and yet, within a few years, he became far more unpopular than Elizabeth had ever been. Quite simply, he did not like the people and the people did not much care for him.

James Stuart, the man, was a strange sight to behold: with a misshapen body, weak knees, a tongue too big for his mouth, afflicted by a constant itch (he never bathed) and a disconcerting habit of nervously fiddling with his codpiece when he got agitated. But, behind the itching, twitching and slavering, James could be manipulative, ruthless and cruel; he was also corrupt, and surrounded himself with male 'favourites'. In fact, the Stuart court was full of toadies and flunkies, many of them imported from north of the border.

James Stuart, the king, was work-shy by nature – he preferred to spend time out in the country at one of his many hunting lodges, rather than attend to state business in London. Academically bright – he liked to think himself a second Solomon – James had intellectual pretensions and was famously dubbed 'the wisest fool in Christendom'. He abhorred smoking, warfare and the occult and even took the time and the trouble to write tomes vehemently denouncing tobacco and witchcraft.

James I (James Stuart) had a questionable claim to the English throne.

But, whereas his Tudor predecessor had courage in spades, James was a physical coward; a man so afraid of assassination he wore body armour day *and* night. In fact, just the sight of swords, daggers and soldiers practising drill made him nervous. Perhaps it was fear of assassination that caused him to dislike public appearances – indeed he hated them so much he once threatened to drop his breeches, saying: ' ...and they shall see my arse also!'

Sir Robert Cecil (1563-1612) – 1st Earl of Salisbury

Robert Cecil was the only surviving son of William Cecil, Lord Burghley, and Mildred Cooke; he took over from his father as Elizabeth's chief minister in 1596 at just thirty-three years of age. A dwarfish hunchback, said to have been damaged in infancy when a nurse dropped him, Robert Cecil – the Earl of Salisbury – was academically clever, cunning, ruthless and witty. He was also a creepy little man. Elizabeth conferred on him the rather cruel nickname 'pygmy' and vandals even daubed 'Toad' on the wall of his home, Hatfield House. All in all, Cecil would have made a good model for *Shakespeare's* Richard III – perhaps he really did.

A story often told about Robert Cecil concerns the queen's final illness in March 1603. Having spent many hours awake – Elizabeth refused to eat, drink or sleep in the days before her death – Chief Minister Cecil finally lost patience and told her that she *must* go to bed. Probably much to his surprise, the ailing queen lashed out with a typically stinging rebuke: 'little man,' she said, '*must* is not a word that is used to princes'. It was a humiliating put-down for the most powerful man in the land – and something that Cecil would not easily forget. Indeed, it was rumoured that a few days later, impatient to hasten the course of history, Robert Cecil literally took matters into his own hands and throttled the dying queen!

After the succession it became clear to King James and Cecil that if the masses ever learned of William Hastings – the secret son of Elizabeth – an Englishman and Tudor heir to the throne, they would find themselves in a very difficult position; possibly facing the prospect of an uprising – especially as the king's initial popularity dwindled. So, James Stuart and Robert Cecil had the strongest of motives – and the power – to ensure that Hastings was obliterated and consigned to eternal oblivion, never to be heard of by the public.

Robert Cecil – 1st Earl of Salisbury, a possible model for Richard III.

The 'indictment' of William Hastings

- Hastings was (potentially) a very serious threat to James himself.
- The fact of Hastings' existence made the legitimacy of the entire Stuart dynasty questionable.
- James' mother Mary, Queen of Scots was executed by Hastings' mother Elizabeth I.
- Hastings was a threat to Robert Cecil's survival.

And so it was that William Hastings became *persona non grata* in his own land.

11

Son of
the Sun

Phaeton – unacknowledged, illegitimate son of the sun
John Florio was Oxford professor of Italian, secretary to the Earl of
Southampton and author of the
first Italian-English dictionary. It
seems he was also a friend of
William Hastings. In March 1591
Florio published his book 'Second
Frutes'. The preface of which contains a commendatory verse entitled 'Phaeton to his friend Florio'
with 'Phaeton' subscribed. Technical and stylistic considerations
have led some scholars to conclude that the 'Phaeton sonnet' is
probably an early work by
Shakespeare's author. For example, a phrase in the fourth line –
'green-lockt summer' – is reminiscent of hyphenations that occur in
many of the sonnets, in *Venus &
Adonis* (1593) and in *The Rape of
Lucrece* (1594). Indeed, it was
precisely for the over-use of
hyphens that *Shakespeare's*
author (Labeo) was lampooned by
his contemporary Joseph Hall.

*En virtute suâ contentus, nobilis arte,
Italus ore, Anglus pectore, vterq; opere.
Floret adhuc, et adhuc florebit: floreat vltra
FLORIVS, hâc specie floridus, optat amans.*

*John Florio, Oxford professor and
friend of Phaeton.*

In Elizabethan and Jacobean times many writers used false names.
However, pseudonyms were not chosen arbitrarily, they always alluded in
some way to the author. Hence, *Phaeton* – a pen name which appeared in
print only once – must have had a special significance for the poet.

In classical mythology, *Phaeton* was the unacknowledged, illegitimate son of the Sun god. In late sixteenth century England, 'The Sun' was a well-known sobriquet of the queen. It would appear, therefore, that only one man could have chosen *Phaeton* as a uniquely appropriate pen name – the unacknowledged, illegitimate the son of 'The Sun' – that is to say, the unacknowledged natural son of Elizabeth I.

The sonnet is written in 'Shakespearean' style – further evidence that the secret son of the queen was the real author of *Shakespeare*. Moreover, the identification of *Phaeton* as Elizabeth's unacknowledged, illegitimate son explains why the pseudonym never appeared in print again: the allusion would have been so clear to anyone versed in mythology, that it would have been much too dangerous to repeat.

Phaeton to his friend Florio

Sweete friend whose name agrees with thy increase,
How fit arivall art thou of the Spring?
For when each branche hath left his flourishing,
And green-lockt Summers shadie pleasures cease:
She makes the Winters stormes repose in peace,
And spends her franchise on each living thing:
The dazies sprout, the little birds doo sing,
Hearbes, gummes, and plants doo vaunt of their release.
So when that all our English witts lay dead,
(Except the Laurell that is ever greene,)
Thou with thy Frutes our barrennes o're- spread,
And set thy flowrie pleasance to be seene.
Sutch frutes, sutch flowrets of moralitie,
Were nere before brought out of Italy.

Phaeton

Phaeton – in Mythology the unacknowleged, illegitimate son of the Sun God.

An empty sieve – symbol of lost virginity?

The painting (page 131) was found rolled-up in an attic in Sienna in 1895. This, the finest version of the so-called 'Sieve' portraits of Elizabeth I, is by Zuccaro (c 1583). It is not known who commissioned the painting, or how it came to be in Italy.

Lines implicit in the design of the Sieve portrait direct the eye to two colourful, brightly illuminated figures standing in the mid-ground behind the queen. The smaller figure in white, beyond, has been identified by Sir Roy Strong as Christopher Hatton. Made Lord Chancellor in 1587, Hatton was a very senior figure at court and a long-standing favourite of Elizabeth; indeed, at the time of the painting he was second only to the Earl of Leicester in the queen's affections.

The fact that the two gaudily clad figures have been given such prominence, implies they have even higher status than Hatton. Hence, the figure on the right with aquiline profile and dark hair, almost certainly represents

'No angel': In 1560 Elizabeth told the Spanish ambassador of her secret – 'I am no angel,' she said. 'I have some affection for Robert Dudley.' Does the empty sieve, shown here, indicate lost virginity? (Zuccaro, 1583)

Leicester – the only courtier of the right age and of higher rank than Hatton, who had such an appearance. But, the key question is the identity of the tall, fair-haired youth – why has he been placed at a prime location with the queen and Leicester? No known courtier, of the right sort of age in 1583, fits the description – yet his conspicuous presence in the picture suggests that he must be someone of very high status.

Elizabeth is shown holding an empty sieve in her left hand – an icon which could represent either virginity or discernment. According to the former interpretation, the virgin of classical myth carried a sieve *full* of water without spilling a drop; by contrast, the sieve held by the queen is completely empty – an image which might imply *loss* of virginity! According to the second interpretation, the sieve represents a challenge to *dis-*

Detail from the Sieve Portrait of Queen Elizabeth. The small child immediately to the left of the tall youth (Hastings) is probably (Sir) Robert Dudley, aged nine in 1583. Hence, the painting shows Leicester with his two sons.

cern hidden meanings. For example, it is noteworthy that the sieve lies along an axis delineated by Leicester's staff. Is this alignment a subtle hint that the sieve's emptiness is linked to Leicester, perhaps because he was responsible for the queen's loss of virginity?

Furthermore, Elizabeth's horizontal eye-line passes through the heads of the two courtiers and her right eye, the centre of the sieve and the head of the young courtier form an isosceles triangle – an implicit symmetry at the centre of the painting which connects the queen, the young man and the sieve. The triangular link makes sense if the youth is associated with the queen's loss of virginity – because *he* is her son by Leicester.

It appears that the key message encrypted in the portrait is that the famous Virgin Queen is not a true virgin! It is supremely ironic that a painting supposedly depicting Elizabeth's virgin status, shows her with her secret son and his father. Seen in that light, the portrait is an example of the Elizabethan fascination with the issue of 'appearance and reality' – how things seem, in contrast with how they are. Reality hidden by a mask.

Like many pictures of that era, the painting is riddled with arcane symbolic meaning. For example, an important function of the picture is to present the queen as an empress – the columns represent empire. Indeed, Elizabeth's imperial ambitions are made explicit by ships, painted on the globe, which are sailing westwards to the New World. It is noteworthy that Leicester's lower left leg is pointing directly at the vessels on the globe and that the right leg of the youth is pointing towards North America. Is this a pictorial reference to Raleigh's expedition to the New World, which took place in 1584? Is it also a subtle hint that the young man intended to take part in the great adventure and that he would soon be bound for America himself?

A mysterious young courtier

Is this (detail) a portrait of William Hastings at the age of majority? According to the inscription in the top left corner, the sitter was twenty-one in 1583 – which means he was born in 1562, the same year as Hastings. The high quality of the painting and the richness of the sitter's attire, with sword, imply that he is a courtier; sumptuary laws meant that apparel directly correlated to social status. It has been suggested, moreover, that the painting is by Zuccaro – the artist who, in the same year, painted the Sieve portrait. The picture's present location and ownership is unknown to the author.

There cannot have been many courtiers born in 1562 who resembled this particular individual – yet the sitter's identity is a mystery. The hair is similar to that of the young courtier in the Sieve portrait, although the nose is less prominent – perhaps the result of 'cosmetic' portraiture. Of special interest is the obfuscated inscription in the top right corner. The question is: if the aim was simply to hide the text, why wasn't it just erased and over-painted? It seems that someone took the time and trouble to purposely obscure the letters. If the concealment was intentional, two questions arise:

- What was so secret about this courtier – at just twenty-one years of age – to warrant the inclusion of a deliberately concealed inscription in his portrait?
- What does the inscription say?

It is reasonable to suppose that the distorted inscription in some way identifies the sitter, in which case his identity is secret. The question is: Why?

The unknown Garter Knight

Historians have long been puzzled by the painting known as Eliza Triumphans and have been unable to agree about the occasion to which it relates. That in itself is strange. How could there have been such an (apparently) important event – which the painting seems to depict – yet no known historical occasion corresponds with it?

The processional order was determined by status; thus, the six men in front of the queen are all of the highest rank, each is wearing the insignia of Garter Knight – pendant with dragon and St George and garter below the left knee bearing the motto: *Honi soit qui mal y pense* (Evil be to him who evil thinks). The presence of the queen with so many Garter Knights and courtiers suggests the painting represents an important event – the question is *what*?

The identities of the people in the procession are crucial for any attempt at interpretation. Five of the six knights in front of the queen have been identified by Sir Roy Strong, although one has not. From the left they are the Lords: Sheffield, Howard, Cumberland, Hunsdon, 'unknown' and Shrewsbury. Immediately in the foreground is a seventh Garter Knight, the Earl of Worcester. In *The Cult of Elizabeth*, Strong discusses in detail the identification of each knight, however, in the case of the unknown knight he says: 'Then comes a puzzle, a dreamy young man in white...'.

Strong lists all those Garter Knights, of about the right age, who might fit the description: Northumberland (37) Lord Howard de Walden (39) the Earl of Sussex (26) Lord Cobham (33) and Lord Scrope (33) – but concludes that,

Eliza Triumphans (1598-1600, by Robert Peake) is the most famous painting of the Virgin Queen in procession – it is also the most enigmatic – a very complex image whose meaning continues to elude art historians. As usual in the late 1590s, Elizabeth is shown in the mask of youth. The 'unknown knight' is fifth from the left in the procession.

although the quality of the image is poor, none of the above noblemen resemble the 'unknown' knight; Strong even suggests that the mystery of his identity might never be solved.

The name of every Garter Knight is known, right back to the order's inception in 1348, and there are only two dozen at any time, so it is very odd indeed that a Garter Knight – especially one placed at a prime location in such an important painting – is unidentifiable.

Furthermore it is also very strange that, unlike all the other knights in the picture, the unknown knight's garter is hidden in deep shadow and only a tiny part of the pendant is visible. Surely, anybody wearing such prestigious emblems would want them to be seen clearly? So why are these highly elite status-symbols all but concealed *only* in the case of the unknown knight?

Nothing happens in Elizabethan paintings 'by accident', which means the garter and pendant were almost certainly obscured *intentionally*. Moreover, it is very suspicious that the unknown knight has been placed at such an important location – *immediately* in front of the queen – where only those of the very highest status are positioned.

The most logical explanation for these mysteries is that the Garter Knight is unknown – yet of the highest rank, because he is, in fact, the secret son of the Virgin Queen, William Hastings.

Despite the poor quality of the images – and an interval of about fifteen years between them – there is a distinct similarity between the young courtier in the Sieve painting (right) and the unknown knight in the procession picture (left). The evidence suggests that these two figures, at prime locations in important paintings with the queen, represent the same individual – the secret son of Elizabeth I – William Hastings.

12

The Shakespeare Codes

During Elizabeth's reign the security of the realm was under threat both from abroad – the two great continental powers France and Spain – and at home, from the sectarian divide between Protestants and Catholics. Largely in response to those threats and assassination plots against the queen, censorship and punishment were harsh and draconian.

Partly because thinkers and writers had secrets to hide and partly because spies, informers and conspirators needed to communicate with each other secretly, the study of cryptography became a serious pursuit. As mentioned previously, the most notorious example of contemporary code-breaking led directly to the execution of Mary, Queen of Scots in 1587. So, at a time when secret knowledge could literally be a matter of life and death, it was natural that those who knew of William Hastings, the secret royal author, should hide their knowledge – for future generations – in text that alluded to the real author under a pseudonym.

The commonest techniques of encryption are *substitution* and *transposition*. In the former method code replaces plain text. For example, a very simple substitution code might replace 'A' with 'Z', 'B' with 'Y', 'C' with 'X', etc – substituting letters according to a fixed rule. That is to say, substitution is a *formulaic* process. With transposition, however, letters of plain text are simply rearranged amongst themselves to make anagrams. Thus, transposition is the most obvious way to encrypt messages without using formulas – which might be lost or fall into the wrong hands. That is why the anagrammatic method was used to encode messages about Hastings.

The secret hidden by the *Shakespeare* hoax was treason to make public at the time and so in order to enhance security, Hastings and his contemporaries constructed their anagrams (mainly) as two-dimensional structures. Unlike the familiar linear anagrams, non-linear anagrams – as the name implies – do not consist of words arranged in a line.

The solutions – or 'keys' – that link the clues to the answers consist of interlocking horizontal and vertical words, arranged in a two-dimensional array rather like *Scrabble*. But, because there is no general formula, each anagram must be solved individually by a process of informed trial and error. In the words of their creators, the anagrams are 'wit tests' – a description which would not be appropriate with a formulaic method of encryption, since no 'wit test' is involved in simply using a formula.

Anagram sources

It has been assumed that every line in verses that refer to 'Shakespeare', during the period when commendatory verse was written (1590-1650), is an anagram if it contains the letters of 'Hastings'. With well over 250 solutions so far, not all included in this book, the assumption has proven good. However, errors could arise due to:

- Inconsistent spelling.*
- Word meanings changed since the seventeenth century.
- Typographical errors made by printers.
  (in original copy and reprints).
- Error by the source author.
- Mistakes in reconstruction.

The commonest differences from modern spelling are the redundant 'e' at the end of many words ending with consonants (deepe, knowne, looke, minde, passe, whome etc) and the doubling of certain consonants especially 'd', 'g', 'l', 'n', 's' & 't' (hidd, dogges, royall, sonn, witt etc). Moreover, the past participle was often written 'd' rather than 'ed' – eg 'walk'd' instead of 'walked' etc. Punctuation tended to be erratic also; sometimes with too many commas, sometimes too few and apostrophes were not used as they are today. As with the spelling, there was no consistency.

The following requirements impose tight restrictions on anagram solutions, and thereby help to exclude spurious results.

The anagrams must:

- Use Shakespeare-related texts (e.g. dedications, verses, 1623 Folio, sonnets etc) with original spelling.

- Not use words or phrases unknown in the seventeenth century.

* Orthography only became standardised after the publication of Dr Samuel Johnson's great dictionary in 1755. The source texts from which anagrams are constructed *must* use the original spelling and punctuation; in fact, most have been taken from the *Shakespeare Allusions* book – Ed C. Mansfield Ingelby Trubner & Co 1874.

- Not contradict each other or known historical fact.

- Be constructed from single lines of text (there are a few exceptions).

- Collectively tell a coherent story.

- Be consistent with variations in seventeenth century spelling.

- Be exact – no surplus or missing letters.

- Make logical, contextual and grammatical sense.

Solving non-linear anagrams

Non-linear anagrams have three parts: 1.**The Clue** – the line of source text. 2. **The Key** – a two-dimensional, Scrabble-like structure which uses all the letters of the clue, with intersecting words reading horizontally and vertically. 3. **The Answer** – the correct sequence of words taken from the key.

For example, the first line of Ben Jonson's 1623 Folio commendatory verse reads: 'To draw no envy (Shakespeare) on thy name,' – that is the clue. The key, with a vertical 'spine' spelling-out SHAKESPEARE, is:

```
        W A S
          T H Y
            A N Y
            K
            E     N
V E N D O R S     O
            P O E T
        H   E
            A
            R
      N A M E
```

With the answer: *Shakespeare, thy vendor's name (he was not any poet)*

Which uses exactly the same punctuation as the clue. The key could have been constructed with the spine horizontal; however, with a vertical spine, most of the words in the key are horizontal – which simply makes it easier to read.

The factors involved in discovering anagram solutions are experience, intuition, specific details of history and an awareness of the words likely to occur in secret messages about a hidden author. Gradually, a 'vocabulary' accumulates that contains certain key words – a lexicon which common sense suggests is likely to have been used by the anagram makers, viz: Hastings, William, hid, hides, hidden, code, name, poet, verse, play, poetry, poem, clue, answer, wit, test, solve, believe, uncover, true, truth, author, writer, wrote, secret, ruse, anagram, riddle, message, lie, false *etc*. Clearly, it is vital to take account of variations in seventeenth century spelling and meaning.

Sometimes the location of an anagram can hint at the solution. For example, line 2 in Jonson's verse *To the Reader* – on the very first page of the 1623 Folio reads: 'It was for gentle Shakespeare cut;' referring to Droeshout's engraving on the title page, opposite the verse. First, 'Shakespeare' is removed from the line (thereby reducing the number of letters from which to construct a solution) and arranged as a vertical 'spine':

S
H
A
K
E
S
P
E
A
R
E

Which leaves: IT WAS FOR GENTLE CUT; these letters are then randomly rearranged, and moved around until a combination of chance, imagination and knowledge suggests an appropriate arrangement of logically connected words. For example, FACE and WRONG can be found within the above letters – which suggests an anagram stating that the Droeshout engraving is the 'wrong face'. Hence, the aim is to construct a meaningful, exact statement involving that idea from the remaining letters. By finding a few more logically connected, inter-locking words amongst these letters – TITLE, PUT and HERE – the key can be assembled, viz:

With the answer:
Shakespeare's title; wrong face put here.

The solution makes perfect contextual sense as it appears directly opposite the Droeshout engraving and Shakespeare's title.

Of course, because words intersect in the key, there are always more letters in answers than in clues; so, someone good at solving ordinary linear anagrams, probably wouldn't be able to 'see' the non-linear solutions, firstly because the answer contains extra letters that do not appear in the clue itself and secondly because keys are two-dimensional.

```
              S
          H E R E
              A
              K
              E
              S
              P U T
      F A C E
              A
          W R O N G
    T I T L E
              S
```

Hence, non-linear anagrams are, in general, more secure than linear ones.

Often the spine, which forms the core of the key, is 'Hastings'; however, sometimes there is no 'obvious' spine word and in those cases the anagrams tend to be more difficult to solve. For example, in Jonson's folio verse *To the Reader*, line 5: 'O, could he but have drawne his wit' contains no obvious spine word, although key words in the 'anagram vocabulary' appear: CODE, AUTHOR, TRUE and HID. These suggest a solution which states that the text is a code, and the true author is hidden. The key is:

The answer: *True author was hid, now believe this code*

It is important to be aware that one clue can contain several exact answers. The greatest exponent of such 'multiple' solutions, Ben Jonson, created one particular clue – the last line of his folio commendatory verse – that reads: 'And despaires day, but for thy volumes light.' which has more than twenty exact solutions. For example, we notice that the 'anagram vocabulary' words: ANAGRAM, SOLVE and HIDDEN appear in the clue – which suggests an answer referring to a hidden anagram. Indeed, the solution, with spine word ANAGRAMS, has the key (right):

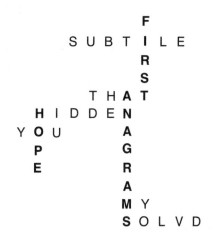

The answer: *Hope that you solv'd my subtile, hidden anagrams first.*

Some solutions contain messages that indicate the presence of an anagram. For example, a line in one source reads: 'This truth, the glad rememberance I must love'. Letters of the anagram vocabulary words: MESSAGE, TRUTH and UNCOVER appear in the line, hinting at a solution that involves uncovering truth in a message.

The key is:

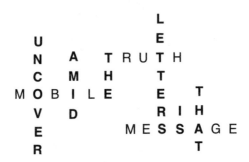

The answer: *Uncover the truth, that message is amid mobile letters.*

Another source, a sonnet in a painting, has the line: 'are all the physicke that my harmes redresse.' Which contains the anagram vocabulary words: HID, SECRET, SHAKESPEARE, PLAYES. The key, with spine SHAKE-SPEARE, is:

```
                    S
                    H
                    A
                    K
        H E R       E
                    S         M
            H       P L A Y E S
        T I T L     E
            D       A         A
                    R         R
              S E C R E T
                              H
                              E
                    M Y
```

The answer: *Hid my Shakespeare title here. They are my secret playes*

13

Man of Letters

Like many associated with the world of theatre, Ben Jonson was no saint. He even killed a man in a duel but was pardoned by claiming 'benefit of clergy', which simply meant he could read the Bible in Latin. By way of chastisement his thumb was branded with the letter 'T' – a permanent reminder that next time he would be sent to Tyburn, the notorious place of execution for murderers and traitors.

Educated at Westminster School, the erudite Jonson was a brilliant scholar and a man who did not suffer fools at all. A soldier and bricklayer, not a university graduate, he was notoriously short-tempered and quarrelsome and took pleasure in deliberately starting fights and arguments. An overbearing extrovert with a towering ego, and a law unto himself, Jonson was imprisoned twice for his part in writing plays that vexed the authorities.

Ben Jonson never wrote of 'Shakespeare' during the Stratford man's lifetime.

In common with a number of contemporary writers and actors, he worked for a time as a secret agent in the dangerous world of espionage – it was always likely that a man with his temperament and intellectual capabilities would be talent-spotted by the spy-masters. And so, in the capacity of 'intelligencer' – or secret agent – he would certainly have been familiar with the various methods of cryptography.

It is *assumed* by scholars that Jonson was, for many years, a friend and colleague of William Shakspere. It has been suggested, furthermore, that there was a 'falling out' between them during the so-called 'war of the poets' around 1600 – a schism in the London theatre world alluded to in *Hamlet*. It is extremely strange, therefore, that Jonson had nothing whatsoever to say about the man from Stratford during William Shakspere's lifetime. Nevertheless, having written more about 'Shakespeare' than any of the author's other contemporaries, it seems appropriate to begin by examining Jonson's curious little verse *To the Reader* – the very first text in the 1623 Folio.

To the Reader

This figure, that thou here seest put,
It was for gentle Shakespeare cut;
Wherein the graver had a strife
with Nature, to out doo the life:
O, could he but have drawne his wit
As well in brasse, as he hath hit
His face, the Print would then surpasse
All, that was ever writ in brasse.
But, since he cannot, Reader, looke
Not on his picture, but his Booke.

B.I.

It is surprising that a writer of Jonson's capabilities, regarded as second only to Shakespeare's author, should pen rather mediocre lines for a verse in such an important location, opposite the title page of the 1623 Folio – the magnum opus. It was suggested long ago that the verse is (potentially) a prime site for secret messages and, indeed, there is a non-linear anagram in every line.

For the sake of clarity and simplicity, only 'clues' (in quotes) and corresponding 'answers' (in italics) appear in the following text. Complete solutions, with keys, are given in the Appendix.

Line 1: 'This figure, that thou here seest put,' 30
(1) *Issue huge test, hath put it here, for the future* 38
The very first line in the 1623 Folio hints at the existence of a huge test.

Remarkably, line 2: 'It was for gentle Shakespeare cut;' yields at least sixteen exact solutions:
(2) *Shakespeare; we left clues for giant test*
Corroborating the first anagram. Clues for the 'giant test' are hidden in the Folio text.

And

(3) *Few knowe page has test; or clues stare in face*

Confirming the first two anagrams that a test has been set – and an indication that clues have been left in the verse.

And

(4) *Tis the page for clues; seeke after answers*

Another hint that anagrams have been deliberately hidden in the verse.

And

(5) *Get first clue; Shakespeare was not genius*

The first statement that the Stratford man was an impostor.

And

(6) *Left clue; Shakespeare is not stage writer*

Another indication that William Shakspere was not the playwright.

And

(7) *Left clues; Hastings wrote Shake Speare*

And

(8) *Test clue; Shakespeare worke of Hastings*

And

(9) *Hastings was author; lie kept secret safe*

Acknowledges the existence of a 'lie' which kept the authorship secret secure.

And

(10) *Shakespeare; few let out Hastings' secret*

There are no contemporary records of rumours about *Shakespeare's* secret author.

And

(11) *Hastings was poet; seeke here after clues*

Another hint that clues have been left in the verse.

And

(12) *Hastings was true poet; seeke after clues*

And

(13) *Hastings is at Petworth; seek after clues*

Present tense implies Hastings is buried at Petworth.

And

(14) *Shakespeare's title; wrong face put here*

And

(15) *True Shakespeare face; it hangs at Wilton*

If Droeshout's engraving depicts the wrong face, where is the right one? Anagram 15 provides the answer. Unfortunately, a serious fire at Wilton in 1647 destroyed much of the original house. It is therefore likely that the picture alluded to in the anagram was consumed by the conflagration.

And

(16) *Shakespeare; left huge secret at Wilton*

Again suggesting a very important link between 'Shakespeare' and Wilton.

Mr. WILLIAM
SHAKESPEARES
COMEDIES,
HISTORIES, &
TRAGEDIES.

Published according to the True Originall Copies.

LONDON
Printed by Isaac Iaggard, and Ed. Blount. 1623

The title page of the 1623 Folio, with Droeshout's engraving and Shakespeare's title above. According to anagram 14, this face – which is the best-attested of all the alleged portraits of 'Shakespeare' – is not a true likeness of the author.

And the linear anagram: **(17)** HASTINGS TRUE POET; SKEW REAL FACE

Which seems to suggest that the Droeshout engraving might be a distortion of the real author's face.

Line 3: 'Wherein the graver had a strife'
(18) *The right answer has hid here ever after*

Line 4: 'with Nature, to out-doo the life:'
(19) *The true author, often hid-out at: Wilton*

There is a long-standing tradition that *Shakespeare's* author spent time at Wilton House, near Salisbury. The owner was Mary (Sidney) Herbert, Countess of Pembroke, daughter of Robert Dudley's sister Mary. Hence, William Hastings and the Countess were cousins. In other words *Shakespeare's* author was 'family', which probably explains why the 1623 Folio was dedicated to Mary's sons, William and Phillip Herbert – the Earls of Pembroke and Montgomery.

Line 5: 'O, could he but have drawne his wit'
(20) *True author was hid, now believe this code*
Confirmation that the verse is a code and that the real author was hidden.

Line 6: 'As well in brasse, as he hath hit'
(21) *That has this as the answer, is reliable*
Another example of a self-referential anagram.

Line 7: 'His face, the print would then surpasse'
(22) *The clue that hides this answer, is left on purpose*
A further indication that the anagrams are deliberate constructs.

Line 8: 'All, that was ever writ in brasse.'
(23) *Witt liberates, what answer reveals*
A motif for all the anagrams.

Line 9: 'But, since he cannot, reader, looke':
(24) *Learne construction, breake the code*
Another self-referential anagram, further evidence the code is deliberate.

14

The Monumental Hoax

With so many anagrams in Jonson's verse, one would expect to find further examples in other 'key texts' associated with 'Shakespeare'; in particular, verses on the gravestone and monument in Holy Trinity Church. Scrutiny of those texts reveals the following:

The gravestone curse (without abbreviations)

> Good frend for Jesus sake forbeare,
> To digg the dust encloased heare:
> Bleste be the man that spares thes stones,
> And curst be he that moves my bones.

Line 2: 'To digg the dust encloased heare:'
(25) *Curse has hidden code: set the test long ago*
Confirmation that the gravestone curse is in fact a code.

And
(26) *Hastings: secret code doth elude the Age*

Line 4: 'And curst be he that moves my bones'
is the linear anagram
(27) SHABBY MONUMENT DOTH SAVE SECRET
So corroborating a hint in the monument verse: '...whom envious death hath plast within this monument'. The Stratford Monument was the obvious place to hide secrets about 'Shakespeare' – indeed, it seems that was its real purpose.

Also, the non-linear anagrams:
(28) *Shabby monument saves the secret codes*

And
(29) *Destroy shabby monument. Save the codes*

And
(30) *Hath set verse code on the shabby monument*

The Shakespeare Monument in Holy Trinity Church, Stratford

The Shakespeare Monument, which was installed on the north wall of the chancel of Holy Trinity Church, some time between April 1616 and November 1623, was referred to by both Leonard Digges and Ben Jonson as a 'moniment'. There was (and is) no such word as 'moniment' – yet Jonson had the 'i' printed in bold, as if to emphasise the misspelling. In a commendatory verse to 'Shakespeare', Digges says '...when time dissolves thy Stratford moniment' – a hint that the 'moniment' was not meant to last forever.

Many have been very disappointed by the effigy, including orthodox scholars, regarding the depiction of the great 'Shakespeare' as nothing less than a travesty – a response very similar to reactions to the Droeshout engraving in the 1623 Folio. The verse inscribed beneath the bust, written here without abbreviations, reads:

> Stay passenger, why goest thou by so fast,
> Read if thou canst, whom envious death hath plast
> With in this monument Shakspeare: with whome
> Quick nature dide whose name doth deck this tombe
> Far more then cost: sieh* all that he hath writt,
> Leaves living art, but page, to serve his witt.

The first line: 'Stay passenger, why goest thou by so fast?' seems to suggest that the reader should take time to study the verse carefully – perhaps because the text contains hidden meaning. Indeed, lines 2/3 pose a challenge: 'Read <u>if thou canst</u>, whom envious death hath plast <u>with in</u> this monument...' However, the monument isn't big enough to hold a body and, in any case, the author is (supposedly) buried in the grave nearby, so naturally, the question arises: what is (or was) 'with in' the monument?

Line 1: 'Stay passenger, why goest thou by so fast,'
(31) *Suggests, by thy answer, the poet test was easy for you*

Line 2: 'Read if thou canst, whom envious death hath plast'
(32) *Hath hid shadowe author's name, in the vaults of this cenotaph*
('cenotaph', from the Greek, means 'empty tomb'.)

Line 3: 'With in this monument Shakspeare: with whome,'
(33) *The name with in shews who is the impostor, then: unmaske*

Line 4: 'Quick nature dide whose name doth deck this tombe,':

(34) *Hidd Tudor Queene's bastard sonne within, make time to checke*

An indication that Hastings was the illegitimate son of Elizabeth I.

Line 5* – spelling mistake?

Line 6: 'Leaves living art, but page, to serve his witt'

(35) *Pass wit test, believe Hastings, everliving author*

(The term 'everliving' denotes a dead poet.)

And

(36) *See Hastings' grave, tis in vestibule vault, Petworth*

The line also yields the linear anagram:

(37) GRAVITAS VITAL, BELIEVE W HASTINGS, TRUE POET

The Shakespeare Monument in Holy Trinity Church, Stratford.

Ben Jonson's enigmatic commendatory verse in the 1623 Folio

This rather odd verse seems to contain many strange, allusive hints and double meanings. It is noteworthy that in the title 'The Author' and 'Mr William Shakespeare' appear in different fonts and very different type sizes –perhaps a subtle hint that they refer to different people.

After a few odd, digressive lines Jonson starts the eulogy proper:

'I therefore will begin. Soule of the age!

The applause! delight! the wonder of our stage!'

Words of the highest praise – which is very surprising, in view of the fact that Jonson never once referred to a William Shakspere – 'the wonder of our stage!' – during the Stratford man's lifetime. It is also rather disconcerting to find that, even after reading this lengthy verse, one's knowledge of

*Line 5 is thought to contain a spelling mistake, 'sieh' probably should read 'sith'.

To the memory of my beloved,
The AVTHOR
Mr. WIlliam Shakespeare
And
what he hath left us.

To draw no envy (Shakespeare) on thy name,
Am I thus ample to they booke, and fame:
While I confesse thy writings to be such,
As neither Man, nor Muse can praise too much;
Tis true, and all mens suffrage; but these wayes
Were not the paths I meant unto thy praise:
For seeliest ignorance on these may light,
Which, when it sounds at best, but eccho's right;
Or blinde affection, which doth ne're advance
The truth, but gropes, and urgeth all by chance;
Or crafty malice, might pretend this praise,
And thinke to ruine, where it seem'd to raise;
These are as some infamous baud, or whore,
Should praise a matron. What could hurt her more?
But thou art proofe against them, and indeed
Above th' ill fortune of them or the need.
I therefore will begin. Soule of the age!
The applause! delight! The wonder of our stage!
My Shakespeare rise; I will not lodge thee by
Chaucer or Spenser or bid Beaumont lye
A little further to make thee a roome:
Thou art a moniment without a tombe,
And art alive still, while thy booke doth live
And we have wits to read, and praise to give.
That I not mixe thee so my braine excuses;
I meane with great, but disproportion'd muses:
For if I thought my judgemment were of yeeres
I should commit thee surely with thy peeres
And tell how farre thou didst our Lily out-shine,
Or sporting Kid or Marlowe's mighty line.
And though thou hadst small Latine and lesse Greeke,
From thence to honour thee, I would not seeke
For names; but call forth thund'ring Aeschilus
Euripides, and Sophocles to us,
Paccuvius, Accius, him of Cordova dead,
To life againe, to heare thy Buskin tread,
And shake a stage: Or when thy sockes were on
Leave thee alone for the comparison.
Of all that insolent Greece or haughtie Rome
Sent forth, or sincedid from their ashes come.

Triumph, my Britaine, thou hast one to showe,
To whom all scenes of Europe homage owe.
He was not of an age, but for all time!
And all the Muses still were in their prime,
When like Apollo he came forth to warme
Our eares, or like a Mercury to charme!
Nature her selfe was proud of his designes,
And joy'd to weare the dressing of his lines!
Which were so richly spun, and woven so fit,
As, since, she will vouchsafe no other wit.
The merry Greeke tart Aristophanes,
Neat Terence, witty Plautus, now not please;
But antiquated, and deserted lye
As they were not of Natures family.
Yet must I not give Nature all: Thy art,
My gentle Shakespeare, must enjoy a part.
For though the Poets matter, Nature be,
His art doth give the fashion. And, that he,
Who casts to write a living line, must sweat,
(Such as thine are) and strike the second heat
Upon the Muses anvile: turne the same,
(And himselfe with it) that he thinkes to frame;
Or for the lawrell, he may he may gaine a scorne,
For a good poets made, as well as borne.
And such wert thou. Looke how the fathers face
Lives in his issue, even so, the race
Of Shakespeares minde, and manners brightly shines
In his well tomed, and true filed lines:
In each of which, he seemes to shake a lance,
As brandish't at the eyes of ignorance.
Sweet swan of Avon! What a sight it were
To see thee in our waters yet appeare,
And make those flights upon the bankes of Thames,
That so did take Eliza, and our James!
But stay, I see thee in the Hemisphere
Advanc'd, and made a constellation there!
Shine forth, thou starre of poets, and with rage,
Or influence, chide, or cheere the drooping stage;
Which, since thy flight fro hence, hath mourn'd like night,
And despaires day, but for thy volumes light.

Shakespeare's author is little enhanced. Although the text seems to say a lot, as biography it is curiously uninformative. Apart from stating that the author was a great writer – which we can gauge from the works for ourselves – the text reveals almost nothing of personal significance about the man himself.

In fact, the verse is riddled with anagrams that refer to Hastings:

The first line contains a non-linear anagram which indicates that the name appearing on the title page – 'Shakespeare' – is the name of the man who sold the works, not the name of the poet.

Line 1: 'To draw no envy (Shakespeare) on thy name,'
(38) *Shakespeare, thy vendor's name (he was not any poet)*

Line 5 is the first that contains the letters of Hastings' name:
' 'Tis true, and all mens suffrage. But these wayes'

Which yields two non-linear anagrams:
(39) *Hastings was the true writer, but freely used false names.*

And
(40) *The future beware, Hastings used many false name titles.*
William Hastings used several false names.

Line 7: 'For seeliest Ignorance on these may light,'
(41) *Martin Marprelate, tis the cryptic code of Hastings*
Martin Marprelate was the pseudonym of a satirical Puritan writer who railed against the bishops in a series of seven tracts published in 1588/1589. It seems that Marprelate's author had access to very personal information about the bishops, and used it to such effect that the Archbishop of Canterbury ordered a nation-wide manhunt to apprehend the author, together with those responsible for printing the works. The secret mobile was eventually found near to Manchester, together with the printers. It is very strange indeed that, after all the effort that went into tracking down the author – and even though it seems the authorities were only one step away from apprehending him – Martin Marprelate himself was never captured and publicly identified.

Line 18: 'The applause! delight! the wonder of our stage!':
(42) *Hastings lodged at Petworth House after the plagues*
The plagues were probably those of 1592-94 which resulted in closure of the London theatres for two years.

Line 19: 'My Shakespeare rise; I will not lodge thee by'
(43) *Hastings wrote plays; libertine yokel he solde them*
Ben Jonson describes the Stratford man as 'libertine yokel'.

And a second anagram:
(44) *Yes; Shake speare he solde poetry by William Hastings*
Confirming that 'libertine yokel' in the previous solution refers to 'Shakespeare', the vendor of the works.

Line 31: 'And though thou <u>ha</u>d<u>st</u> small Lat<u>in</u>e, and lesse <u>G</u>reeke,' with the letters 'hasting' spelt in sequence (small Latine, and lesse Greeke – a Jonsonian joke?). One of the most famous lines written about 'Shakespeare'.

(45) *Hastings learned languages, skilled mother, taught method*
Which explains how *Shakespeare's* author acquired knowledge of several languages.

And
(46) *Hastings, dreaded like hell, language lessons mother taught*
Perhaps not very surprising in view of who his mother was!

Line 48: 'And joy'd to weare the dressing of his lines!'
(47) *The whore wife Jane Daniel soe endors'd Hastings' joy!*
Jane Daniel (nee Jeanne de la Kethulle) a francophone Huguenot, came to England c 1588 and was employed by Frances Walsingham, Essex's wife, as a lady-in-waiting. Jane probably knew Christopher Mountjoy – another Huguenot – with whom Shakspere lodged in 1604. Thus, a probable link exists between Hastings and Shakspere through Jane Daniel and Mountjoy. As a result of Jane's relationship with Hastings it is possible to identify the 'Fair Youth' of the sonnets as Robert Devereux, the Earl of Essex – William Hastings' stepbrother. Thus, Hastings (the Poet), Jane Daniel (the 'Dark Lady') and Essex (the 'Fair Youth') formed the triangular relationship alluded to in the sonnets. Indeed, the late sonnets indicate that the Poet and the 'Fair Youth' had sexual relations with the 'Dark Lady' – and Jane Daniel had two sons called William and Devereux, presumably named after the respective fathers.

Line 51: 'The merry Greeke, tart Aristophanes,'
(48) *Regret, the anagrams here, shake posterity*
Recognition of the likely impact that the anagrams would make in the future.

And
(49) *Regret, Shakespeare name, is theatre story*

And
(50) *Rearrange here, 'tis key, to theatre poets name*

And
(51) *Rate, Shakespeare poetry, Hastings merrit*
('merrit' was a contemporary spelling.)

Line 59: 'Who casts to write a living line, must sweat,'
(52) *We set the wit test, now uncover, William Hastings' name*
Another solution that refers to a 'wit test'. Jonson's clue mentions a 'living line' – what does that mean? Is a 'living line' one in which the letters are moved around, as though 'alive', to create hidden messages – a subtle reference, perhaps, to the anagram method itself?

Line 67: 'Of Shakespeare's minde, and manners brightly shines'
(53) *Shakespeare's name is foil sorry, Hastings' name has been hidden*

And
(54) *Hastings is hidden by Marprelate namesake, no bishop's friend*
The Marprelate texts contain very personal, satirical attacks against the bishops; hence, Martin Marprelate was 'no bishop's friend'.

Line 70: 'As brandish't at the eyes of ignorance'
(55) *Actor had beene seen in Stratford by Hastings*
During his late teens and twenties (~ 1580-1588) William Hastings probably travelled widely in England and northern Europe as an actor/spy with Lord Leicester's Men, his father's play troupe. Records show that Leicester's Men visited Stratford sometime in 1587. It is therefore likely that Hastings (perhaps already using the code name Shake-speare) met William Shakspere in Stratford on that occasion. It was probably the coincidence of Shakspere's name and Hastings' code word that led to their professional relationship. After all, William was a very common forename and Shakespeare (with its many variants) was common throughout Warwickshire – so the 'coincidence' of their meeting was hardly improbable.

Line 71: 'Sweet swan of Avon! what a sight it were'
(56) *We swear an oath! The Sweet Swan of Avon is Hastings*
'Sweet swan of Avon ...' – one of the best known phrases written about

'Shakespeare' – is a key piece of evidence used by traditionalists in support of the Stratford man's authorship claim. The line is also a partial linear anagram:

(57) *FEW OWN A VAST NOSE! WHAT A SIGHT IT WERE*
Another example of Jonsonian wit – a derogatory comment hidden inside a compliment – implying that Hastings had a large, prominent nose (like his parents) and possibly a long neck (like a swan).

Line 77: 'Shine forth, thou starre of poets, and with rage' is the linear anagram:
(58) *HASTINGS HONED OUR FIRES, FOR HEAT, AT PETWORTH*
Suggests that William Hastings might have used the ideas of others for inspiration; perhaps he attended the secret meetings – the 'wit matches' – that took place at the famous Mermaid Tavern in Bread Street, London on the first Friday of each month.

The line also contains the non-linear anagram:
(59) *Hastings wrote the parts, for friends, at Petworth House*
Which implies that some of the plays were originally written for amateurs – perhaps even female actors, who were not allowed on the professional stage in those days.

The last line of Jonson's verse: 'And **despaires** day, **bu**t <u>for thy</u> volum<u>es</u> <u>light</u>.' contains more than twenty exact solutions – the largest multiple anagram found to date.

First, a simple linear solution:
(60) *PROVIDE HASTINGS' DEATH, BY MY LUST FOR A DUEL*
A remarkable admission, but entirely consistent with Jonson's pugnacious reputation – indeed, it is Jonson through and through.

And the non-linear anagrams:
(61) *By my poetry riddle, you have at last found Hastings here*
The letters of DARESBURY, after Lady Daresbury (bold type) and FORTYEIGHT (underlined) appear in sequence in the clue. Both words are the spines of keys, viz:

(62) *Set duel trap for Hastings, Lady Daresbury the motive*
Which again suggests that Lady Daresbury (Jane Daniel) was William Hastings' mistress, the 'Dark Lady' of the sonnets. However, the 'Dark Lady'

sonnets are highly defamatory; hence the publication of *Shake-speares Sonnets* in May 1609 was used to entrap Hastings in a duel.

And

(63) *Sad murder at fortyeight, but Hastings' playes liv'd on*
Indicating that William Hastings was *killed* in 1610, when he was forty-eight years old.

And

(64) *By my riddle, you have found out Hastings is Marprelate.*

And

(65) *Let me give you the proofe, Hastings is Dudley's bastard*

And

(66) *You have solv'd my poetry, Hastings is bastard of Dudley*
Confirming the assertion that William Hastings was the illegitimate son of Robert Dudley, the Earl of Leicester.

And

(67) *By my best riddle, you have found the Hastings' play parts*
A hint that there are many anagrams in this line – 'my best riddle' – implying also the existence of anagrams that refer to characters in the plays.

And

(68) *Murder'd spy Polonius hid, given fatal stabs by Hamlet*
Which describes the precise circumstances in which Polonius was killed by Hamlet.

And

(69) *You solv'd this playe, Hamlet is bastard son of Gertrude*
A remarkable revelation, which makes sense of an unsolved mystery at the heart of *Hamlet*: why didn't the prince immediately become king on the death of his father? The answer, it seems, is that although Hamlet was royal, he was illegitimate and therefore could not ascend the throne – just like his creator. Furthermore, Hamlet's illegitimacy raises the intriguing possibility that he was in fact the son of 'Uncle' Claudius – which might explain his notorious 'delay'; critics have long wondered why the Prince did not murder Claudius as soon as he discovered the truth about his father's murder.

And

(70) *My deftly made riddles, prove truths about Hastings.*

And

(71) *Bye your attempt, you have solv'd riddles for Hastings*

And

(72) *Hope that you solv'd my subtile, hidden anagrams first*

A truly astonishing achievement by Jonson – to have incorporated so many correlating and meaningful anagrams in just one line!

15

Shakespeare's Shadow

John Benson & William Marshall*

Stratfordians point out that, in the decades following Shakspere's death, his authorship of the works was never questioned. But, in fact, within a few years of publication of the First Folio there were indications, in print, that 'Shakespeare' wasn't what he seemed to be. One of the most significant hints appeared in 1640 when a very strange verse and engraving was included in *Poems by Wil. Shake-speare.*

The verse by John Benson is a pastiche of part of Ben Jonson's commendatory poem in the 1623 Folio. Astonishingly, the first line is *both* a statement *and* a question! 'This shadowe is renowned Shakespear's?' Benson is clearly questioning the image in Marshall's engraving calling it a 'shadowe' (cf the inscription on the Wilton Monument). Moreover, the words 'applause' and 'delight', that appear

This Shadowe is renowned Shakespear's? Soule of th'age
The applause? delight? the wonder of the Stage.
Nature her selfe, was proud of his designes
And joy'd to weare the dressing of his lines;
The learned will Confess, his works are such,
As neither man, nor Muse, can prayse to much
For ever live thy fame, the world to tell;
Thy like, no age, shall ever paralell.

in Jonson's folio verse, are also questioned, which is very odd if there was nothing 'questionable' about the author. In view of the fact that Benson and

---

* It is noteworthy that the verse and engraving are seldom – if ever – discussed or even mentioned in books by orthodox scholars.

Marshall were contemporaries of people who had known 'Shakespeare' personally, the crucial issue is: what could possibly have *motivated* Benson & Marshall to question the image of 'Shakespeare' *if* the Stratford man was indeed the real author? No other writer's image was 'questioned' in this way, so why was 'Shakespeare' singled out for special treatment?

Furthermore, the image itself is suspicious: the figure is shown *holding* a sprig of laurel – the symbol of a poet – the leaves are not worn as a crown, which is how poets were usually depicted. Is that because 'Shakespeare's shadow' is only a 'mask' and, as such, he does not have the right to wear the laurel crown?

One final point: the first line of the verse: 'This shadowe is renowned Shakespear's? soule of th' age' is a non-linear anagram with answer:

(73) *Hidden Hastings wrote the workes hee us'd Shakespeare so as to foole*

Another first line anagram, in text about 'Shakespeare', that refers to Hastings.

Leonard Digges

Son of the mathematician Thomas Digges, Leonard was one of four contemporaries of *Shakespeare's* author to write commendatory verse in the 1623 Folio. Digges incorporated a non-linear anagram in the first line:

Line 1: 'Shake-speare, at length thy pious fellowes give'
(74) *Hastings wrote the Shakespeare playes, he gave life soul*

TO THE MEMORIE
of the deceaſed Authour Maiſter
W. SHAKESPEARE.

Shakespeare, at length thy pious fellowes give
The world the workes: thy workes, by which out live
Thy tombe, thy name must when that stone is rent,
And Time dissolves thy Stratford Moniment*...

L. Digges

And in another verse about 'Shakespeare' by Digges (See Page 160):
Line 2: 'This truth, the glad rememberance I must love':
(75) *Uncover the truth, that message is amid mobile letters*

A self-referential anagram, which alludes to the method of solution, i.e. letters are moved about – 'mobile letters' – until appropriate words appear.

And

(76) *Uncover the truth, Hamlet is made to resemble Hastings*

Which confirms what many have thought: that Hamlet is a reflection of the author himself. It seems that if we want to know what Hastings was like, as a person, we can gain some insight by studying his most intimate and enigmatic creation.

Line 13: 'One phrase from Greekes, nor Latines, imitate'

(77) *Shake-speare title, Hastings got it free, from manor name*

The 'Shakespeare' title was derived from a non-linear anagram of 'Stoake Parke Manor House'. Perhaps noticing that the last three letters of 'house' spell 'use', Hastings realised that a name could be extracted from the name of the place where he grew up: 'Stoake Parke Manor House'. The full title is a non-linear anagram, which suggests the use of 'Shake-Speare':

> **Upon Master Shakespeare,
> the deceased author, and his poems
> (1640)**
>
> Poets are borne not made, when I would prove
> This truth the glad rememberance I must love
> Of never dying Shakespeare, who alone,
> Is argument enough to make that one.
>
> L. Digges

Only the first part of the verse is shown here.

(78) *Use manor so to take Shake-Speare*

Shake and Speare appear as *separate* words in the key, hence the hyphenation of Shake-speare.

Line 18: 'Is pure his owne, plot, language exquisite'

(79) *Hastings, genius, he was ex pupil to glorious Queene*

Corroborates Jonson's anagrams, which claim that Hastings was taught by his mother.

Line 27: 'Then vanish upstart writers to each stage,'

(80) *Curse on Hastings' grave at Petworth, hath set it as test*

Shakspere's gravestone, in Holy Trinity Church, is yet another puzzle:

- Why – as early as the eighteenth century – was it necessary to replace the original gravestone with a *copy*?

- Why is there no name inscribed?
- Why is the stone only a fraction of the usual length?

The anagram implies a possible resolution. It seems that Hastings' grave at Petworth was probably sealed in the eighteenth century, when the truth of Shakespeare's authorship became known to a few people, as evidence on the monument at Wilton suggests. It was probably decided to replace Shakspere's original gravestone, at Stratford, with the curse-inscribed stone from Hastings' grave at Petworth. The intention was to make it easier for anyone who solved the curse to relate it to the monument on the wall overlooking the grave in Holy Trinity. Of course, on transferring the gravestone to Stratford, William Hastings' name had to be cut off the top, which would explain why the stone now on Shakspere's grave is *both* nameless *and* unusually short.

Line 39: 'Of richer veines, prime judgements that have far'd'
(81) *Hastings even made search drive for Jesuit, Father Campion*
This solution provides evidence that William Hastings was working as a spy for his father, Leicester, in 1580/81. Anthony Munday, the poet, playwright and secret agent, is known to have worked for Leicester. Indeed, Munday was involved in the pursuit of Edmund Campion, and his name has been associated with 'Shakespeare' – so it's possible he acted as a mentor to Leicester's son. It seems Munday was a man of extreme contrasts – writing delicate poetry one minute, torturing people the next!

Line 64: 'Shall passe true currant to succeeding age.'
(82) *Hastings' death in duel regall cause. Pure Scots curse*
An indication that James I ordered Hastings' death. The clue itself seems to hint at a message that has been left for the future. It is noteworthy that Hastings died in his forty-eighth year in 1610 and that in the very same year, in June, King James made his eldest son, Henry, the Prince of Wales – the title bestowed upon the heir to the throne.

Line 65: 'But why doe I dead Shakespeare's praise recite?'
(83) *Shakespeare's diaries? Copy buried deepe at Petworth*
What exactly is meant by 'Shakespeare's diaries'? Were they original manuscripts of the works written in Hastings' own hand – or some sort of personal record of his life? Either way, if the 'Shakespeare diaries' *are* ever unearthed it would be a finding of the utmost historic and literary significance.

John Warren – In preface to: *Shakespeare's poems* (1640)

Line 1: 'What, lofty Shakespeare, art againe reviv'd?'

(84) *Shakespeare diary? Have left it, in grave, at Petworth*

Another first line anagram about Hastings, and a further indication that diaries of some sort were buried with him at Petworth.

Line 5: 'These learned poems amongst thine after-birth,'

(85) *Hastings' name, set behinde the Stratford poet-memorial*

Corroborates hints in the monument verse and the anagrams therein, that the name of the true author has been hidden 'within' the monument.

And

(86) *Marprelate is Hastings' name, the honest bishop feared it*

Further evidence that Hastings wrote the satirical Puritan tracts attacking the bishops.

Line 9: 'Let carping Momus barke and bite his fill,'

(87) *Shakespeare, bumbling mimic and illiterate oaf*

Which is precisely how many Anti-Stratfordians regard the rustic William Shakspere. The anagram brings to mind Jonson's *Poet Ape* (an 'ape' is a

---

Of Mr. William Shakespeare

What, lofty Shakespeare, art againe revived?
And Virbius like now show's thy selfe twise liv'd,
Tis (Benson's) love that thus to thee is showne,
    The labours his, the glory still thine owne.
These learned poems amongst thine after-birth,
That makes thy name immortall on the earth,
    Will make the learned still admire to see,
    The Muses gifts so fully infused on thee.
Let carping Momus barke and bite his fill,
And ignorant Davus slight the learned skill:
Yet those who know the worth of thy desert,
And with true judgement can discerne thy art,
    Will be admirers of thy high tun'd straine,
    Amongst whose number let me still remaine.

(Preface to Shakespeare's poems 1640)

---

mimic) and his satirical portrait of the Stratford man as the rustic clown Sogliardo. The phrase 'illiterate oaf' is consistent with the impression created by Shakspere's 'signatures' and the fact that, according to records from the Belott vs Mountjoy lawsuit in 1612, he was unsure of his age.

And
(88) *Bible trick is true, Hastings left code name in psalm*
Which presumably refers to the forty-sixth psalm, since 'shake' is the forty-sixth word from the beginning and, excluding 'selah', 'speare' is the forty-sixth word from the end. It seems that Hastings worked on the authorised version of the Bible, a masterpiece long regarded as the 'other' great work of English literature. Hastings would have been in his 46th year in 1607/08 at the time when the psalms were (probably) being prepared. Work on the authorised version took six years from 1604 to 1610. The psalms are located at about the mid-point of the Bible – corresponding to about 1607 if the translators worked in sequence at a steady rate. William Shakspere did not reach his forty-sixth year until 1609/10 – so, under those assumptions, the 'timing' of the work on the psalms does not correspond with his age. The surreptitious inclusion of 'Shake' and 'Speare' – which do not appear in earlier versions of Psalm 46 – probably took place whilst work was in progress, rather than in 1610 when the project was completed.

Line 13 'Will be admirers of thy high tun'd straine,'
(89) *Hint, William Hastings murder'd bye fortyeight*
Consistent with Jonson's anagram, in the last line of his folio commendatory verse, that William Hastings was killed by the age of forty-eight in 1610.

Line 14 'Amongst whose number let me still remaine.'
(90) *To mourne the loss remember William Hastings' name*
Continuing the sense of the preceding solution.

John Milton – An epitaph on the admirable dramaticke poet, W. Shakespeare (1630).

Line 8: 'hast built thy selfe a lasting monument'
(91) *Hastings, the bashful Milton salutes thy name*

Line 9: 'For whilst to th'shame of slow-endeavouring Art'
(92) *So few heard of Hastings who out-shone trite rivals. Milton*
Confirmation that Hastings was unknown to the general public.

Line 14: 'Dost make us marble with too much conceiving,'
(93) *Breake church monument to view Hastings code, Milton*
Which is consistent with anagrams in the last line of the gravestone curse.

John Milton, 1630
An epitaph on the admirable dramaticke poet

W. Shakespeare

What neede my Shakespeare for his honour'd bones,
The labour of an Age, in piled stones
Or that his hallow'd Reliques should be hid
Under a starre-y pointing Pyramid?
Dear sonne of Memory, great Heire of Fame,
What needst thou such dull witnesse of thy Name?
Thou in our wnder and astonishment
Hast built thy selfe a lasting Monument:
For whilst to th' shame of slow-endevouring Art
Thy easie numbers flow, and that each part,
Hath from the leaves of thy unvalued booke,
Those Delphicke lines with deepe impression tooke
The thou our fancy of her selfe bereaving,
And so sepulcher'd in such pompe dost lie
That Kings for such a tombe would wish to die.

Line 16: 'That kings for such a tombe would wish to die.'
(94) *Hastings life cut short oh but what workes he did. Milton*
Confirmation that William Hastings did not die from natural causes.

J. M. S. 1632

(J.M.S. is an unknown author. Owing to its length, a facsimile of the text is not included here.)

Line 1: 'A mind reflecting ages past, whose cleere'
(95) *Free code's deep secret, get William Hastings' name*
Another first line anagram, referring to Hastings, in verse about *Shakespeare*.

Line 2: 'And equall surface can make things appeare'
(96) *Anagram clue Hastings' face appeared like queene's*
An indication that Hastings looked like his mother.

Line 6: 'Rowle backe the heavens, blow ope the iron gates'

(97) *Believe Hastings wrote the book, not clowne Shake-speare*

Line 21: 'Enlive their pale trunkes, that the present age'
(98) *Hint, put Hastings' eleven letter Shake Speare title here*

Line 71: 'And more then nature takes, our hands shall give'
(99) *Hastings' anagrams reveal honest, untolde naked truth*
The truth about Hastings never became public.

John Weever – Ad Gulielmum Shakespeare (To William Shakespeare) 1595

Line 1: 'Honie tong'd Shakespeare, when I saw thine issue,'

(100) *See who is heere, 'tis unknowne Hastings, Shakes-peare hides*

Yet another first line anagram in text addressed to 'Shakespeare' that refers to Hastings.

Line 10: 'Their sugred tongues, and power attractive beuty'

(101) *Tis true, Hastings taught to pen court poetry by Edward de Vere*

The phrase 'court poetry' almost certainly refers to verse written in sonnet style. It

> ### John Weever (1595)
> ### Ad Gulielmum Shakespeare
>
> Honie-tong'd Shakespeare, when I saw thine issue,
> I swore Apollo got them and none other,
> Their rosie-tainted features cloth'd in tissue,
> Some heaven born goddesse said to be their mother:
> Rose-checkt Adonis with his amber tresses,
> Faire fire-hot Venus charming him to love her,
> Chaste Lucretia virgine-like her dresses,
> Prowd lust-stung Tarquine seeking still to prove her:
> Romeo_Richard: more, whose names I know not,
> Their sugred tongues, and power attractive beuty
> Say they are saints, although that sts they shew not
> For thousands vowes to them subjective dutie:
> They burn in love thy children Shakespear het the,
> Go, wo thy Muse more Nymphith brood beget them.

seems that Edward de Vere, the Earl of Oxford, an acknowledged poet twelve years William Hastings' senior, was his poetry tutor.

William Davenant – Remembrance of Master William Shakespeare. (1637)

Verse 1, line 1: 'Beware (delighted poets!) when you sing'
(102) *Hastings buried deeply in Petworth (now go see!)*
Another first line anagram referring to Hastings.

Verse 2, line 1: 'Each tree, whose thick, and spreading growth hath made,'
(103) *When accident, hath damag'd Hastings, he wrote, Shake-speare worke*

Is D'Avenant suggesting that an accident triggered Hastings' writing? It is noteworthy that the author of *Shake-speares Sonnets* indicates, on three occasions, that he is lame. Was the lameness caused by the accident?

Verse 2, line 2: 'Rather a night beneath the boughs, than shade,'
(104) *Hastings thought, that the braine, had beene shatter'd*
Implying that Hastings suffered a severe head injury – did it cause a personality change, did it 'free-up' his latent writing ability?

Verse 3, line 2: 'Long since (alas!) to such a swift decay;'
(105) *Hastings' (costly!) fall; was due to sea accident*
D'Avenant's anagrams appear to be telling a consistent story: William Hastings suffered a serious head injury through an accident at sea – a 'costly fall' – a phrase which suggests there were lasting consequences. What were the long-term effects? Lameness, headaches, bouts of madness? Periods of uncontrollable creative genius? Did the injury leave Hastings in permanent pain, necessitating the use of analgesics – opiates perhaps?

In rememberance of Mr William Shakespeare

Ode

1.
Beware (delighted poets!) when you sing
To welcome Nature in the early spring;
Your numerous feet not tread
The banks of Avon; for each flowre
(As it nere knew a sunne or showre)
Hangs there, the pensive head.

2.
Each tree, whose thick, and spreading growth hath made,
Rather a night beneath the boughs, than shade,
(Unwilling now to grow)
Lookes like the plume a captive weares,
Whose rifled falls are steept i'th teares
Which from his last rage flow.

3.
The piteous river wept is selfe away
Long since (Alas!) to such a swift decay;
That reach the map; and looke
If you a river there can spie;
And for a river your mock'd Eie,
Will finde a shallow brooke.

Thomas Heywood (1635)
A line from a commendatory verse addressing several poets

Mellifluous Shake-speare, whose inchanting quill

'Mellifluous Shake-speare, whose inchanting Quill'
(106) *Helpeful clue, William Hastings sonn of queen is Shake-speare*
The anagram says it all.

Hugh Holland – Commendatory verse in the 1623 Folio.

Line 1: 'Those hands, which you so clapt, go now, and wring'
(107) *Hastings, was author incognito, who had code word, on plays*
Another first line anagram about Hastings. It seems that just as many of the *Shakespeare* characters assume a disguise, so their creator appeared *incognito* also.

Line 12: '(Deaths publique tyring-house) the *nuncius* is.' where *nuncius* is 'message' in Latin – suggesting that a message is hidden in the bracketed text, hence: 'Deaths publique tyring-house':

Vpon the Lines and Life of the Famous
Scenicke Poet, Maſter **William**
SHAKESPEARE.

Those hands which you so clapt, go now, and wring
You Britaines brave; for done are Shakespeares days:
His dayes are done, that made the dainty playes,
Which made the Globe of heav'n earth to ring.
Dry'de is that veine, dry'd is the Thespian spring,
Turn'd all to teares, and Phoebus clouds his rayes:
That corp's, that coffin now besticke those bayes,
Which crown'd him poet first, then poets king.
If tragedies might any prologue have,
All those he made, would scarse make one to this:
Where Fame, now that he gone is to grave
(Deaths publique tyring-house) the nuncius is.
For though his line of life went soone about.
The life yet of his lines shall never out.

Hugh Holland – Commendatory verse
in the 1623 Folio.

(108) *Birth by queene put-out Lady Hastings*

Which suggests that Lady Hastings, a woman without children of her own, had the responsibility for bringing up the queen's secret child foisted on to her.

Michael Drayton   (1627)

Shakespeare thou hadst as smooth a Comicke vaine,
Fitting the socke, and in thy natural braine,
As strong conception, and as Cleere a rage,
As any one that trafiqu'd with the stage.

In the last line: 'As any one that trafiqu'd with the stage.'
(109) *Story was that queene hid infant at the Hastings'*
Corroborating the previous anagram, that a child of the queen was hidden by the Hastings family.

16

To All The World
Must Die

Shake-speares Sonnets (1609):
Title page & Thomas Thorpe's dedication

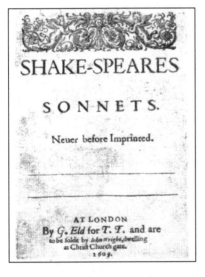

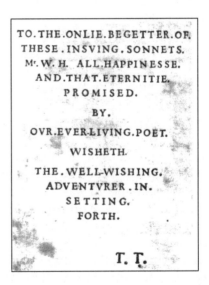

The title page of *Shake-speares Sonnets* and, with it, probably the most mysterious dedication in history. The style is lapidary, with stops after each word, like inscriptions on stone tablets. The text has been initialled by the publisher Thomas Thorpe.

The dedication raises some obvious questions:

- Who was the mysterious M^r. W.H.?
- If M^r. W.H. sought complete anonymity, why did Thorpe include the initials?
- If M^r. W.H. did not seek anonymity, why did Thorpe not name him?

A common misunderstanding is to suppose that Thorpe's text *dedicates* the sonnets to M^r. W.H.. At one level, the 'dedication' is a private message from Thorpe to the poet, which is partly why it is difficult to understand. On inspection the dedication yields three linear anagrams, each referring to Hastings. The first three lines:

'To. the. onlie. begetter. of. these. insuing. sonnets. M^r. W.H. all. happinesse.' *

becomes:
(110) BRINGE HELP TO WILLIAM HASTINGS THE UNSEENE POET OF THESE SONNETS

The second part: 'And. that. eternitie. promised. by. our. ever-living. poet. wisheth.' yields:
(111) PRIVATE POETRY BELIEVE UN-WED TIMID HASTINGS HEIR TO THRONE

The final part: 'The. well-wishing. adventurer. in. setting. forth.' is:
(112) HASTINGS LEFT THE TRUE VIRGIN IN THE NEW-WORLD

An obvious allusion to Virginia, the name given to the first English colonies in North America in honour of the 'virgin' queen. The anagram implies that Elizabeth I was not a true virgin and that William Hastings, her son, visited the New World when the Virginia colonies were named by Sir Walter Raleigh in 1584. In this context, it is noteworthy that in the Sieve portrait, which was probably painted in 1583 – just before the expedition – there are subtle hints that the young courtier, standing next to Leicester, is going to take part in the voyage to the New World.

The Tempest alludes to the wrecking of the *Sea Venture*, in a storm near Bermuda in 1609. However, information about the incident did not reach the public domain until many years after the play was written – so the question arises as to how the author knew details about events on the voyage. The last words of Thorpe's sonnet dedication: '... wisheth the well-wishing adventurer in setting forth.' might hint at the answer.

An expedition to the New World departed London on May 15th, 1609 leaving Falmouth in Cornwall on June 2nd. The precise timing of the registration of the sonnets, May 20th, is consistent with the possibility that M^r. W.H. – William Hastings – took part in the expedition to the New World

---

* the solution does not include the superscript 'r'

(along with about 500 other brave souls) and that he witnessed the storm and shipwreck himself. That would explain why, as Keats pointed out, the description of the storm, at the start of the play, is so good – the dramatist experienced it himself.

Examples of anagrams in *Shake-speares Sonnets* (1609 edition)

Shake-speares Sonnets contain many non-linear anagrams; some of them were included by the publisher, Thomas Thorpe – those whose solutions include the initials 'T.T.', just as he subscribed the dedication. Many more anagrams have been incorporated in sonnets by Hastings himself.

Anagrams left in sonnets by Thomas Thorpe:

Sonnet 10, line 6: 'That gainst thy selfe thou stickst
not to conspire,'
(113) *You cotton so soon, the fact is Shakespeare is*
Hastings' title   TT
(In this context, 'cotton' = 'succeed' and 'so soon' = 'four hundred years'! N. B. the phrase 'to cotton on', which is not the same as 'cotton', is relatively modern.)

Sonnet 52, line 2: 'Can bring him to his sweet up-locked
treasure,'
(114) *Shake-Speare public code words, true name*
is Hastings   TT

Sonnet 89, line 3: 'Speake of my lamenesse, and I straight will halt:' indicates that Shakespeare's author was lame.
(115) *William Hastings himself, named ploy: Shakespeare   TT*

Sonnet 97, line 14: 'That leaves looke pale, dreading the winter's neere.'
(116) *Hidden Hastings. He even wrote Shake Speare worke,*
all alone   TT

Sonnet 108, line 3: 'What's new to speake, what now to register,'
(117) *We know, Hastings is poet, who wrote Shake-speare   TT*

Sonnet 147, line 6: 'Angry that his prescriptions are not kept'
(118) *Hastings is Shakespeare poet sorry can't print   TT*

Examples of sonnet anagrams by Hastings himself

Sonnet 2, line 8: 'Were an all-eating shame, and thriftlesse praise.'
(119) *Please arrange letters, find William Hastings' name here.*

Sonnet 10, line 11: 'Be as thy presence is gracious and kind,'
(120) *Hastings is bounded in secrecy, in Shakespeare*

The most famous sonnet, number 18, contains at least six anagrams relating to Hastings:

Line 3: 'Rough windes do shake the darling buds of Maie,'
(121) *Disguised Hastings hidd name, but looke here for answer*

Line 6: 'And often is his gold complexion dimm'd,'
(122) *Hastings' name in complex code, fooled dim minds*

Line 8: 'By chance, or natures changing course untrim'd:'
(123) *Hastings' name: not by chance recurring, but through code*

Line 12: 'When in eternall lines to time thou grow'st,' – hints at a hidden message.
(124) *Get truth not lie, William Hastings wrote the sonnet*

Line 14: 'So long lives this, and this gives life to thee.'
(125) *Hastings lives in hiding, solve the tests hee left to fool*

Sonnet 37, line 8: 'I make my love ingrafted to this store:'
'ingrafted to this store:' – suggests a hidden message.
(126) *Hastings is hid: move letters to looke for my name*
Sonnet 76 lines 7 & 8: Excluding the last two sonnets (which do not thematically belong with the others) this is the mid-point of the sequence as Thorpe published it. The middle lines of the sonnet are:
'That every word doth almost tel my name, / Shewing their birth, and where they did proceed?'

Which seems to be a strong hint that the poet's name has been hidden in these lines, at the very centre of the sequence – a natural place to conceal it. William Hastings' name is indeed hidden here, together with the names of Thomas Thorpe and Edward de Vere. The lines yield the following non-linear solution:

(127) *William Hastings and Thomas Thorpe had been shewn how to write the poetry, the lyric method, by Edward de Vere*

Which corroborates anagram 101: 'Tis true: Hastings taught to pen court poetry by Edward de Vere'. It is astonishing that the *full* names of William Hastings, Thomas Thorpe *and* Edward de Vere, all appear together in the two lines at the centre of the sonnet sequence. It seems that de Vere was the poetry tutor to *both* Hastings and Thorpe. Hence, the phrase 'our ever-living poet' – in the sonnet dedication – refers to Edward de Vere, the deceased tutor of Hastings and Thorpe.

Sonnet 87, line 14: 'In sleepe a king, but waking no such matter.'
(128) *Hastings is unknowne page, claims to be the true king.*
William Hastings was the king England never knew.

Sonnet 89, line 4: 'Against thy reasons making no defence.'
(129) *Find the key to encode Hastings' name in anagrams.*

Line 5: 'Thou canst not (love) disgrace me halfe so ill,'
(130) *Hastings has left name in code, so (solve it) collect truth*

Line 6: 'To set a forme upon desired change,'
(131) *For true name of the poet, read Hastings' code*

Line 7: 'As ile my selfe disgrace, knowing thy wil,'
(132) *Seek ye well, find codes, William Hastings is angry*

It is hardly surprising that William Hastings was angry in view of the fact that he had to live his entire life in hiding, because his mother would never *officially* acknowledge his existence.

No sad true lover find my grave to weep there

The full name of Petworth Church contains a fortuitous anagram that identifies the location of Hastings' grave – which probably explains why he chose to be buried there. In addition, one of the anagrams in line 2 of Jonson's *To the Reader* hints that there are 'clues' to be found at Petworth: 'Hastings is at Petworth; seek after clues'. The full title of Petworth Church (old spelling) is: 'Saint Marye the Virgine's Church, Petworth' with the non-linear solution:

(133) *Mr Hastings is here in the vestiary, Petworth Church*

Joseph Hall (1574 – 1656)

Joseph Hall was well-known for writing satirical verse about contemporaries. His father, John Hall of Ashby-de-la-Zouch, was employed by Henry Hastings as an argent, so it's very likely that Joseph knew William Hastings personally in his youth, and that is how he came to know the 'Shakespeare secret' at an early age – he was only twenty-three when the verse was published. After spending many years at Cambridge, Hall was appointed chaplain to James I and eventually became the Bishop of Exeter.

Line 1: 'Labeo is whip't, and laughs me in the face.'
(134) *The name of William Hastings, has beene put in code.*
Yet another first line anagram referring to Hastings.

Line 3: 'Gird but the Cynick's helmet on his head,'
(135) *Let mee but teach you the trick, Hastings is hidden*

Line 5: 'Long as the craftie Cuttle lieth sure'
(136) *Hastings is true author Hall left secret clue*
By including his name, Hall effectively signed the anagram.

> Labeo is whip't, and laughs me in the face.
> Why? For I smite and hide the galled place,
> Gird but the Cynick's helmet on his head,
> Care he for Talus or the flayle of lead?
> Long as the craftie Cuttle lieth sure
> In the black Cloud of his thick vomiture;
> Who list complaine of wronged faith or fame
> When he may shift it to anothers name?

This verse by Hall which strongly hints at a hidden author, was published in 1597.

17

The
Royal Spy

A mysterious epigram

John Davies, a poet and writer from Hereford, dedicated epigram 159 in his book *The scourge of Folly* to *'Our English Terence: Mr Will. Shake-speare'*. In common with much that contemporaries wrote about 'Shakespeare', these lines have long been a cause of puzzlement and controversy.

> **John Davies of Hereford (abt 1611) in The scourge of folly**
>
> **To our English Terence, Mr Will Shake-speare.**
>
> Some say (good Will) which I, in sport, do sing,
> Had'st thou not plaid some Kingly parts in sport,
> Thou hadst bin a companion for a king;
> And, beene a king among the meaner sort.
> Some others raile; but, raile as they thinke fit,
> Thou hast no rayling, but, a raigning wit:
> And honesty thou sow'st, which they do reape,
> So, to increase their stocke which they do keepe.

Line 1: 'Some say (good Will) which I, in sport, do sing,'
(137) *William Hastings, is (good) spy, who code word, is hiding*

Another first line anagram referring to Hastings and, significantly, an indication that he was involved in espionage.

And Line 2: 'Had'st thou not plaid some kingly parts in sport,'
(138) *Tis truth, Hastings pay'd impostor to take plaies to London*

It is clear that William Hastings could not appear as 'himself' in the public playhouses; in any case he had onerous work to do as a secret agent. It was therefore necessary to use a 'mask' – the Stratford man – who literally acted as *Shakespeare's* author in the London theatres. In fact, the use of literary impostors was not unusual in the sixteenth century; Sir Thomas Moore, Lord Chancellor to Henry VIII, used a man called William Ross as the mask for *Responsio ad convitia Martini Lutheri* (1523) – a scurrilous attack on the founder of Protestantism, Martin Luther.

Sir Arundel Talbot

This miniature portrait (right) was made in Venice by Isaac Oliver and dated 'May 13th 1596' by the artist himself.

Historians do not know of anyone actually called 'Arundel Talbot' – but they suggest that the name might have been derived from the sitter's ancestors.

On the back of Oliver's miniature, written in a small neat hand, is a statement in Latin claiming that the image is a *true* living likeness of 'Arundel Talbot', gilded knight – yet details of the face are unfinished. Why did someone – perhaps the sitter himself – take the unusual step of emphasising, in writing, the accuracy of the portrait?

William Hastings disguised as Sir Arundel Talbot, the famous spy

It is noteworthy that very few Englishmen were allowed to visit Italy in those days, because Italy was the home of Catholicism – so, Arundel Talbot must have been someone 'special'. Furthermore it is highly significant that the miniature was made in Venice, the international centre of espionage at the time, and that 'Sir Arundel Talbot' is itself a non-linear anagram:

(139) *All are blind to our test*

It seems that Sir Arundel Talbot was an English spy, living in Venice in 1596. Moreover, the non-linear structure of the anagram suggests that he was in some way associated with William Hastings.

```
        B           T
A  L  L     A  R  E
        I           S
        N           T  O
        D           U
                    R
```

Of crucial importance is the fact that the Arundel and Talbot families were Hastings' ancestors. The Talbots, of ancient and prestigious pedigree, were related through marriage to the Dudleys – a kinship of which the latter were especially proud – and the Arundels (Howards) were the most powerful Catholic family in England. In fact, Elizabeth Howard (mother of Anne Boleyn) was a grandmother of Elizabeth I. So, it would seem that Oliver's miniature depicts William Hastings *disguised* as the spy Sir Arundel Talbot. It is noteworthy that when the names William Hastings and

Arundel Talbot are combined in a non-linear anagram, they yield the answer:

(140) *William Hastings hid as Arundel Talbot*

Anagram solutions in the last line of Jonson's folio commendatory verse, support the claim that William Hastings used the name Arundel Talbot as a spy, viz:

'And despaires day, but for thy volumes light.'

(141) *Hastings hidd as Arundel Talbot, the very famous spye.*

The anagram implies that Hastings was well-known as Arundel Talbot.

And

(142) *You have freed my poem, Hastings hidd as Arundel Talbot.*

And

(143) *Hastings is hid by spy Arundel Talbot, you deserve fame.*

Line 2 of Milton's verse on 'Shakespeare': 'The labour of an Age, in piled stones'

(144) *Help to find Hastings, go see Arundel Talbot*

By finding Arundel Talbot one finds William Hastings.

And Line 13 'Will be admirers of thy high tun'd straine,'

(145) *Free the myth, Sir Arundel Talbot hid wise Hastings*

Hastings left anagrams in the sonnets that refer to Arundel Talbot

Sonnet 3, line 6: 'Disdaines the tillage of thy husbandry?'

(146) *Is hidden Hastings safely hid by Arundel Talbot?*

Like the clue, the answer is a question.

The famous sonnet 18, line 11: 'Nor shall death brag thou wandr'st in his shade,'

(147) *Learn that Sir Arundel Talbot's shadow, has hid Hastings*

Sonnet 27, line 12: 'Makes blacke night beautious, and her old face new.'

(148) *Break Hastings' code, seek the clue. Find Arundel Talbot was mee*

Sonnet 89, line 9: 'Be absent from thy walkes and in my tongue,'

(149) *Many knowe Arundel Talbot, but few my name Hastings*

Confirming one of Jonson's anagrams, which implies that the name Arundel Talbot was well known at the time – 'the very famous spye' – and yet there are no known extant records referring to anyone called Arundel Talbot.

Sonnet 100, line 4: 'Darkning thy powre to lend base subjects light.'
(150) *Break the code. The spy Arundel Talbot is just Hastings in wig*
Which again suggests that the miniature of Arundel Talbot is Hastings disguised.

And, in the preface to: Shakespeare's poems (1640) by John Warren.
Line 9: 'Let carping Momus barke and bite his fill,'
(151) *Arundel Talbot name is fib, simple trick of Hastings*

Got you the truth?

I am indebted to Kate Vereker, my research assistant, for drawing attention to an epigram by Ben Jonson (No 29) addressed to 'Sir Annual Tilter'. In view of Jonson's well-known satirical wit, it is a very distinct possibility that this name alludes to Sir Arundel Talbot. Indeed, on inspection, the second line of the epigram yields a non-linear anagram that refers to William Hastings:

'And thou, right guiltless, may'st plead to it, why?'
(152) *William Hastings, is hidd, as the royal spye, got you the truth?*

The phrase 'royal spye' implies that Sir Arundel Talbot was the queen's personal secret agent, probably charged with obtaining information about everyone and everything – including (especially) the most senior courtiers and ministers.

It is highly significant that *The Merchant of Venice* was written some time between summer 1596 and summer 1598 – just after the miniature of 'Sir Arundel Talbot' was painted in Venice. In fact, the play refers to the names of families living there at the time and in March 1596, two of months before the miniature was painted, a couple of Danish students – Rosencrantz and Guildenstern – were enrolled at Padua University, not far from Venice.

Famous for its liberal attitude, the university attracted scholars from all over the continent; it was the only Italian university to admit English Protestants. Padua was home to the best school of medicine and anatomy in Europe and Galileo, the famous mathematician, scientist and astronomer was working there at the time. For an intellectual spy, like William Hastings, the university would have been a focal point, and might have provided an opportunity for study. Indeed, it is possible that in the guise of Arundel Talbot he attended lectures by Galileo himself. Moreover, Venice, Padua, Verona and Mantua are located within a few miles of each other and each appears as a location in *Shakespeare* plays: *The Merchant of Venice, Romeo and Juliet* (Verona & Mantua), *Two Gentlemen of Verona* and *The Taming of the Shrew* (Padua).

Furthermore, spying is a key theme in *Hamlet*:

- Rosencrantz and Guildenstern are used by Claudius to spy on Hamlet.
- Polonius sends Reynaldo to spy on Laertes in Paris.
- Polonius and Claudius spy on Hamlet and Ophelia.
- Horatio spies on Claudius during 'the mousetrap'.
- Hamlet spies on Claudius at prayer.
- Polonius spies on Hamlet & Gertrude in the queen's chamber.
- Hamlet and Horatio spy on Ophelia's funeral.
- Claudius tells Gertrude to keep a watch over Hamlet after Ophelia's funeral.

The average rate at which the *Shakespeare* works were written, over a twenty-year period, was only about 150 words per day – a rate which allowed the author plenty of time for other professional activities. It seems that, William Hastings was a secret agent 'by day' and an amateur dramatist 'by night'. It was probably through his employment as the 'royal spy' that he gained his special insights into human behaviour. Thus Hastings had a significant advantage over other dramatists, even those writers who were 'ordinary' spies like Jonson, Marlowe and Munday. He did not need to 'guess' how those in the highest echelons behaved, since he was in a privileged position to observe them at close quarters. His view was comprehensive and panoramic, encompassing all of society. So, in the guise of Arundel Talbot, Hastings had access to a vast range of secret information, including much that was highly sensitive – which might explain how he acquired material ranging from personal details of the bishops, that appear in the Marprelate tracts, to the precise circumstances of Edmund Campion's interrogation.

The queen's secret hound

There appears to be very good evidence that Hastings was engaged in espionage and that one of the code names he used as a secret agent was 'Arundel Talbot'. In the capacity of royal spy, Hastings acted as the special agent of the queen, almost certainly reporting to her directly. Elizabeth knew that 'secret knowledge is the key to power' and that she had to keep a very close eye on everyone, even very senior ministers such as Lord Burghley and the spy-chief Sir Francis Walsingham. So, in the guise of Sir Arundel Talbot, William Hastings was the queen's eyes, ears and nose – the royal watchdog.

A summary of key points

- It seems that no such person as 'Sir Arundel Talbot' appears in the historical archive.
- Sixteenth century Venice was the international centre of trade – and espionage; hence, an Englishman using a false name in Venice was almost certainly a spy.
- 'Sir Arundel Talbot' is a non-linear anagram – the type used to encode information about Hastings:
  'Sir Arundel Talbot' = 'all are blind to our test'.
- The last line of Jonson's 1623 folio commendatory verse contains three non-linear anagrams that identify William Hastings as Arundel Talbot.
- The first line of John Davies' epigram yields a non-linear anagram which identifies Hastings as a spy.
- An anagram by Hastings himself, in sonnet 89, alludes to his well-known code name 'Arundel Talbot'. Many more anagrams link Hastings with Arundel Talbot.
- Talbot and Arundel were the names of Hastings' ancestors.
- *The Merchant of Venice* was almost certainly written between summer 1596 and summer 1598. The play refers to specific locations in Venice and the names of families living there at the time.
- Two Danish students (Rosencrantz & Guildenstern) were enrolled at Padua University in March 1596. Rosencrantz & Guildenstern are the names of two Danish students that appear in *Hamlet* a few years later.
- Padua, Venice, Verona and Mantua are situated within a few miles of each other in northern Italy – each is a location in at least one *Shakespeare* play.
- Jonson's anagram, in epigram 29 to Sir Annual Tilter, indentifies Hastings as the 'royal spye'.
- 'Talbot' was a breed of dog – a type of bloodhound, now extinct – that was used in the sixteenth century for hunting. Talbot was therefore a particularly appropriate name for a secret agent, sniffing-out information. Furthermore, the 'dog' was an iconic symbol sometimes used to represent a spy.

Edmund Spenser (1552? – 1599)

In his *Teares of the Muses* (1595) Edmund Spenser alludes to a contemporary writer as 'our gentle Willy'. In those days, 'gentle' usually referred to someone of noble birth, which suggests that 'Willy' was not the Stratford man, since he was base-born.

Line 1: 'But that same gentle spirit, from whose pen'

(153) *True name of the poet is Hastings, set problem as wit test*

Edmund Spenser (1595) in Teares of the Muses

But that same gentle spirit, from whose pen
Large streames of honnie and sweete nectar flowe,
Scorning the boldness of such base-borne men
Which dare their follies forth so rashlie throwe,
Doth rather choose to sit in idle cell
Than so him selfe to mockerie to sell.

Line 2: 'Large streames of honnie and sweete nectar flowe,'

(154) *Real name of Hastings was left in secret code, now free the answer*

Line 3: 'Scorning the boldnes of such base-borne men'

(155) *Hastings is noble-borne code has not been secure from me*

This implies that Spenser himself cracked Hastings' code. The phrase 'base-borne men' stands in marked contrast to the 'gentle spirit' of line 1.

In 1594 Spenser completed his *Colin Clouts* poem, a work in which several contemporary authors are alluded to by pseudonyms. One of the writers, identified by Spenser as *Aetion*, is thought to refer to Shakespeare's author. The line in question is:

'And there, though last not least is Aetion,'

(156) *Learn that Hastings, uses the Aetion title, so to hide*

Aetion means 'Eagle man' – a pseudonym that probably alluded to Hastings' bird-like appearance. In common with his parents it seems he had a large, aquiline nose – as suggested also by Jonson's anagram in his folio commendatory verse, the famous line: 'Sweet swan of Avon!...' which becomes: *'Few own a vast nose! what a sight it were'*.

In 1579 Edmund Spenser was working for the Earl of Leicester, so it is possible that William Hastings met the poet at that time. Regarded by many as the greatest poet of the age – contemporaries called him 'the prince of poets' – Spenser spent much of his adult life as a servant of the crown in Ireland. But in the mid 1590s he returned to London and worked for about a year, at Essex House, in The Strand. The timing suggests that since he was writing for the Earl of Essex ('Fair Youth' of the sonnets) Spenser was the anonymous 'rival poet' alluded to in the middle of the sonnet sequence. Edmund Spenser died on January 13th 1599 – just a few weeks after returning to England – and was buried in Westminster Abbey. It seems that the funeral was probably paid for by Spenser's former patron, Robert Devereux, the Earl of Essex.

Some anagrams in the 1623 Folio

The following is a tiny sample of anagram solutions taken from the 1623 Folio:

The wounded name

The following lines appear in Hamlet's dying speech:
'Oh good Horatio, what a wounded name,
(Things standing thus unknowne) shall live behind me.'
The expression 'wounded name' seems to be an allusion to the author's real name, since **Hasting**s contains 'a sting' – a wound – and can therefore be considered a 'wounded' name. Furthermore, the line: '(Things standing thus unknowne) shall live behind me' is the non-linear anagram:

(157) *Believe the hint (unknowne) William Hastings is hidden genius.*
Presumably, 'the hint' refers to the 'wounded name' in the previous line.

In *Much Ado About Nothing* (Act II Sc ii) Beatrice asks Benedick to come to dinner. On repeating her words aloud, Benedick realises they contain a double meaning. The line reads:
'Ha, 'against my <u>will I am</u> sent to bid you come into dinner': there's a double meaning in that:'

'William' is spelt in sequence – an occurrence unique in the entire canon, as is the phrase 'double meaning', though there are many double meanings in *Shakespeare*. In fact, the part of the line: 'Ha, against my will I am sent to bid you come into dinner' is a non-linear anagram containing both 'William Hastings' and 'double meaning':

(158) *The double meaning is code, William Hastings wrote in anonymity*

So, there is literally a 'double meaning' in the line.

Othello, AII Sc1, pg 824, line 94:
'One that excels the quirkes of blazoning pens,'.

This line, a 'needle' in the folio haystack, is unique in that 'hastings' appears in sequence, together with the letters of 'shakespeare' and 'queen elizabeth'. It can be shown, by frequency analysis, that such a combination, even in a book as large as the folio – with well-over 100,000 lines – is very unlikely to occur by chance. Moreover, the line in question has been altered. In the first edition of *Othello*, which was published in 1622, the year before the First Folio, the corresponding line reads: 'One that excels the blasoning pens,'. But in the folio edition 'quirkes of' has been added and 'blasoning' is spelt with a 'z'. It is highly likely that it was the folio editors themselves who made these changes, since it is very improbable that they found a new version of the play, from which to correct and update, between 1622 and the folio's publication in 1623.

The following are some of the non-linear anagram solutions that occur in the line:
(159) *Next clue took prize, Hastings is son of queene Elizabeth*

And

(160) *Birth of son got queene Elizabeth sicknesse, no poxe at all*
A very important anagram, corroborating one of the fundamental claims in this book that Queen Elizabeth gave birth to a son at Hampton Court Palace in October 1562, and that the illness she experienced at that time was not smallpox.

And

(161) *Expose Hastings' link to queene, secret son of Elizabeth*

And

(162) *Proof not luck, expose Hastings queene Elizabeth's son*

And

(163) *Eloquent sonne of Elizabeth, got Shakespeare lexicon*
It seems that contemporaries were aware of Hastings' very extensive vocabulary (up to 40,000 words). The acquisition of a vast personal lexicon was an astonishing achievement in itself, especially in view of the fact that the first English dictionary – of just 2,500 'difficult' words – was not published until 1604. However, some of the finest private libraries in England – the

ones at Petworth and Wilton, perhaps Lord Burghley's very extensive library, the Earl of Leicester's personal library and the queen's vast collection of books – would probably all have been available and, together, provided the literary resources from which Hastings built the *Shakespeare* lexicon.

And

(164) *Next link to queene, Hastings spoke French to Elizabeth*

It is ironic that the 'mother' tongue (literally) of the greatest English writer was French! Did Hastings address his mother in French because it was the international language of the aristocracy – or because it gave Hastings' conversations with his mother a degree of privacy? Perhaps he regarded French as a more refined language than English – perhaps it was a combination of reasons. Whatever, the insight offered by this anagram confirms Professor Lefranc's opinion, that Shakespeare's author understood cultured and colloquial French. Perhaps that is only to be expected: as Elizabeth's tutor, Roger Ascham, said she spoke French and Italian as well as she spoke English.

And

(165) *Next link to queene, poet Hastings actor son of Elizabeth*

Which supports a view, held by many actors, that *Shakespeare's* author had been a player himself. However, acting was a very lowly form of employment and would certainly have been seen as a shameful occupation for the son of the queen!

And

(166) *Next linke to queene, Hastings poet of Elizabeth's court*

Confirming that William Hastings was the resident court poet.

18

A Mysterious 'Persian' Lady

The pregnant Virgin Queen with a representation
of her secret son!

A Mysterious 'Persian' Lady

This painting (c 1590-1600 by Marcus Gheeraedts II) of a so-called 'Persian Lady' – the headdress is a Persian style – with a weeping stag, has elicited much controversy over the years. The cartouche in the lower right corner contains a sonnet. At least four points suggest that the Persian Lady is meant to represent Elizabeth I:

1. The tree has been identified by Sir Roy Strong as a common walnut: *Juglans regia* – where Juglans is walnut and regia is a royal dwelling, in Latin. The tree represents the lady's family – a hint, through the botanical name, that she is royal.

2: The dress is very unusual, the first example of an English woman wearing Persian costume. No lady at court would dare to pre-empt or upstage the queen – as far as fashion was concerned, Elizabeth was the one and only trend setter. As the first example of a lady in 'Persian' costume it suggests the model might be the queen herself.

3: Two eighteenth century art historians, George Vertue and Horace Walpole, identified the Persian Lady as Queen Elizabeth – based on documentary evidence from the seventeenth century.

4. Two non-linear anagrams in the sonnet indicate that the queen is Hastings' mother.

It seems that the painting shows Elizabeth, as she would have appeared in the autumn of 1562 – pregnant. The picture, which is retrospective, was not painted from life. The Persian Lady's face was the artist's 'guess' at the queen's appearance when she was about twenty-nine years old. The sonnet is an expression of her private thoughts:

> The restles swallow fits my restles minde,
> In still revivinge still renewinge wronges;
> her Just complaintes of cruelly unkinde,
> are all the Musique, that my life prolonges.
>
> With pensive thoughtes my weeping stagg I crowne,
> whose Melancholy teares my cares Expresse;
> hes Teares in sylence, and my sighes unknowne
> are all the physicke that my harmes redresse.
>
> My onely hope was in this goodly tree,
> which I did plant in love bringe up in care;
> but all in vanie, for now to late I see
> the shales be mine, the kernels others are.
>
> My Musique may be plaintes, my physique teares
> If this be all the fruite my love tree beares.

On inspection, the verse yields the following non-linear anagrams:

Line 4: 'are all the Musique, that my life prolonges.'

(167) *Queen is mother of Hastings, poem truly tells all.*

Line 5: 'With pensive thoughtes my weeping stagg* I crowne,'

(168) *The weeping stagg is Hastings, now uncover the wit test in my poem*

The weeping stag is a symbolic representation of Hastings himself, grieving (probably) at the injustice of his plight as the unknown, unacknowledged son of the queen.

Line 7: 'Hes teares in sylence, and my sighes unknowne'

(169) *My name is Hastings, key shewn here encodes answer in clue*

```
              N  A  M  E
              N  Y
              S
    S  H  E   W  N
              E
       H  E   R  E
       A         N           K
    I  S         C  L  U  E  E
       T         O           Y
       I  N      D
       N         E
       G         S
       S
```

The key has been included here because it is explicitly referred to in the answer. It seems that Hastings himself thought of the anagrams as having three parts:

Clue – the line of source text

Key – the non-linear, Scrabble-like structure

Answer – the anagram solution extracted from the key

Line 8: 'are all the physicke that my harmes redresse.'

(170) *Hid my Shakespeare title here. They are my secret playes*

Hastings acknowledges the *Shakespeare* plays as his secret.

---

* There is a weeping stag in *As You Like It*.

Line 9: 'My onely hope was in this goodly tree,'
(171) *Hastings wisely denys poem, to royal mother*
Another indication that the queen is Hastings' mother.

Latin epithets appear in the painting, one associated with the stag reads: 'Dolor est medicina e dollori' – 'grief is medicine for grief' – while one on the tree reads: 'Injusti justa querela' which translates as: 'a just complaint of injustice' – presumably this was Hastings expressing grievance at the treatment he received from his mother.

Phaeton revisited
The sonnet in Florio's *Second Frutes* (1591) shows that Hastings had devised the anagram method before 1591, that very few knew about it and that he was already using the code names 'Shakespeare' and 'Arundel Talbot'.

Phaëton to his friend *Florio.*

Sweete friend whose name agrees with thy increase,
How fit a rivall art thou of the Spring?
For when each branche hath left his flourishing,
And green-lockt Summers shadie pleasures cease:
She makes the Winters stormes repose in peace,
And spends her franchise on each living thing:
The dazies sprout, the little birds doo sing,
Heerbes, gummes, and plants doo vaunt of their release.
So when that all our English Witts lay dead,
(Except the Laurell that is euer greene,)
Thou with thy Frutes our barrennes o're-spread,
And set thy florerie pleasaunce to be seene.
Such frutes, such flowrets of moralitie,
Were nere before brought out of Italy.

Phaëton.

Line 1: 'Sweete friend whose name agrees with thy increase,'
(172) *Hastings set the wit test, few were aware code hides my name in heere*
Another first line anagram that refers to Hastings.

Line 4: 'And green-lockt Sommers shadie pleasures cease:'
(173) *More riddle clues: Hastings uses Shake-speare as code name*
A hyphen appears in both clue and answer.

Line 7: 'The dazies sprout, the little birds doo sing,'
(174) *Tis true, lie hidd poet Hastings, Elizabeth Tudor's son*
Another anagram indicating that Hastings was the son of the queen.

Line 8: 'Hearbes, gummes, and plants doo vaunt of their release.'

(175) *Here, verse proves, Hastings hides as famous name Arundel Talbot.*

Another indication that Hastings was well known, at the time, by the pseudonym 'Arundel Talbot'.

Anagrams in the Wilton Monument inscription

The Shakespeare statue, in the Wilton Monument, points to the first line – an *adapted* quotation from the 1623 folio version of *Macbeth*, viz:

'Life's but a walking SHADOW'

The corresponding line in the folio reads:

'Life's but a walking shadow, a poore player,'

Three questions arise: why has the line been changed, why is the statue pointing to it and why is the word 'shadow' immediately below the statue's finger, picked-out in capitals?

It seems the line was altered so as to create a non-linear anagram.

'Life's but a walking shadow'

(176) *As few know Hastings was all but hid*

Yet another first line anagram referring to Hastings, in text relating to Shakespeare.

Also: LIFE, PLAYER and STAGE have been inscribed in capitals – why?

The letters comprising all the capitalised words form non-linear anagrams:

(177) *False poet hid wise royall sage*

And

(178) *The false poet was paid regally*

Which suggests that Shakspere was well paid by Hastings to act as his mask; that would explain the puzzle of the Stratford man's considerable earnings – 'paid regally' – a major source of income that does not appear in the archive. Thus, William Shakspere was able to spend money on property, land, tithes and commodities at a rate far greater than his (probable) income as an actor, 'playwright' and play-manager would have allowed.

And

(179) *Greedy false poet was the alias*

The documented facts of William Shakspere's life strongly support the assertion that he was greedy and uncharitable. During times of famine, in the late 1590s, he hoarded grain so as to inflate the price while his Stratford neighbours starved. And records show that, although wealthy, he consistently failed to donate anything to the poor in either Stratford or London. It seems to have been a case of 'like father, like son' – John Shakspere was a usurer who charged exorbitant interest rates.

The Wilton monument anagrams are significant because:

1. They suggest that a few people, in the mid-eighteenth century, knew the 'Shakespeare secret' and how to construct non-linear anagrams.

2. They corroborate the link between Hastings and Wilton as suggested by other anagrams: *To the Reader*, Line 2: 'True Shakespeare face; it hangs at Wilton' and 'Shakespeare; left huge secret at Wilton' and in line 4: 'The true author, often hid-out: at Wilton'.

Stratford graffiti

These initials are inscribed on the external wall of Holy Trinity Church, Stratford, almost exactly behind the Shakespeare Monument. The figures below read 1833.

It might just be coincidence, of course, but the presence of these particular initials in such a significant location, behind the Stratford memorial, suggests that some people knew the truth about 'Shakespeare' as recently as the nineteenth century – indeed, it is possible that a few are privy to the secret even now.

Insignia at Hampton Court

The insignia here are carved on the stairs to the King's apartments at Hampton Court.

It is noteworthy that the initials 'W H' appear in three significant locations: By the main door of St Giles Church, Stoke Poges, where Hastings was raised; behind the monument, on the exterior wall of Holy Trinity Church, Stratford – where anagrams indicate that Hastings' name is hidden; and at Hampton Court Palace – where Hastings was born. The probability that those particular initials would appear, by chance, in all three locations is thousands to one against.

A pair of Williams

In the entire canon there are only two fictional parts named *William*; unlike most of the characters in the plays, they were inventions of the author himself. One of them, a bumbling yokel who appears in *As You Like It*, lives in the Forest of Arden a few miles north of Stratford. The other, in *The Merry Wives of Windsor*, is the schoolboy William Page. Are these parts allusions to the author and his mask?

In view of the fact that the roles were creations of the playwright himself, it is tempting to think that William Shakspere, the rustic from Stratford-upon-Avon, near the Forest of Arden, is alluded to as the country bumpkin and that the schoolboy, growing up in the Windsor area, represents the author as a child. It is worthy of note that the latter's surname is Page and that young William Hastings was a pageboy living near Windsor in the household of his uncle. Furthermore, it has been noticed that when places named in the plays are plotted on a map of England, a cluster appears in the Windsor area, although there is nothing in the vicinity of Stratford.

19

Summary Questions

This chapter summarises key points through a series of questions:

1. What was the mystery illness that caused the queen to suddenly cut short her summer progress in August 1562? When gravely ill at Hampton Court in October of the same year, why did she insist – several times – that Dr Burcot's diagnosis of smallpox was wrong? Why did the queen's ladies-in-waiting agree that the illness was not smallpox?

2. Why did the miserly queen, at the height of her illness, give instructions to pay Tamworth – Robert Dudley's personal body groom – £500 pa (a yearly fortune) in the event of her death? Why was an obscure servant like Tamworth in the queen's mind at that difficult time; what had he done for Elizabeth to merit such untypical generosity?

3. Why did the queen declare in front of several witnesses, one month after the illness of 1562, that Robert Dudley 'was beholden to her' because for his sake she had 'passed the pikes'?

4. Why did stories begin to circulate, in the early 1560s, that Elizabeth and Dudley had a sexual relationship and that the queen had a secret child? Why – *even* in the face of the death penalty – did people continue to spread rumours about a secret royal child?

5. Why did the queen, in a letter to the Speaker of the House of Commons in February 1563, state that her 'illness' (she *never* referred to it as pox) was 'God's chastisement'?

6. Why must Elizabeth's 'illness' of 1562 never be mentioned in her presence?

7. Why were several people executed at Norwich in 1570 for claiming that the queen had a child – yet many other rumourmongers 'only' had their tongues and ears cut off?

8. Why did Elizabeth stipulate that, when she died her body must not be opened for embalming?

9. Why did the queen consistently refuse to name a successor?

10. Why were more of *Shakespeare's* plays performed at Elizabeth's court than those of any other playwright?

11. The queen sent Dr Haywood to the Tower for life, simply for referring to the deposition scene in *Richard II* – why did she not deal with the man who actually wrote the play at least as severely?

12. Why did none of the highly educated courtiers (Bacon, Raleigh, Cecil etc) who saw the *Shakespeare* plays, ever mention the brilliant dramatist from Stratford?

13. How did the Stratford yokel, William Shakspere, acquire by far the largest vocabulary of any contemporary writer at a time before the first English dictionary and when books were expensive luxuries?

14. How did Shakspere, without drawing attention to himself, acquire a profound insight into the mind-set of people in the highest echelons of society?

15. Why was a Danish prince of such importance to the author that he wrote a 41/2 hour play on the subject?

16. Why did 'Shakespeare' write more about 'dangerous' subjects like history and politics than any other playwright of the age?

17. Why did the Garter King of Arms refer to Shakspere of Stratford as a mere 'player' in 1596 when two very famous poems (*Venus & Adonis* and *The Rape of Lucrece*) had already appeared in print under *Shakespeare's* name?

18. How was the commoner William Shakspere able to break the strict social etiquette of the times, by writing very personal sonnets to a young aristocrat?

20. Who was the mysterious 'M^r. W.H.' identified by Thomas Thorpe, 1609, as the 'onlie begetter' of *Shake-speares Sonnets*?

21. Why did colleagues never refer to 'Shakespeare' in personal terms? Why, during his lifetime, did nobody ever identify the Stratford man as a poet, playwright or author?

22. Why did 'Shakespeare' never write commendatory verse about any colleague, even though it was common practice to do so?

23. In an age when collaboration amongst playwrights was the norm, why did *Shakespeare's* author collaborate so little?

24. Why did Shakspere suddenly stop writing and retire to Stratford (c 1610/11) whilst still at the height of his powers?

25. Why are there no letters, manuscripts or any other documents in the author's own hand, yet hand written items by many of his non-literary contemporaries have survived to the present?

26. Why does it appear that the six alleged signatures of 'Shakespeare' have been written by two different people? Why would a (supposedly) famous writer, like Shakspere, have a legal clerk sign a document as important as his will?

27. Why did William Shakspere make no attempt to save *any* of his literary works?

28. Why did the Stratford man, supposedly a professional writer who used hundreds of sources to write his plays, make no mention of books in his will? Why has no evidence of his personal library ever been found?

29. According to his will, Shakspere regarded actors as his 'fellows', rather than poets and playwrights. Why did he leave nothing at all to members of the *literati* and why did the will make no reference to an aristocratic patron, e.g. Southampton?

30. Why are many contemporary references to 'Shakespeare' allusive, as though hinting at something that cannot be made explicit (e.g. Edwards, Hall, Jonson, Spenser and Benson)?

31. How did Shakspere escape punishment (not even questioned!) for his authorship of *Richard II* – the seditious play, used to incite rebellion, that so angered the queen?

32. Someone as talented as *Shakespeare's* author must have aroused envy in a few of his rivals. Why did nobody have anything derogatory to say about the yokel dramatist?

33. Why was the author of *Shake-speares Sonnets* so sure of total oblivion after death, that he could state categorically in sonnet 81: 'Though I (once gone) to all the world must die'?

34. What is (or was) 'plast with in' the Stratford monument?

35. Why did both Jonson and Digges use the word 'moniment' in reference to the Stratford Monument and why did Jonson have the 'i' printed in bold type?

36. On the death of a poet or playwright it was customary for colleagues to write eulogies. Why was nothing at all written about William Shakspere, by the *literati*, when he died in 1616?

37. Why was the 1623 Folio dedicated to William and Philip Herbert rather than the Earl of Southampton – the alleged 'Shakspere' patron?

38. If Shakspere did not write *Shakespeare*, why did someone – especially in an age renowned for its gossips – ever reveal 'the secret' after the real author's death?

39. Why did Edmund Campion use the pseudonym 'Hastings' when travelling incognito in 1581? Why did he fail to explain the choice of name when questioned about it at his trial?

40. Shakspere vigorously pursued debtors for petty claims. Why did he not seek redress when his name was forged by unscrupulous publishers?

41. Why did Ben Jonson, in his 1623 Folio commendatory verse, describe 'Shakespeare' as 'starre of poets', 'the wonder of our stage' and 'soule of the age' when he never mentioned the name 'Shakespeare' during the Stratford man's lifetime?

42. Why are the vast majority (85%) of dialect words in the *Shakespeare* plays of Yorkish origin?

43. Traditionalists suggest that Shakspere was on nodding terms with the aristocracy and the *intelligencia*. But if that was true why, in the twenty-odd years of his professional career, did none of his eminent contemporaries ever refer to the brilliant dramatist?

44. Having gone to extraordinary lengths to capture the satirical Puritan writer 'Martin Marprelate', why did the search end as soon as the printers of the tracts were caught? Why was the author never publicly identified?

45. What caused the sudden death of William Shakspere in April 1616?

46. Why was the name 'Shake-speare' hyphenated on many of the earliest published works?

47. Why are the subjects of the *Shakespeare* plays, in general, very different to those of rivals?

48. Why did John Benson explicitly question 'Shakespeare's' image in his prefatory encomium to the 1640 edition of *Poems by Wil. Shake-speare*?

49. Why is the Droeshout engraving on the title page of the 1623 Folio so badly executed? Why is there nothing – inscription or symbol, as in the engravings of contemporaries – to show that the sitter is a writer?

50. Why did Jonson preface the 1623 Folio with his mediocre 'To the Reader' – an apparently superfluous verse that explains what everyone can see: the image on the facing page depicts William Shakespeare?

51. Who was the 'unknown' Garter Knight in the procession picture, Eliza Triumphans? Why has such a highly-ranked nobleman never been identified? Why, in his case only, has the garter and chain been deliberately obscured?

52. Why is the sieve, held by Elizabeth I in the portrait of that name, empty? Who was the young man standing behind her? Why does he resemble the unknown Garter Knight?

53. Why, even when the Stratford man was at the height of his fame, was *Shakespeare's* name missing from a list of over thirty poets and playwrights covering the years 1600-1615?

54. Why would a common playwright pen a drama (*Macbeth*) with much to cause the new Scots king serious discomfort?

55. How did the Stratford man know of two Danish students enrolled at Padua University in March 1596, named Rosencrantz and Guildensterne, just like the students who appear in *Hamlet* a few years later?

56. How did William Shakspere know details of Elsinore (Hamlet's Castle) and the topography of its environs?

57. Why did a landlubber like Shakspere include so many precise references to the sea and seafaring in his works?

58. Why didn't the secret service 'talent-spot' (as they had Jonson, Marlowe and Munday) an extremely eloquent writer/actor like Shakspere?

59. How did a man as talented and remarkable as 'Shakespeare', manage to avoid the close attention and scrutiny of *all* his literary colleagues and rivals – why does he appear to have made no *personal* impression on any of them? Why are there no quotations by the author himself that have survived?

60. If Shakspere put his name in Psalm 46 in 1610 – when 46 years old – why was he unsure of his age just two years later in the Bellot-Mountjoy law suit?

61. Why did the people of Stratford – especially William Shakspere's relatives and close friends – remain silent about the famous poet and playwright in their midst?

62. Why was it necessary, as early as the eighteenth century, to replace the gravestone at Holy Trinity Church with a *copy* of the original? Why is there no name inscribed on it and why is the stone unusually short?

63. Why did no member of Shakspere's family purchase a copy of the 1623 Folio?

64. Why are certain words picked-out in capital letters on the Shakespeare Monument at Wilton, yet no words are capitalised on the monument at Poet's Corner?

65. If the case for orthodoxy is watertight, why have so many famous individuals – notably writers and actors – doubted the Stratford man's authorship?

66. Why does *every* line of inquiry – starting with William Shakspere – lead to a problem?

20

In Sleep
A King...

It is very curious that none of Shakspere's literary contemporaries ever drew attention to the strangeness of the individual in their midst: a man with no track-record as a sonneteer, yet (apparently) commissioned to write very personal sonnets to an aristocratic youth; an author who outshone everyone – but no colleague referred to him *personally* when he was alive. The 'soule of the age' – yet, as a personality, someone who makes the impression of a cipher. A man from a deeply rural background, but a dramatist who specialised in writing about the upper echelons of society; an author whose plays were shown at court more frequently than those of any other playwright – apparently the queen's favourite – yet no courtier ever mentioned him. No envious rival drew attention to the unprecedented royal 'patronage', or to the fact that the author had achieved many successes on the London stage. And when William Shakspere escaped the inquiry in the aftermath of the Essex rebellion in 1601 – without even being questioned about his authorship of *Richard II* – none of those playwrights who had been jailed for their plays, openly questioned the unbelievably lenient and seemingly biased treatment of the yokel from Warwickshire.

The silence is most strange, especially from someone as bright, outspoken and argumentative as Ben Jonson, a dramatist who had been imprisoned himself for the plays he wrote. Moreover, if Jonson's coruscating tribute to the author in the 1623 Folio is honest and accurate, it must have been abundantly clear to all who knew the Stratford man that he was utterly exceptional. Yet none of those who supposedly worked with Shakspere, and knew him well, had anything to say about the 'phenomenon' amongst them.

Apart from occasional reference to 'the works of Shakespeare' – *which certainly does not count as personal biography* – it is very odd that the astonishingly articulate playwright, walking dictionary, human encyclopaedia and brilliant wit, apparently made no impression at all on anyone that ever met him! At least, nobody thought it worthwhile to write down anything he said – which is curious, in view of the fact that many of those who came into contact with him were writers themselves. Furthermore, except for the Belott-Mountjoy lawsuit in 1612, when William Shakspere, of Stratford, appeared as a witness, there are no recorded utterances from the man himself. That such a talented individual failed to make a memorable impact on *any* of his colleagues, whilst he was alive – and the strange silence of the author *himself* – is, to say the least, very odd.

If William Shakspere, of Stratford, was the true author of *Shakespeare*, it should be possible, using *only* the documented facts of his life, to show that he wrote the works. It is not possible to do so, however, because no contemporary documents have been found that specifically identify him as a writer. Therefore, it is unsurprising that the Stratford man's assumed authorship creates so many problems and that, as a dramatist, he presents an enigma – which even orthodox scholars acknowledge. In view of that acknowledgement, it seems strange that the academics have failed to take the next logical step and question the traditional attribution. However, the reason for their failure to do so is clear: it is not in the professional interests of scholars to challenge the tradition in which they have been raised. But by insisting on the absolute validity of the traditional attribution, the academics have left themselves no escape; they are forced to defend orthodoxy – *at all cost* – to save face and reputation.

Nevertheless, the difficulties will not go away. There are too many problems and unanswered questions in what 'ought' to be the straightforward story about a playwright from the sticks; yet *nothing* is straightforward. For example, it's hardly credible that all the contemporary documentary evidence, directly linking the Stratford man to the writing of *Shakespeare*, went missing 'accidentally'. It's also very suspicious that every personal detail, which might have cast light on the alleged author, has been erased from the archive. Indeed, the mysterious dearth of evidence suggests that William Shakspere was either the most perversely secretive individual in literary history, or else he was not really the author of the works attributed to him. But if Shakspere *was* obsessively secretive – even going to the trouble of suppressing *every* link with the writings – why did he allow his name to appear on the published works?

Monumental folly

The most probable explanation for the total absence of 'hard' evidence is that documents, explicitly connecting the Stratford man to a writing career, never existed in the first place. The only (literally) solid link between Shakspere and *Shakespeare* is the monument in Holy Trinity. Quite simply, if the memorial is not what it seems to be, the tradition of the rustic genius from Stratford is a hoax. In fact, evidence strongly indicates that the monument is indeed a folly. Both Jonson and Digges wrote of the Stratford Monument as a moniment – Jonson emphasising the misspelling by having the 'i' printed in bold type – yet there is (and was) no such thing as a 'moniment'. So what *motivated* both of them to use a non-existent word? It looks like a very strong hint that the 'moniment' is not a monument in the usual sense.

In addition, the monument verse says: 'Read if thou canst whom envious death hath plast with in this monument Shakespeare...'. This cannot be right, since Shakspere is buried in the nearby grave and, in any case, the monument is too small to hold a body. The logical conclusion is that whatever is meant by Shakespeare 'with in' the monument, cannot be the man (Shakspere) buried in the grave. Thus, the curious phrase 'Read <u>if thou canst</u>' is a very strong hint that there is a secret in the verse itself. That is made more credible still by the fact that if 'Shakespeare' is a hoax, the Stratford Monument would be THE obvious place to hide the truth – which makes the bogus word 'moniment' seem all the more suspicious. Indeed, it appears that a phoney word is being used, very pointedly, as a label for the poet-memorial – probably because the monument, like the alleged writer, is a fake.

Furthermore, if the Stratford man was the real author's mask, it is very difficult to see how he could have fooled the entire London literati for over twenty years. Many of those with whom he must have come into contact were university educated 'gentlemen', a group of writers who particularly disliked upstart yokels of Shakspere's ilk. They would have been very wary of the Warwickshire rustic, and would surely have seen through any deception on his part. Hence, if Shakspere was an impostor, it is virtually certain that some of the more perceptive members of the *literati* knew the truth.

In that case four questions arise:

Q: Why did they keep the secret?
A: It was treason to claim the queen had a child.

Q: Why did they hide it?
A: To preserve the story for posterity.

Q: How did they hide it?
A: Mainly in non-linear anagrams.

Q: Where did they hide it?
A: In text associated with *Shakespeare*

To shield themselves from discovery by government officials, contemporaries used an anagrammatic method of encryption which they called 'keys' – a technique invented by Hastings himself that was almost certainly unknown to cryptographers (generally) at the time. Members of the nobility who knew the 'great secret' remained totally silent, not only because they depended on the queen for preferment and patronage, but because no sane aristocrat would be willing to risk his or her life – and heritage – simply to embarrass and humiliate the monarch. After all, revelation of the royal secret was treason; fear of execution kept *everyone* in check.

Analysis of evidence
The assertion that the unacknowledged, illegitimate son of Elizabeth I and Robert Dudley was the secret author of *Shakespeare* is supported by three very distinct kinds of evidence:

1. The rationale.
2. Circumstantial evidence.
3. The large number of exact, coherent anagrams.

1. The rationale

- In view of the author's eloquence, extensive knowledge and deep insight into the highest echelons of society, who could have had a better mother, mentor and tutor than the son of the polymath, polyglot queen?

- Who had stronger personal and political reasons to conceal her illegitimate child than the unmarried Virgin Queen?

- A highly deceptive individual – capable of telling the 'Big Lie' – Elizabeth knew from personal experience that honesty is (often) the worst policy.

- Who had greater power to keep secrets permanently hidden than the monarch?

- Who had more compelling reason to write in sonnet 81: 'Though I (once gone) to all the world must die' and in sonnet 72: 'my name be buried where my body is' – than the secret heir to the throne?

- Who had better reason to use the pen name *Phaeton* – the unacknowledged, illegitimate Son of the Sun God – than the illegitimate son of (The Sun) Elizabeth I?

- Who could have gained greater knowledge and deeper

insight into the mind-set of the nobility than the royal spy Arundel Talbot?

• Who had a more powerful motive to eliminate the unacknowledged heir to the throne, and obliterate all record of him, than James I and his Chief Minister Robert Cecil?

• Who had greater power and better reason to maintain the *Shakespeare* secret – long after the author's death – than James I and the ensuing Stuart dynasty?

2. Circumstantial evidence

• The unexplained illness of Elizabeth I during her summer progress, in August 1562.

• Anomalies and mysteries concerning the queen's near-fatal illness at Hampton Court, in October 1562.

• Incorrect diagnosis of Elizabeth's illness by Dr Burcot.

• The queen's very pointed remarks to Robert Dudley, in front of witnesses, a month after the illness.

• Elizabeth's (intended) huge annual payment to Tamworth, Dudley's body groom, in the event of her death.

• The queen's letter to the Speaker of the House of Commons, in February 1563, referring to her recent 'illness' as God's chastisement.

• Stories about a secret royal child that emerged in the early 1560s, which continued to circulate for more than twenty years – even though rumourmongers faced very harsh punishments including the death penalty.

• The execution of several people at Norwich, in 1570, who claimed the queen had a child – a sure sign that the condemned weren't simply ordinary gossips.

• Mysteries at St Giles Church, Stoke Poges: a vicar without a known CV who left within a year of appointment in 1562/63;

records that began in March 1563 – much later than two adjacent parishes; very old superposed initials W H & W + P carved by the church door.

- Paintings: 1. An unidentified garter knight located immediately in front of the queen in an important procession picture. 2. The (empty) Sieve portrait of Elizabeth I – (loss of virginity) with unknown courtier. 3. The portrait of a mysterious courtier, of exactly the right age, with an undecoded inscription. 4. The miniature of an individual called by the (false) name 'Sir Arundel Talbot'. 5. The mysterious 'Persian' Lady portrait with inscribed sonnet.

- The significance of certain lines in *Shake-speares Sonnets*, which suggest deep secrecy about the author himself; in particular: the poet knows that after death he *must* be lost to posterity and that his name will be buried with his body.

- Verses by contemporaries which allude to *Shakespeare's* author (specifically: the poet of *Venus & Adonis* and *The Rape of Lucrece*) as a concealed aristocrat.

3. The anagrams
Three assertions recur many times in the anagram solutions:
- Hastings was the real author of *Shakespeare*.
- Hastings was hidden.
- Hastings was the son of the Queen.

Chance or design?
The case presented in this book hinges largely, although not exclusively, on whether the anagrams are the result of chance or design. The key question of chance vs. design is addressed by examining general and specific points:

General points:
- If the anagrams are random coincidences, many names other than Hastings ought to give rise to a similarly large number of apparently meaningful messages, in the same texts, using the same method of anagram construction.

- It should be possible to make apparently meaningful exact anagrams, referring to Hastings, in text where it is *certain* that nothing has been deliberately hidden *at the same frequency of occurrence* as in contemporary texts referring to *Shakespeare*.

- Many anagrams split into pairs of correlating clauses e.g. 'curse has hidden code; set the test long ago'. Such precise correlation is very unlikely to occur by chance.

- The very high frequency at which anagrams about Hastings appear in first lines of text referring to 'Shakespeare' – which would certainly not be expected if the anagrams were random occurences.

- Solutions that make 'self-referential' statements and anagrams in appropriate locations are also very unlikely to occur by accident, viz: 'few knowe page has test; or clues stare in face', ''tis the page for clues; seek after answers', 'Shakespeare's title; wrong face put here' – all in the second line of *To the Reader*. And 'regret the anagrams, here, shake posterity', 'hope that you solv'd my subtile hidden anagrams, first' – the latter in the final line of Jonson's Folio commendatory verse. These are just a few examples of solutions of the self-referential type.

Specific points

The issue of whether the anagrams are due to chance can also be resolved by focusing on specific points; namely, well-known texts associated with 'Shakespeare' and his work:

1. The gravestone curse.
2. The Stratford Monument verse.
3. Jonson's prefatory verse *To the Reader* in the 1623 folio.
4. Jonson's commendatory verse in the 1623 folio.
5. Needle in the haystack – a uniquely special line in the 1623 folio version of *Othello*.

If the traditional attribution is right *there is nothing to hide about Shakespeare's authorship* – by definition. However, scrutiny of the above texts shows that all of them contain information encrypted in the same way.

1. The gravestone curse

The secret messages encoded in the gravestone curse have a threefold purpose:

- To show that the curse is a code and that 'Shakespeare' is a hoax – line 2.
- To name the real author – line 2.
- To indicate that the monument overlooking the grave contains a secret – line 4.

Messages hidden within the gravestone curse would certainly not be expected if orthodoxy was right. The fact that meaningful, coherent and appropriate statements *are* encoded in the text is therefore highly significant. In particular, one of the anagrams in line 2 states that the curse is a test which hides a code: 'curse has hidden code; set the test long ago' – a self-referential anagram and an indication that the anagram-maker thought it would be a long time before the code was broken. Furthermore, anagrams in the last line hint that the 'shabby monument', on the wall overlooking the grave, is (or was) the repository of secret codes.

2. The Stratford Monument verse

The monument and inscribed verse are not what they might appear to be:

- line 1 is an instruction and a question: 'Stay passenger, why goest thou by so fast?' which suggests there is more to the text than meets the eye – a hint that the verse requires careful study, not just a brief perusal.

- line 2 presents a challenge: 'Read <u>if thou canst</u> whom envious death hath plast <u>within</u> this monument'. The conditional instruction 'Read if thou canst' implies a logical contradiction – unless it means that the verse is some sort of test, with encrypted information. The text itself prompts the question: what is <u>within</u> the monument?

- Leonard Digges referred to the Stratford 'moniment' in his commendatory verse. Ben Jonson similarly used the word 'moniment' and even had the 'i' printed in bold type. It is noteworthy that a muniment is a document which proves the rights to something – like a title deed. Hence, 'moniment' might be a hybrid – the first part of <u>mon</u>ument and the last part of mun<u>iment</u>. Is this a hint that the moniment contains (or contained) a document proving 'the authorial rights' to *Shakespeare*?

- Anagrams referring to the monument: **A. In the gravestone curse**, the last line yields the linear anagram: 'SHABBY MONUMENT DOTH SAVE SECRET', and the non-linear anagrams: 'Verse on shabby bust meant as decoy method.', 'Hath set verse code on the shabby monument.', 'Shabby monument saves the secret codes.' and 'Destroy shabby monument. Save the codes' **B. In the monument verse**: line 2 becomes: 'Hath hid shadowe author's name, in the vaults of this cenotaph', line 3 yields: 'The name with in shews who is the impostor, then: unmaske' and line 4: 'Hidd Tudor Queene's bastard sonne within, make time to checke' **C. In John Warren's preface to Shakespeare's Poems (1640)** 'Hastings' name set behinde, the Stratford poet-memorial' **D. In Milton's verse** 'Break church monument to view Hastings' code, Milton'.

Anagrams in the monument verse indicate that the real author's name is hidden 'within', that he is the illegitimate son of the Tudor queen, that he is the true poet, that his real name is W. Hastings and that he is buried in a vault at Petworth. In addition, it seems that the monument is (or was) the repository for 'hard' evidence that proves the true authorship of *Shakespeare*. Commonsense suggests that the monument was the most obvious place to hide *material* evidence that categorically identifies the real author. However, the monument was repaired twice in the eighteenth century so it is possible – if not probable – that whatever was originally 'plast with in' was found on one of those occasions. If so, someone probably uncovered the 'Shakespeare' secret at the time of the repairs – but, owing to its very sensitive nature, had to remain silent.

3. To the Reader

Ben Jonson's prefatory 1623 Folio verse *To the Reader* seems superfluous: do we really need a rather mediocre ten-line poem to tell us that the Droeshout engraving, with Shakespeare's title emblazoned above, depicts the author? The verse itself is hardly worthy of a second-rate poet, let alone the great Ben Jonson and yet it has been given pride of place, preceding even the title page. However, if Jonson knew something about the authorship of *Shakespeare* that he dare not explicitly reveal, *To the Reader* would have been an obvious place to hide it. Indeed, close inspection shows that the verse *is* much more than just a second-rate rhyme. *To the Reader* is a key – like a Rosetta stone – that helps to unlock the 'Shakespeare Codes' by providing exemplars which illustrate the anagram method used in the folio text.

To the Reader has five main functions:

- To indicate that a 'huge test' exists – line 1.

- To state that 'Shakespeare' was not the true author – line 2.

- To show that clues have been deliberately left in the verse.

- To demonstrate that non-linear anagrams are the method of encryption.

- To name the real author (at least seven times) – line 2.

Anagrams *directly* identifying the author can only have been hidden in line 2 – 'It was for gentle Shakespeare cut;' – since this is the only line containing the letters of 'Shakespeare'. Indeed, anagrams in line 2:

- Indicate that Shakspere was not the true playwright.

- Identify Hastings as the real author/ writer/ poet.

- Confirm the existence of a 'lie' which concealed the truth about 'Shakespeare'.

- Imply that Hastings is buried at Petworth.

- Indicate that the face in the Droeshout engraving is false and that the author's true portrait is (or was) at Wilton.

It is extremely unlikely that sixteen exact anagrams, all using the same punctuation, would appear by chance in just the second line of the book! Moreover, if the anagrams *are* random occurrences, there should be no significant bias towards them appearing in one line rather than another. In other words, sixteen anagrams in line 2 – with only one anagram in each of the other lines – is a distribution far from that typical of randomness. Furthermore, it is highly improbable that all the remaining lines in the verse would each contain exact, meaningful solutions – viz:

1: 'This figure that thou here seest put':
    Issue huge test, hath put it here, for the future

3: 'Wherein the graver had a strife':
   The right answer has hid here ever after

4: 'with Nature, to out-doo the life:':
   The true author, often hid-out: at Wilton

5: 'O, could he but have drawne his wit':
   True author was hid, now believe this code

6: 'As well in brasse, as he hath hit':
   That has this as the answer, is reliable

7: 'His face, the print would then surpasse':
   The clue that hides this answer, is left on purpose

8: 'All, that was ever writ in brasse':
   Witt liberates, what answer reveals

9: 'But, since he cannot, reader, looke':
   Learne construction, breake the code

4. Jonson's commendatory verse in the 1623 Folio

In view of the fact that Jonson's verse is eighty lines long, it is surprisingly uninformative about the *man* who wrote *Shakespeare*. Indeed, the text seems to conceal more than it reveals, with many subtle hints and allusions at hidden meanings. Once again, it would be very surprising to find coherent secret messages in the verse, *if* the Stratford man was *Shakespeare's* author. So the presence of more than fifty exact anagrams in the text, is very powerful evidence that the real author was hidden. Here are some of the solutions, in a slightly modified order:

> *Shakespeare, thy vendor's name (he was not any poet)*
> *Hastings was the true writer, but freely used false names*
> *The future beware, Hastings used many false name titles*
> *Martin Marprelate, tis the cryptic code, of Hastings*
> *Hastings is hidden by Marprelate namesake, no bishop's friend*
> *By my riddle you have found out, Hastings is Marprelate*
> *Regret the anagrams, here, shake posterity*
> *Regret, Shakespeare name, is theatre story*
> *Hastings learned languages, skilled mother, taught method*
> *Hastings dreaded, like hell, language lessons mother taught*

> *We swear an oath! the sweet swan of Avon is Hastings*
> *We set the wit test, now uncover, William Hastings' name*
> *Actor had been seen in Stratford by Hastings*
> > *(Actor = William Shakspere)*
> *Hastings lodged at Petworth house after the plagues*
> *Hastings wrote the parts, for friends, at Petworth house*
> *The whore-wife Jane Daniel, soe endors'd Hastings' joy!*
> *Set duel trap for Hastings, Lady Daresbury the motive*
> *Provide Hastings' death, by my lust for a duel*
> *Sad murder at fortyeight, but Hastings' playes liv'd on*
> *Let me give you the proofe, Hastings is Dudley's bastard*
> *Hastings hidd as Arundel Talbot, the very famous spye*
> *Hastings is hid by spy Arundel Talbot, you deserve fame*
> *You have freed my poem, Hastings hidd as Arundel Talbot*
> *My deftly made riddles, prove truths about Hastings*
> *Hope that you solv'd my subtile hidden anagrams, first*

5. Needle in the haystack

The *only* line in the 1623 Folio that contains 'Hastings' in the correct sequence of letters, along with the letters of 'Queen Elizabeth' and 'Shakespeare', appears in *Othello* Act 2 Sc 1, viz: 'One that excels the quirkes of blazoning pens,'. However, in the first published edition of the play, in 1622, the corresponding line reads: 'One that excels the blasoning pens,'. It is virtually certain that the folio editors were responsible for the alterations. Without the addition of 'quirkes of' and the change of spelling from 'blasoning' to 'blazoning', there would be no 'Queen Elizabeth' or 'Shakespeare' and no meaningful anagrams. In fact, the line transposes into a number of very important solutions, directly linking Hastings to the queen, viz:

> *Next clue took prize, Hastings is son of Queene Elizabeth*
> *Expose Hastings' link to queene, secret sonne of Elizabeth*
> *Birth of son got queen Elizabeth sickeness, no poxe at all*
> *Proof not luck, expose Hastings son of queen Elizabeth*
> *Eloquent son of Elizabeth, got Shakespeare lexicon*
> *Next link to queen, Hastings poet of Elizabeth's court*
> *Next link to queen, poet Hastings actor son of Elizabeth*
> *Next link to queen, Hastings spoke French to Elizabeth*

It is quite easy to estimate an upper limit for the likelihood that a line with the necessary attributes might occur, at random, somewhere in the folio. The main factors determining the probability are the frequency at which the 'rare' letters Q, X, Z, P & K appear in lines of text, together with the frequency at which 'Hastings' appears in sequence. Analysis of the folio text indicates that the *upper* limit on the probability is about 1 in 5,000.

Clearly, the presence of Q, X, Z, P, K & Hastings in sequence is not suffi-cient in itself to *guarantee* meaningful anagrams – however, the appearance of at least ten exact solutions reduces the chance of random occurrence to a probability far smaller even than 1 in 5,000. Thus, frequency analysis shows that the anagram solutions are very unlikely to be the result of chance. But in any case, it is simply a *fact* that without alterations made by the editors to the 1622 version of *Othello*, the anagrams that appear in the folio version would not exist.

Uncover the truth, Hamlet is made to resemble Hastings
'A little more than kin – and less than kinde'   (1623 Folio spelling)

There seems to be a hint, in Hamlet's first utterance, of an invisible word between kin and kinde ... In fact, the missing four-letter word ('king') raises a question of fundamental importance: as heir to the throne, why didn't Hamlet immediately become king on the death of his father?

A moody prince and university student, Hamlet is an indecisive intellec-tual of questionable mental stability. His father, the king – also called Hamlet, has recently died. Soon after the funeral Hamlet's mother, Queen Gertrude, marries uncle Claudius, the dead king's brother and his murderer. The treasonous act, accomplished by poisoning, is revealed to the prince by his father's ghost, a spirit temporarily released from the bonds of purgatory that, for good or ill, urges Hamlet to seek revenge. Thus, *Hamlet* has been categorised as a so-called 'revenge play', a type of drama fashionable at the time.

However, the prince does not immediately act upon the astonishing supernatural revelation; instead of moving directly against the malefactor, he embarks upon a highly protracted course that brings disaster to almost every-one in his path: Polonius, Ophelia, Laertes, Rosencrantz, Guildenstern, Gertrude and Claudius all succumb to the ineluctable power of a dark mael-strom at the heart of the play. Only Horatio, Hamlet's stooge-like friend, is left to tell the tragic tale of the 'wounded name'. Of course, the play is far more complex than this very brief outline suggests. Among many things – not least musings on the nature of existence – it is concerned with the question of royal succession. Prince Hamlet 'ought' to have been crowned king on the death of his father; but it is the man from the north, young Fortinbras of Norway, who finally claims the Danish throne – much as James VI of Scotland became King of England on the death of Elizabeth I.

'You would pluck out the heart of my mystery' – Hamlet

Hamlet raises two key questions: why was the playwright so concerned about the issue of royal succession – a politically very dangerous subject to handle, when the old queen was nearing the end of her reign? But above all, why did Hamlet – by far the largest part in the canon – have such special significance for his creator? Scholars have long puzzled over the inspiration for this mammoth play: what were the psychological 'demons' that gripped the mind of the dramatist as he wrote this work?

In common with the author of the sonnets, Hamlet states that he has secrets – indeed, that *he* is a mystery. So, the 'resonance' between the enigmatic playwright and his equally enigmatic creation invites a comparison:

Was the author of *Hamlet* likely to have been...

A man with no *known* education, whose parents and close relatives were all illiterate; an individual who, in his youth, had no personal connection with Richard Tarleton (Tarleton = Yorrick – 'the skull' addressed by Hamlet). A yokel who reached maturity with no known access to well-stocked libraries, no association with the court and no known link to the aristocracy. A rustic from Warwickshire with no known connection to Elsinore Castle in Denmark. A yokel who had no clear reason to choose the Danish prince for 'very special' dramatic treatment and with whom he had nothing in common. A rustic who almost certainly spoke in a thick accent and yet, through Hamlet, instructs the players: 'Speak the speech... trippingly on the tongue'. A man who was exceedingly unlikely to have known of two Danish students enrolled at Padua University in March 1596, called Rosencrantz and Guildenstern – the names of Hamlet's student friends?

Or was he more likely to have been...

The secret son of the most intellectually brilliant monarch in British history, who came from a family full of linguists, writers and highly articulate intellectuals. An individual who would have received a first-rate humanist education. A man who was a scholar and a linguist himself (who spoke fluent French and Italian) an actor and spy who probably visited Elsinore in 1586 with his father's play troupe. A court poet who is certain to have known Lord Burghley (the probable model for Polonius) and many scholars, politicians and adventurers of the time. Someone who, in childhood, almost certainly knew Tarleton personally, the clown with Leicester's Men. A man living in Venice as a spy in 1596 when Rosencrantz and Guildenstern were a few miles away at Padua. All in all it seems Hastings made Hamlet in his own image.

A dog's obeyed in office

It is possible that Hastings used some of his plays to sting the conscience of the audience, especially when the audience happened to be the court itself. One wonders, for example, what James I made of the phrase 'a dog's obeyed in office' as he watched *King Lear* from his front-row seat – James Stuart was certainly not stupid! For William Hastings personally, drama might have been a means of 'getting at' certain people, much as Hamlet used *The Mousetrap*, the play within a play, to try and shame uncle Claudius and his mother into admission of guilt. However, Shakespeare's author is not thought of as a satirical writer because, from an orthodox point of view, it is impossible to imagine – in a climate of very harsh censorship – that the lowly Stratford dramatist would have dared to satirise his superiors.

Using insights gleaned as the royal spy, Hastings might have concealed satire in the plays, perhaps making fun of courtiers with jokes accessible to a few insiders only. Certainly no 'ordinary' dramatist would have dared to write plays lampooning his betters at court. But Hastings was very special; he knew that he could get away with satire, just as he knew that he could get away with *Richard II* and just as he knew he could get away with the scurrilous Marprelate tracts – because, as the unacknowledged son of the queen, he did not exist! It seems he had everyone over a barrel, including his mother.

The contents of some of the *Shakespeare* plays imply serious questions about the status of the author. A prime example is *Macbeth*, a drama which contains much that seems calculated to cause King James the greatest discomfort: drawn daggers, reference to the king's touch, witchcraft and terrible bloody murders – including the murder of children enacted on stage. But James was squeamish, terrified of swords and unsheathed daggers, denied the power of the king's touch and condemned witchcraft and the occult as nonsense. The playwright appears to have purposely chosen subject matter likely to anger, frighten and provoke his sovereign. What was he trying to do, get himself sent to the Tower? It is hard to believe that a dramatist of genius, with an eye to his liberty and future prospects – with knowledge of the monarch's personal insecurities – would have dared to write such a work. Indeed, it is the very disturbing content of the 'Scottish play' – at least from the perspective of King James – which is the main reason to doubt that *any* ordinary dramatist could have written it.

In view of the politically sensitive content of several plays, and the strict censorship in force at the time, one would certainly have expected to find the author in deep trouble on more than one occasion – and yet the Stratford man was *never* questioned about *any* of his work. The inability of orthodoxy to convincingly explain how and why Shakspere escaped official censure – on a number of occasions – is one of the most powerful arguments against the traditional attribution.

Furthermore, an unlettered yokel from the sticks, like Shakspere, could not possibly have 'protected' a hidden aristocratic dramatist from the authorities. A rustic impostor could not have defended the author from the law of the land *and* the wrath of the queen in a case as serious as *Richard II*. Indeed, it is difficult to see how the Stratford man was persuaded to put his name on a work that was so dangerous. But *uniquely* in Hastings' case, Shakspere knew he was untouchable because by hiding the real author from the public he was doing the government's job. Hence, with guaranteed immunity from the authorities, and very generous remuneration, William Shakspere became William Hastings' official mask.

Shakespeare, bumbling mimic and illiterate oaf

The evidence presented in this book makes it abundantly clear that *Shakespeare* was simply a title, a name that appeared on works which were in all other respects anonymous. In fact, the Stratford man *himself* never claimed to have written them. However, it would still have been possible for William Shakspere to argue that the works published under his name were *his* – not because he wrote them, but because he *owned* them! The ownership of otherwise anonymous text was all that mattered.

One of the most important reasons why the Stratford man was chosen as Hastings' mask – apart from the coincidence of his name and Hastings' code name – was that he was *unable* to write! Shakspere's illiteracy *guaranteed* there would be no letters, manuscripts or any other documents written in his hand. Of course, that has made it impossible to compare the quality and style of the published work with the quality and style of his 'normal' everyday prose. Such a comparison, had it been possible, would have provided very good evidence as to whether or not Shakspere was *capable* of writing *Shakespeare*. It was therefore vital for security that Hastings' mask could not write – an inference which is supported by anagram solution 87: 'Shakespeare, bumbling mimic and illiterate oaf'.

It was always very difficult to see how a genius of 'Shakespeare's' magnitude, could have completely escaped the attention of the cognoscenti and literati, throughout his lifetime. It was equally difficult to see how someone with an important central role for many years in the London theatres, 'The Wonder of the Stage', could have passed away in 1616 totally unnoticed by every single one of his former colleagues.

Final anagrams

The name of the place where William Hastings grew up – Stoake Parke Manor House – is a non-linear anagram which not only instructs the solver to take the name 'Shake Speare': ▶

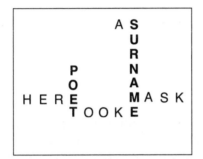

(78) *Use manor so to take Shake Speare*

... but also indicates exactly how 'Shakespeare' is to be used:

(180) *Tooke surname here as poet mask:*

Astonishing!

Some of the most compelling evidence that the real author was hidden by a mask – a decoy – is provided by the author's contemporaries: Thomas Edwards, Joseph Hall and Thomas Thorpe.

Thomas Edwards (1595) from an envoy in Narcissus ▶

This verse is about as explicit as it gets concerning the truth about Shakespeare's author. 'Adon deftly masking...' can only mean that the

Adon deafly (deftly) masking through
Stately tropes rich conceited,
Shewed he well deserved to.
Loves delight on him to gaze,
And had not love her self entreated,
Other nymphs had sent him bays.

Eke in purple robes distained,
Amidst the Centre of this clime,
I have heard say doth remain,
One whose power floweth far,
That should have been of our rhyme
The only object and the star.

Well could his bewitching pen,
Done the Muses objects to us,
Although he differs much from men,
Tilting under Friaries,
Yet his golden art might woo us,
To have honored him with bays.

author of the poem *Venus & Adonis* (1593) was hidden by a front-man, because the real poet was a nobleman who could not be identified – as verse two makes clear. Moreover, the penultimate line – 'Yet his golden art might woo us,' – is a non-linear anagram with answer:

(181) *Lie hides Hastings, now you got my truth*

Indeed!

Joseph Hall (1597): In referring to the author of *Venus & Adonis* as a crafty cuttlefish hiding in thick black clouds of ink, Hall makes it clear that the real poet is concealed and, by way of secret confirmation, includes anagrams that refer to the real author:

> Labeo is whip't, and laughs me in the face.
> Why? For I smite and hide the galled place,
> Gird but the Cynick's helmet on his head,
> Care he for Talus or the flayle of lead?
> Long as the craftie Cuttle lieth sure
> In the black Cloud of his thick vomiture;
> Who list complaine of wronged faith or fame
> When he may shift it to anothers name?

Line 1: 'Labeo is whip't, and laughs me in the face.'
(134) *The name of William Hastings, has beene put in code.*

Line 3: 'Gird but the Cynick's helmet on his head,'
(135) *Let mee but teach you the trick, Hastings is hidden*

Line 5: 'Long as the craftie cuttle lieth sure'
(136) *Hastings is true author Hall left secret clue*

The fact that Hall refers to Hastings as Labeo is highly significant, since the real Labeo was a Roman lawyer and an aristocrat. There are many legal terms and references in the canon, yet Shakspere had no known connection with the legal profession. However, it was almost de rigueur that young noblemen studied law, so the many precise legal terms and references in *Shakespeare* are strong circumstantial evidence that the author was of the aristocracy.

Thomas Thorpe's (1609) dedication to M^r. W.H. the 'onlie begetter' of *Shake-speares Sonnets*:

TO. THE. ONLIE. BEGETTER. OF.
THESE. INSUING. SONNETS.
M^r. W. H. ALL. HAPPINESSE.

Which, as indicated previously, is the linear anagram:
(110) BRINGE HELP TO WILLIAM HASTINGS THE UNSEENE POET OF THESE SONNETS

It is clear that Edwards, Hall and Thorpe were not referring to a man called 'Shakespeare' as the author of works published under that title. Edwards says 'Adon' is 'deftly masking', Hall says 'Labeo' is hiding like a crafty cuttlefish and Thorpe says that the 'onlie begetter' of the sonnets is a Mr W. H.. Moreover, each of them left anagrams in their texts identifying Hastings as the hidden poet – a combination of evidence which argues very powerfully against Stratfordian orthodoxy. In addition, the poet himself indicates in the sonnets that his name will be lost to posterity – hence his *real* name is not the name that appears on the published works.

One of the most remarkable features of the anagrams is that not only does every line with the letters of Hastings' name yield an exact, meaningful statement, but that so many of them say the same thing: Hastings was hidden. Indeed, it is the consistency of meaning that argues very strongly against the anagrams being chance. Quite simply, (chance) anagrams would yield incoherent statements – a 'collective message' would not emerge from a large number of random solutions.

To the Reader

I hope that by bringing William Hastings into the public domain, this book satisfies the entreaty in Thorpe's anagram – and that it does justice to all those who took the trouble to leave encrypted messages in texts alluding to Shakespeare.

In my opinion, the combination of thesis and evidence presented here is the most compelling, complete and logically satisfying of all the attempts that have been made to resolve the Authorship Controversy. It seems to me that this case answers all the major questions – and many more besides – whereas orthodoxy, by contrast, answers none convincingly; in fact, it raises many imponderable difficulties – problems that should not exist if William Shakspere actually wrote the works attributed to him.

After six years of research I honestly find it impossible to imagine a better solution to the authorship mystery than the assertion that William Hastings, secret son of Elizabeth I and Robert Dudley, was the real author of Shakespeare – but then, as the writer, I am biased. So it is now for you, the reader, to assess the evidence, ponder the arguments and form your own conclusion...

APPENDIX

Appendix

FULL ANAGRAM SOLUTIONS
The following are the complete solutions of non-linear anagrams referred to in the text. Some solutions have more than one key structure and certain words have more than one possible spelling; however, for the sake of clarity and simplicity, the alternatives have not been included here.

The format is:

    Clue: Line of original source text - in quotes
    Key: Non-linear structure of interlocking horizontal and vertical* words (*Vertical words in bold type)
    Answer: Correct sequence of words extracted from the key - in italics

Line 1: 'This figure, that thou here seest put,'

```
            T
            H  A  T  H
         T  E  S  T

            F  O  R
         P  U  T
         I  T
         H  U  G  E
      H  E  R  E
   I  S  S  U  E
```

(1) Issue huge test, hath put it here, for the future

Line 2: 'It was for gentle Shakespeare cut;'

And...

```
          S                                        A
          H                                        N
          A                              T  I      S
          K                    C                   W
          E                    L               A   E
    T  E  S  T                 U     T         F  O  R
          P                    E     H         T     S
       W  E  A  R        P  A  G  E     S  E  E  K  E
          A                                        R
          R
    C  L  U  E  S
          E
          F  O  R
 G  I  A  N  T
```

(2) Shakespeare; we left clues for giant test

(4) Tis the page for clues; seeke after answers

And...

And...

```
             K                 W
          I  N                 A           G  E  T
             O  R           S  H  A  K  E
       F  E  W                    N  O  T
    H        A  E                 F  I  R  S  T
    A     P  C  L  U  E  S     C  L  U  E
    S  T  A  R  E                    S  P  E  A  R  E
          G
       T  E  S  T
```

(3) Few knowe page has test; or clues stare in face

(5) Get first clue: Shake-speare was not genius

And...

```
                              W
                    S       R
                    T       I  S
                    A       T
                    G       E
                S P E A R E
                H
                A
                K
        C L U E
            E
            F
      N O T
```

(6) Left clue; Shakespeare is not stage writer

And...

```
                              W
                              O  F
                              R
                S H A K E
                          A   E
                T E S T
                          I           C
                          N           L
                          G           U
                          S P E A R E
```

(8) Test clue; Shakespeare worke of Hastings

And...

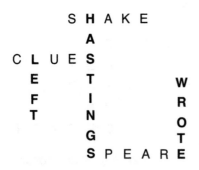

```
                S H A K E
                A
        C L U E S
            E   T       W
            F   I       R
            T   N       O
                G       T
                S P E A R E
```

(7) Left clues; Hastings wrote Shake Speare

And...

```
        A U T H O R
                S A F E
                    S E C R E T
        K E P T
            L I E
                N
                G
        W A S
```

(9) Hastings was author; lie kept secret safe

And...

```
 S  H  A  K  E
 A              F
 S  P  E  A  R  E
O  U  T           W
 I
 N
 G              L
 S  E  C  R  E  T
                T
```

(10) Shakespeare; few let out Hastings secret

And...

```
           H
           A
  W  A  S
           T
           I        A     C
           N     P  F     L
           G     O  T  R  U  E
           S  E  E  K  E     E
                 T  R     S
```

(12) Hastings was true poet; seeke after clues

And...

```
                 P
                 O
        H  E  R  E
        A        T
 W  A  S
        T
        I     C     A
        N     L     F
        G     U     T
        S  E  E  K  E
                    R
```

(11) Hastings was poet; seeke here after clues

And...

```
         A
 P  E  T  W  O  R  T  H
                     A
                     S  E  E  K
              A  F  T  E  R
                     I  S
                     N
                     G
        C  L  U  E  S
```

(13) Hastings is at Petworth; seek after clues

```
        S                          And...
        H E R E
        A
        K                                    S  W  I  L  T  O  N
        E                                    H  U  G  E
        S                                    A        F
        P U T                                K     A  T
F A C   E                                    E
        A                                    S  E  C  R  E  T
      W R O N G                              P
T I T L E                                    E
        S                                    A
                                             R
(14) Shakespeare's title; wrong                E
face put here
                                  (16) Shakespeare; left huge
                                  secret at Wilton
And...

        W
        I T
        L
        T R U E                   Line 3: 'Wherein the graver had a
    S   O                         strife'
    H A N G S
F A C   E                                 H
    K                                     E V E R
    E                                     R        I
    S                           A F T E R          G
    P                                              H I D
    E                                              T H E
    A T                                            A
    R                                     A  N  S  W  E  R
    E
                                  (18) The right answer has hid here
(15) True Shakespeare face; it    ever after
hangs at Wilton
```

Line 4: 'with Nature, to out-doo the life:'

```
            O
            F
        A T T H E
        O U T E
W I L T O N
        H I D
        O
        T R U E
```

(19) The true author: often hid-out, at Wilton

Line 5: 'O, could he but have drawne his wit':

```
                W
                A
        T H I S   C
A U T H O R     N O W
        U   H     D
        B E L I E V E
            D
```

(20) True author was hid, now believe this code

Line 6: 'As well in brasse, as he hath hit'

```
H A S
  N
A S
  W           T H A T
  E           H     H
  R E L I A B L E   I S
                    S
```

(21) That has this as the answer, is reliable

Line 7: 'His face, the print would then surpasse'

```
                        P
                        U
        C               R
        L E F T         P
        U       H       O N
A N S W E R     A       S
                T H E
                I
                D
                E
        T H I S
            S
```

(22) The clue that hides this answer, is left on purpose

Line 8: 'All, that was ever writ in brasse.':

```
                L
                I
                B
A N S W E R     E R
                R
                A
W H A T         T
I       R E V E A L S
T       S
T
```

(23) Witt liberates, what answer reveals

Line 9: 'But, since he cannot, reader, looke':

```
        L
    B R E A K E
        A
C O N S R U C T I O N
O       N       H
D       E       E
E
```

(24) Learne construction, breake the code

ANAGRAMS IN THE GRAVESTONE CURSE

Line 2: 'To digg the dust encloased heare:'

```
        H
        A
    C U R S E
A G O
    D
  T E S T
      E
      T H E
      I
      D
      D
      E
    L O N G
```

(25) Curse has hidden code: set the test long ago

And...

```
D O T H
    A
    S
    T H E
    I
    N
    G
    S E C R E T
      O       L
      D       U
    A G E     D
              E
```

(26) Hastings' secret code: doth elude the Age

Line 4: 'And curst be he that moves my bones'

```
            M
            O
            N
            U
    T       M
    H
S E C R E T
    O       N
    D       T
    E
    S A V E S
            H
            A
            B
            B
            Y
```

(28) Shabby monument saves the secret codes

Also...

```
                S
                H
                A
      C         B
      O    M    B
      D E S T R O Y
  T H E         N
      S A V E   U
                M
                E
                N
                T
```

(29) Destroy shabby monument. Save the codes

And...

```
          M
      C O D E
      O N
  S     T   U
  H A T H   M
  A   V E R S E
  B         N
  B     S E T
  Y
```

(30) Hath set verse code on the shabby monument

THE MONUMENT VERSE

Line 1: 'Stay passenger, why goest thou by so fast,'

```
        A
        N
        S
         W A S
      T E S T
  F O R   H
          E A S Y
          Y O U
              G
              G
      P O E T
          S   B
          T H Y
          S
```

(31) Suggests, by thy answer, the poet test was easy for you

Line 2: 'Read if thou canst, whom envious death hath plast'

```
  T           C
S H A D O W E
E           I N
            O F
      V A U L T S   T
            A     H A T H
          N   P   H I D
          A U T H O R S
          M
          E
```

(32) Hath hid shadowe author's name, in the vaults of this cenotaph

Line 3: 'With in this monument Shakespeare: with whom,'

```
        U
    I   N
        M
        A
        S
        K
    T H E N

        T H E
W I T H
N A M E
        I
        M
        P
W H O       I
    S H E W S
    T
    O
    R
```

(33) The name with in shews who is the imposter, then: unmaske

Line 4: 'Quick nature dide whose name doth deck this tombe,'

```
        S
        O   B
W I T H I N   A   T O
  Q U E E N E S H I D D
C H E C K E   T   M
            M A K E
    T U D O R
            D
```

(34) Hidd Tudor Queene's bastard sonne within, make time to checke

Line 6: 'Leaves living art, but page, to serve his witt'.

```
B               A U T H O R
E                       A
L                   P A S S
I                       T
E                       
V                   W I T
E V E R L I V I N G
                    G
                T E S T
```

(35) Pass wit test, believe Hastings, everliving author

And...

```
            V
G R A V E
            S
    P E T W O R T H
    I               A
    B       T I S
V A U L T           T
    L               I
    E           I N
                    G
                S E E
```

(36) See Hastings' grave, tis in vestibule vault, Petworth

JONSON'S FOLIO VERSE ANAGRAMS

Line 1: 'To draw no envy
(Shakespeare) on thy name,'

```
            W  A  S
               T  H  Y
               A  N  Y
               K
               E        N
V  E  N  D  O  R  S     O
               P  O  E  T
            H  E
               A
               R
         N  A  M  E
```

*(38) Shakespeare, thy vendor's
name (he was not any poet)*

And...

```
                        U
                  F     S
      B  E  W  A  R  E
                  L     D
                  S
            T  H  E
               A
               S
   F  U  T  U  R  E
         T  I  T  L  E  S
         N  A  M  E
         G     A
         S     N
               Y
```

*(40) The future beware, Hastings
used many false name titles.*

Line 5: 'Tis true, and all mens
suffrage. But these wayes'

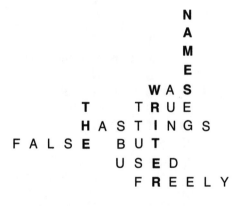

```
                  N
                  A
                  M
                  E
               W  A  S
      T        T  R  U  E
      H  A  S  T  I  N  G  S
F  A  L  S  E     B  U  T
         U  S  E  D
         F  R  E  E  L  Y
```

*(39) Hastings was the true writer,
but freely used false names*

Line 7: 'For seeliest Ignorance
on these may light'

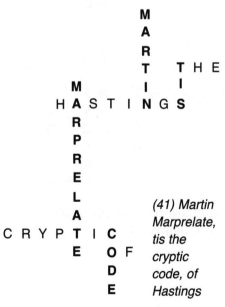

```
                  M
                  A
                  R
                  T        T  H  E
            M     I        I
   H  A  S  T  I  N  G  S
            R
            P
            R
            E
            L
            A
C  R  Y  P  T  I  C
            E     O  F
                  D
                  E
```

*(41) Martin
Marprelate,
tis the
cryptic
code, of
Hastings*

Line 18: 'The applause! delight!
the wonder of our stage!'

And...

```
              A
P E T W O R T H
              A F T E R
    H O U S E
              T H E
              I
              N
      L O D G E D
  P L A G U E S
```

*(42) Hastings lodged at Petworth
House after the plagues*

```
                  H E
W I L L I A M
          Y E S
              T
              I
              N         S O L D E
              G         H
              S P E A R
              O         K
              E         E
              T
              R
            B Y
```

*(44) Yes, Shake speare; he solde
poetry by William Hastings*

And...

```
            H E
            A
            S
    W R O T E
            I
L I B E R T I N E
    H   G Y
    E   S O L D E
    M   K
        E
      P L A Y S
```

*(43) Hastings wrote plays; libertine
yokel, he solde them*

Line 31: 'And though thou <u>hadst</u>
small Lat<u>ine</u>, and lesse <u>Greeke</u>

```
                  H
                  A
                  S
          T       T
          A S K I L L E D
          U       N
  L A N G U A G E S
          H       S
  M E T H O D
          O
          T
          H
          E
L E A R N E D
```

*(45) Hastings learned languages,
skilled mother, taught method*

And...

```
            D
            R
M O T H E R
            A           H
            D           A
    L E S S O N S       S
            D           T       T
          H   L I K E A          A
          E       N     R        U
          L A N G U A G E        G
          L       S     M        H
                        T
```

*(46) Hastings, dreaded like hell,
language lessons mother taught*

Line 51: 'The merry Greeke,
tart Aristophanes,'

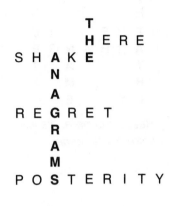

```
                        T
                    H E R E
      S H A K E
                N
                A
      R E G R E T
                R
                A
                M
      P O S T E R I T Y
```

*(48) Regret, the anagrams
here, shake posterity*

Line 47: 'And joy'd to weare the
dressing of his lines!'

```
          W I F E
          H
        S O E
          R
      T H E
      D A N I E L
        T     N
        S     D
        T     O
        I     R
      J A N E S
      O   S   D
      Y
```

*(47) The whore wife Jane Daniel
soe endors'd Hastings' joy!'*

And...

```
              S T O R Y
          T H E A T R E
          N A M E
          K
          R E G R E T
        I S
          P
          E
          A
          R
          E
```

*(49) Regret, Shakespeare name,
is theatre story*

Appendix

And...

```
        T I S
        H                   P
    H E R E           T O
R E A R R A N G E     E
        T           A     T
        R           M     S
    K E Y           E
```

*(50) Rearrange here, 'tis key,
to theatre poets name*

And...

```
                    H
            R A T E
                    S H A K E
                    T
    M E R R I T
                    N
                    G
                    S P E A R E
                    O
                    E
                    T
                    R
                    Y
```

*(51) Rate, Shakespeare poetry,
Hastings merrit*

Line 59: 'Who casts to write a living line, must sweat,'

```
        T               U
        H A S T I N G S           N O W
    S E T               C             A
                        O   W I L L I A M
                        V     I       W E
                    T E S T
                        R
```

(52) We set the wit test, now uncover, William Hastings' name

Line 67: 'Of Shakespeare's minde, and manners brightly shines'

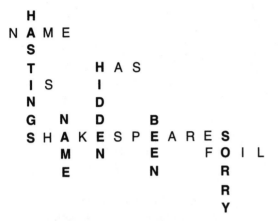

(53) Shakespeare's name is foil sorry, Hastings' name has been hidden

And...

(54) Hastings' is hidden by Marprelate namesake, no bishop's friend

Line 70: 'As brandish't at the eyes of ignorance'

(55) Actor had beene seen in Stratford by Hastings

Line 71: 'Sweet swan of Avon! what a sight it were'

(56) We swear an oath! The Sweet Swan of Avon is Hastings

233

Line 77: 'Shine forth, though starre of poets, and with rage'

(59) Hastings wrote the parts, for friends at Petworth House

Line 80:

(62) Set duel trap for Hastings, Lady Daresbury the motive

Line 80 - the last line: 'And despaires day, but for thy volumes light'

(61) By my poetry riddle, you have at last found Hastings here

And...

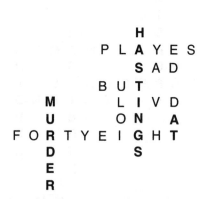

(63) Sad murder at fortyeight, but Hastings' playes liv'd on

Line 80:

```
        B
  M Y
  A
  R I D D L E
  P S
  R           F
H A V E         O U T
  L       Y O U
  H A S T I N G S
  T           D
  E
```

(64) By my riddle you have found out, Hastings is Marprelate

And...

```
                D
                U
                D
                L
  B         M   E
  A         Y
H A S T I N G S
  T     S   I
  A         V
  R       L E T
  D Y       H
  P R O O F E
        U
```

(65) Let me give you the proofe, Hastings is Dudley's bastard

Line 80:

```
                  D
  H               U
B A S T A R D     D
  I S             L
  T               E
  I               Y O U
  N         H       F
  G P       A
  S O L V D
    E       E
    T
    R
M Y
```

(66) You have solv'd my poetry, Hastings is bastard of Dudley

And...

```
                M
              B Y
R I D D L E   E
              S
              T H E
              A
              S
              T
          F O U N D
              G
        P A R T S
      L
  H A V E
  Y O U
```

(67) By my best riddle, you have found the Hastings' play parts

And...

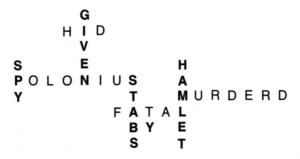

(68) Murder'd spy Polonius hid, given fatal stabs by Hamlet

And...

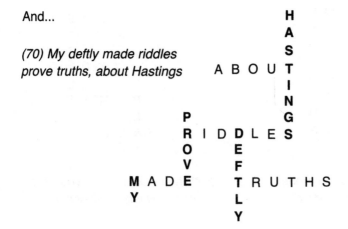

(69) You solv'd this playe, Hamlet is bastard son of Gertrude

And...

(70) My deftly made riddles prove truths, about Hastings

And...

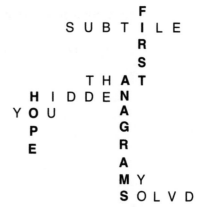

And...

```
B Y E         A                           F
F O R         T               S U B T I L E
  U           T                           R
  R I D D L E S                           S
            M                     T H A T
            P             H I D D E N
    H A S T I N G S   Y O U         A
            Y O U         P         G
              L           E         R
        H A V E                     A
            D                       M Y
                                    S O L V D
```

(71) Bye your attempt, you have solv'd riddles for Hastings

(72) Hope that you solv'd my subtile, hidden anagrams first

JOHN BENSON (1640)

Line 1 'This shadowe is renowned Shakespear's? soul of th' age'

```
                  S
                T O
        W       H
      F O O L E
      R               W
S H A K E S P E A R E
      E               O       A
      S       H A S T I N G S
              I       E
          U S D
              D
            H E E
              N
```

(73) Hidden Hastings wrote the workes hee us'd Shakespeare so as to foole

LEONARD DIGGES 1623 Folio commendatory verse

Line 1 'Shake-speare, at length thy pious fellowes give'

```
H A S T I N G S
            H E
        G A V E
            K
    L I F E
            S O U L
            P
        T H E
        P L A Y E S
        W R O T E
```

(74) Hastings wrote the Shakespeare playes, he gave life soul

LEONARD DIGGES (1640)

Line 2 'This truth, the glad remem-
brance I must love':

And...

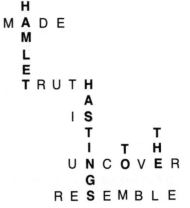

*(75) Uncover the truth, that message
is amid mobile letters*

*(76) Uncover the truth, Hamlet
is made to resemble Hastings*

Line 13: 'One phrase from Greekes, nor Latines, imitate'

(77) Shake-speare title. Hastings got it free, from manor name

A LOCAL HABITATION AND A NAME

The full manor title is a non-linear anagram which yields 'Shake-Speare':

Line 18: 'Is pure his owne, plot, language exquisite'

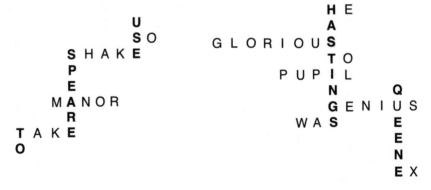

(78) Use manor so to take Shake Speare

(79) Hastings genius, he was ex pupil to glorious Queene

Line 64: 'Shall passe true currant
to succeeding age

```
                                    C
            D E A T H               U
            U         A     P U R E
      C A U S E       S C O T S
      R E G A L L     T         E
                      I N
                      N
                      G
                      S
```

Line 27: 'Then vanish upstart
writers to each stage,'

```
      H A T H
          A T         S
      C U R S E        E
        P E T W O R T H
            I     N
            N         T
            G R A V E
          A S         S
              I T
```

(80) Curse on Hastings' grave at
Petworth, hath set it as test

Line 39: 'Of richer veines, prime
judgements that have far'd'

```
            H
        F A T H E R
      J E S U I T
          T
        D R I V E
      E V E N
          G   M
          S E A R C H
            D   A
            E   M
                P
                I
            F   O R
                N
```

(81) Hastings
even made
search drive, for
Jesuit Father
Campion

(82) Hastings' death in duel regall
cause. Pure Scots curse

Line 65: 'But why doe I dead
Shakespeare's praise recite?'

```
                S
                H
                A
                K
      B U R I E D
                S         C   A
                P E T W O R T H
                E D E E P E
                A         Y
        D I A R I E S
                E
                S
```

(83) Shakespeare's diaries? Copy
buried deepe at Petworth

JOHN WARREN (1640)

Line 1: 'What lofty Shakespeare,
  art againe reviv'd'
And...

*(84) Shakespeare's diary?
Have left it, in grave, at Petworth*

*(86) Marprelate is Hastings' name,
the honest bishop feared it*

Line 5: 'These learned poems
  amongst thine after-birth'

Line 9: 'Let carping Momus barke
  and bite his fill,'

*(85) Hastings' name, set behinde
the Stratford poet-memorial*

*(87) Shakespeare, bumbling mimic
and illiterate oaf*

And...

```
N   H
A   A         T R I C K
M   I         R     O
L E F T       U     D
    B I B L E       E
    I N
    G
    P S A L M
```

(88) Bible trick is true, Hastings left code name in psalm

Line 13: 'Will be admirers of thy high tun'd straine,'

```
                H
                A
                S
        H I N T
            W I L L I A M  M
        B       N          U
F O R T Y E I G H T        R
                S          D
                           E
                           R
                           E
                           D
```

(89) Hint, William Hastings murdered
by fortyeight

Line 14: 'Amongst whose number let me still remaine'

```
        T H E
        N A M E
          S           R
          T           E
      W I L L I A M    M
          N           E
          G           M
    L O S S           B
              T       E
        M O U R N E
```

(90) To mourne the loss remember William Hastings' name

JOHN MILTON (1630)

Line 8: 'hast built thy selfe a
lasting monument'

```
T H Y
N A M E
  S
  T
M I L T O N
  N           B
  G           A
  S A L U T E S
          T H E
            F
            U
            L
```

*(91) Hastings, the bashful Milton
salutes thy name*

Line 14: 'Dost make us marble with
too much conceiving.'

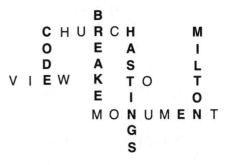

```
            B
C H U R C H       M
O       E   A     I
D       A   S     L
V I E W K   T O   T
        E   I     O
        M O N U M E N T
            G
            S
```

*(93) Breake church monument to
view Hastings code, Milton*

Line 9: 'For whilst to th'shame of
slow-endevouring Art'

```
        W H O
      H E A R D     F
        S H O N E   E
      O U T         W
  R     T R I T E
M I L T O N
  V       G
  A       S O
  L         F
  S
```

*(92) So few heard of Hastings who
out-shone trite rivals. Milton*

Line 16: 'That kings for such a
tombe would wish to die.'

```
        O H
          A
          S
      B U T
        D I D
M I L T O N     W
      I   G W   O
      F     S H O R T
    H E       A   K
        C U T     E
                  S
```

*(94) Hastings life cut short oh but
what workes he did. Milton*

J.M.S. (1632)

(J.M.S. is an unknown author.)

Line 14: 'A mind reflecting ages past, whose cleere'

(95) Free code's deep secret, get William Hastings' name

Line 6: 'Rowle backe the heavens, blow ope the iron gates'

(97) Believe Hastings wrote the book, not clowne Shake-speare

Line 2: 'And equall surface can make things appeare'

(96) Anagram clue Hastings' face appeared like queene's

Line 21: 'Enlive their pale trunkes, that the present age'

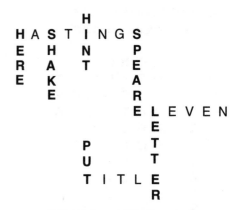

(98) Hint, put Hastings' eleven letter Shake Speare title here

Line 71: 'And more then nature
takes, our hands shall give'

```
              H
R E V E A L
              S
    U N T O L D E
              I
              N A K E D
    A N A G R A M S
    H O N E S T
              R
              U
              T
              H
```

*(99) Hastings' anagrams reveal
honest, untolde naked truth*

John Weever

Line 1: 'Honie-tong'd Shakespeare,
when I saw thine issue,'

```
                        T
                        I
    H A S T I N G S
        W H O
            A
    U N K N O W N E
    H I D E S
        I S
            P
            E
            A
    H E R E
    S E E
```

*(100) See who is here, 'tis
unknowne Hastings,
Shakespeare hides*

Line 10: 'Their sugred tongues, and
power attractive beuty'

```
                    P E N
    E           T O
    D E V E R E
    W           T A U G H T
    A     C O U R T     A
    R         B Y       S
    D                   T R U E
                        I
                        N
                        G
                T I S
```

*(101) Tis true, Hastings taught to pen
court poetry by Edward DeVere*

WILLIAM DAVENANT (1637)

Verse 1, line 1: 'Beware
(delighted poets) when you sing'

```
D   H
E   A       B
E   S   G   U
P E T W O R T H
L   I       I N
Y   N O W E
    G       D
    S E E
```

(102) Hastings buried deeply in
Petworth (now go see!)

Verse 2, line 2: 'Rather a night
beneath the boughs, than shade,'

```
                        B
        H               E
        A           T H E
        S           H   N
        T           O   E
B R A I N E         U
        N           G       H
        G           H       A
        S H A T T E R D
                    H
                    A
                    T
```

(104) Hastings' thought, that the
braine, had been shatter'd

Verse 2, line 1: 'Each tree,
whose thick, and spreading
growth hath made,'

```
                        W
                        H
                W R O T E
        H       O       N
        A       R
        S H A K E
        T       I
H       I
A C C I D E N T
T       G       D
H       S P E A R E
                M
                A
                G
            H E
                D
```

(103) When accident, hath damaged
Hastings, he wrote, Shake-speare work

Verse 3, line 2: 'Long since
(alas!) to such a swift decay;'

```
                H
            W A S
A C C I D E N T
            U   I   F
        S E A   N   A
                G   L
            C O S T L Y
                O
```

(105) Hastings" (costly!) fall;
was due to sea accident

THOMAS HEYWOOD (1635)

Line 24: 'Mellifluous Shake-speare, whose inchanting Quill'

```
                    Q
            C L U E
                U   E   S   O
            H E L P E F U L
                N       E
            H           A
W I L L I A M           R
            S H A K E
            T
            I
    S O N N
            G
        I S
```

(106) Helpful clue, William Hastings sonn of queen is Shakespeare

HUGH HOLLAND (1623 Folio commendatory verse)

Line 1: 'Those hands, which you so clapt, go now, and wring'

Line 12: '(Deaths publique tyring-house) the *nuncius* is.'

(nuncius = message in Latin)

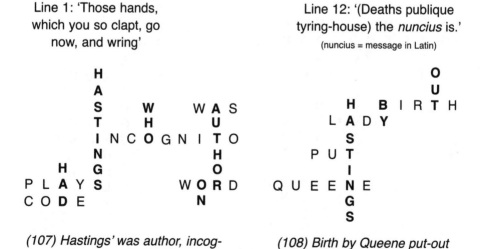

```
        H
        A
        S     W       W A S
        T     H       U
        I N C O G N I T O
        N     G       H
    H   G             O
P L A Y S         W O R D
C O D E               N
```

```
                        O
                        U
            H   B I R T H
        L A D Y
            S
        P U T
            I
Q U E E N E
            G
            S
```

(107) Hastings' was author, incognito, who had code word, on plays

(108) Birth by Queene put-out Lady Hastings

MICHAEL DRAYTON (1627)

The last line: 'As any one that trafiqu'd with the stage.'

```
              T H A T
      Q         A
      U         S T O R Y
  T H E     A T
      E       H I D
    I N F A N T
      E         G
            W A S
```

(109) Story was that Queene hid infant at the Hastings'

ANAGRAMS LEFT IN SONNETS BY THOMAS THORPE (TT)

Sonnet 10, line 6: 'That gainst thy selfe thou stickst not to conspire,'

Sonnet 52, line 2: 'Can bring him to his sweet up-locked treasure'

```
                    T
                    I
        T           T
I   F   H       H   L
S H A K E S P E A R E
    C       O   S
    T           T
                I  S
                N
                G   C
                S O O N
                    T
                    T
                  Y O U
                    N
                          T T
```

(113) You cotton so soon, the fact is
Shakespeare is Hastings' title TT

(114) Shake-Speare public code
words, true name is Hastings TT

Sonnet 89, line 3: 'Speake of my lamenesse and, I straight will halt'

Sonnet 97, line 14: 'That leaves looke pale, dreading the winter's neere.'

```
        W           N
H A S T I N G S      A
        L       H I M S E L F
        L       A   E
        I       K   D
        A       E
        M       S
                P L O Y
                E
                A
                R
                E       T T
```

(115) William Hastings himself named ploy: Shakespeare TT

```
H I D D E N
A L L
S P E A R E
T
I       W R O T E
N A L O N E
G   R
S H A K E
  H E
            T T
```

(116) Hidden Hastings. He even wrote Shake Speare worke, all alone TT

Sonnet 108, line 3: 'What's new to speake, what now to register,'

```
W H O
  A
  S H A K E
  T       N
  I S     O
  N       W E
  G
  S P E A R E
W R O T E
    E
    T       T T
```

(117) 'We know, Hastings is poet, who wrote Shake-Speare' TT

Sonnet 147, line 6: 'Angry that his prescriptions are not kept'

```
        H               P
        A           C   O
        S H A K E S P E A R E
P R I N T       O   N   T
        I       R   T
        N       R
        G       Y       T T
      I S
```

(118) Hastings is Shakespeare poet sorry can't print TT

ANAGRAMS LEFT IN SONNETS BY HASTINGS

Sonnet 2, line 8: 'Were an all-eating shame, and thriftlesse praise.'

```
                        W
                H       I
        L       A P L E A S E
    H E R E     S   L
        T       T F I N D
        T       I   A
        E       N A M E
    A R R A N G E
        S       S
```

(119) Please arrange letters, find William Hastings' name here

Sonnet 10, line 11: 'Be as thy presence is gracious and kind,'

```
    S H A K E
      A
    I S
      T
      I N
    I N
      G   S
      S P E A R E
          C
          R
  B O U N D E D
          C
          Y
```

*(120) Hastings is bounded in secrecy,
in Shake-speare*

Sonnet 18 contains at least six anagrams referring to Hastings:

Line 3: 'Rough wondes do shake
the darling buds of Maie,'

```
              H         F
              A         O
    A N S W E R
    B U T
        H I D D
        N A M E
        G           H
    D I S G U I S E D
                    R
        L O O K E
```

*(121) Hastings hidd name, but
looke here for disguised answer*

Line 6: 'And often is his gold
complexion dimm'd,'

*(122) Hastings' name in complex
code, fooled dim minds*

Line 12: 'When in eternall lines
to time thou grow'st,'

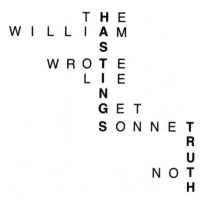

*(124) Get truth not lie, William
Hastings wrote the sonnet*

Line 14: 'So long lives this, and
this gives life to thee.'

*(125) Hastings lives in hiding,
solve the tests hee left to fool*

Line 8: 'By chance, or natures changing
course untrim'd:'

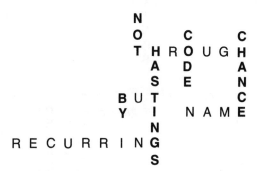

*(123) Hastings' name: not by chance
recurring, but through code*

Sonnet 37, line 8: 'I make my love ingrafted to this store'

(126) Hastings is hid: move letters to looke for my name

Sonnet 87, line 14: 'In sleepe a king, but waking no such matter.'

(128) Hastings is unknowne page, claims to be the true king.

Sonnet 76, lines 7 & 8: 'That every word doth almost tel my name,/Shewing their birth, and where they did proceed?'

Sonnet 89, line 4: 'Against thy reasons making no defence.'

(129) Find the key to encode Hastings' name in anagrams

(127) William Hastings and Thomas Thorpe had been shewn how to write the poetry, the lyric method, by Edward de Vere

Line 5: 'Thou canst not (love) disgrace me half so ill,'

```
H A S
A
S O   C O L L E C T
L E F T     O             R
I N     D             U
N A M E             I T
G                   H
S O L V E
```

(130) Hastings has left name in code, so (solve it) collect truth

Line 6: 'To set a forme upon
desired change'

```
O
F O R     P
E C O D E
N A M E
D     T H E
A
S
T R U E
I
N
G
S
```

*(131) Read the code for Hastings ,
true name of poet*

Line 7: 'As ile my selfe disgrace,
knowing thy wil,'

```
W
Y E
F   L   H
W I L L I A M
N       I S
C O D E S   T
I
A N G R Y
G
S E E K
```

*(132) Seek ye well, find codes,
William Hastings is angry*

'SAINT MARYE THE VIRGINE'S CHURCH, PETWORTH
(old spelling)

```
                                    C
                                    H E R E
                                    U
                                  M R
                        V           C
                I       P E T W O R T H
        H A S T I N G   S
                N       T H E
                        I
                        A
                        R
                        Y
```

(133) Mr Hastings is here in the vestiary, Petworth Church

JOSEPH HALL (1574-1656) – verse published 1597

Line 1: '*Labeo* is whip't, and laughs me in the face.'

```
                C
        H       O F     T
        A       D       H
        S   B E E N E
    P U T           A
    W I L L I A M
    I   N           E
        G
    H A S
```

(134) The name of William Hastings has been put, in code

Line 3: 'Gird but the Cynick's helmet on his head,'

```
            B
    Y O U   H
        T E A C H
            S   L
            T H E   H
            I   T R I C K
            N       D
            G       D
        I S     M E E
                    N
```

(135) Let mee but teach you the trick, Hastings is hidden

Line 5: 'Long as the craftie
cuttle lieth sure'

*(136) Hastings is true author
Hall left secret clue*

Line 2: 'Had'st thou not plaid
some kingly parts in sport,'

*(138) Tis truth, Hastings paide
impostor to take plays
to London*

ANAGRAMS BY JOHN DAVIES in *The scourge of folly.* To 'Our English Terence: Mr Will Shake-speare'.

Line 1: 'Some say (good *Will*)
which I, in sport, do sing,'

```
            W H O
  W I L L I A M
        O   S P Y
        R   T
C O D E     I S     H
            N     I S
            G O O D
            S     I
                  N
                  G
```

*(137) William Hastings, is (good)
spy who code word, is hiding*

SIR ARUNDEL TALBOT

**The name 'Sir Arundel Talbot' is a
non-linear anagram**

```
        B         T
A L L   L   A R E E
        I         S
        N         T O
        D           U
                    R
```

(139) All are blind to our test

255

The names William Hastings
and Arundel Talbot combine to
form the non-linear anagram:

And...

```
    T A L B O T
      R
      U
      N
  H I D
  A   E
  S   L
  T
W I L L I A M
  N
  G
  A S
```

*(140) Williams Hastings hid
as Arundel Talbot*

```
                    F
                    R
          H A V E
                    E
          H I D D
          A   S
          S
      T   T   P
      A R U N D E L
      L       G   M Y
      B       S
    Y O U
          T
```

*(142) You have freed my
poem, Hastings hidd as
Arundel Talbot*

**BEN JONSON'S
COMMENDATORY VERSE
IN THE 1623 FOLIO**

Last line: 'And despaires day,
but for thy volumes light.'

And...

```
      F A M O U S
        R       P
    T   U   A   Y
H A S T I N G S   E
    L   D
    B       V E R Y
    O       L
    T H E
      I
      D
      D
```

*(141) Hastings hidd as Arundel
Talbot, the very famous spye.*

```
              H
              A
          I   S
              T
      T   H I D D
      A R U N D E L
      L       G   S P Y
      B Y     S   E   O
      O           R   U
      T           V
        F A M E
```

*(143) Hastings is hid by spy Arundel
Talbot, you deserve fame.*

MILTON'S VERSE ON SHAKESPEARE

'The labour of an Age, in piled stones'

'Will be admirers of thy high tun'd straine,'

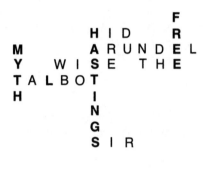

(144) Help to find Hastings, go see Arundel Talbot

(145) Free the myth, Sir Arundel Talbot hid wise Hastings

ANAGRAMS BY HASTINGS LEFT IN SONNETS, RELATING TO ARUNDEL TALBOT

Sonnet 3, line 6: 'Disdaines the tillage of my husbandry?'

Sonnet 18, line 11: 'Nor shall death brag thou wandr'st in his shade,'

(146) Is hidden Hastings safely hid by Arundel Talbot?

(147) Learn that Sir Arundel Talbot's shadow, has hid Hastings

Sonnet 27, line 12: 'Makes blacke night
beautious, and her old face new.'

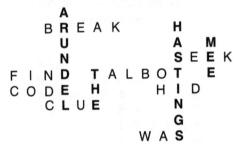

```
        A
B   R   E   A   K           H
        U                   A       M
        N                   S   E   E   K
F   I   N   D   T  A  L  B  O  T     E
C   O   D   E       H       H   I   D
        C   L   U   E       N
                            G
                    W   A   S
```

*(148) Break Hastings' code. Seek the
clue, find Arundel Talbot was mee*

Sonnet 100, line 4: 'Darkning
thy powre to lend
base subjects light.'

```
                        T  H  E
                    B   R  E  A  K
                            S  P  Y
            T   A   L  B  O  T
                    R      W  I  G
            J   U   S  T   N
                    N   H   G
                    D   E  I  S
C   O   D   E           N
            L
```

*(150) Break the code. The
spy Arundel Talbot is just
Hastings in wig*

Sonnet 89, line 9: 'Be absent from thy
walkes and in my tongue,'

```
M   A   N   Y
    R
B   U   T
    N       H
    D   N   A   M   E
    E       S   Y
T   A   L   B   O   T       F
            I           E
        K   N   O   W   E
            G
            S
```

*(149) Many knowe Arundel Talbot, but
few my name Hastings*

JOHN WARREN
In preface to Shakespeare's
poem (1640). Line 9: 'Let
carping Momus barke and
bite his fill,'

```
                H
            A   R   U   N   D   E   L
            S   I   M   P   L   E
T   A   L   B   O   T
R           F   I   B
I           N   A   M   E
C           G
K           I   S
```

*(151) Arundel Talbot name is fib,
simple trick of Hastings*

And though, right guiltless,
may'st plead to it, why?

(152) *William Hastings is hidd*
as the royal spye
Got you the truth?

EDMUND SPENSER

Line 1: 'But that same gentle
spirit, from whose pen'

(153 *True name of poet is Hastings,*
set the problem as wit test

And... line 2: 'Large streames of
honnie and sweete
nectar flowe,'

(154) *Real name of Hastings*
was left in secret code, now
free the answer

And... line 3: 'Scorning the
boldnes of such base-borne men'

(155) *Hastings is noble-borne*
code has not been
secure from me

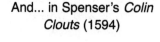

And... in Spenser's *Colin Clouts* (1594)

(156) Learn that, Hastings uses the Aetion title, so to hide

HAMLET (Act V Sc ii)

Hamlet says: '(Things standing thus unknowne) shall live behind me'

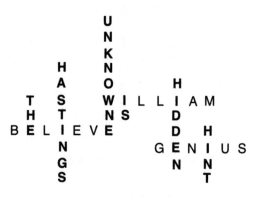

(157) Believe the hint (unknowne) William Hastings is hidden genius

MUCH ADO ABOUT NOTHING

ACT II Sc ii: Benedick says: 'Ha, "against my will I am sent to bid you come into dinner"; there's a double meaning in that:'

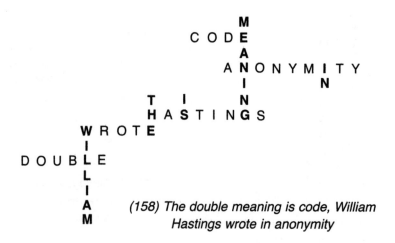

(158) The double meaning is code, William Hastings wrote in anonymity

'One that excels the quirkes of
blazoning pens,'

```
            N E X T
            L
H A S T I N G S
    P R I Z E   O
    C     S A     N
    L     B
Q U E E N E
    E           T O O K
                H     F
```

*(159) Next clue took prize,
Hastings is son of queene
Elizabeth*

And....

```
                Q
                U
                E L I Z A B E T H
H               E X P O S E
A               N
S E C R E T
T               O
L I N K
N
G
S O N
    F
```

*(161) Expose Hastings' link to
queene, secret son of Elizabeth*

And....

```
                P
            N O X
                X
Q U E E N E
A L L
    S I C K N E S S E
    Z           O F
    A T         N
    B I R T H
    E
G O T
    H
```

*(160) Birth of son got queene
Elizabeth sicknesse,
no poxe at all*

And....

```
L
Q U E E N E
    C     L
    K     I
          Z
          A
          B         E
          E         X     N
          T         P R O O F
          H         S O N   T
    H A S T I N G S E
                    E
```

*(162) Proof not luck, expose
Hastings queene Elizabeth's son*

And....

```
              S
              P        G
       L E X I C O N
              A        T
     E        R
   E L O Q U E N T
     I
     Z
   S H A K E
     B
 S O N N E
   F     T
         H
```

*(163) Eloquent sonne of Elizabeth,
got Shakespeare lexicon*

And....

```
       Q U E E N E
            L
       L I N K
            Z
       H A S T I N G S
            B    O    E
       S    E         X
     P O E T    A C T O R
       N    H            F
```

*(165) Next link to queene, poet
Hastings actor son of Elizabeth*

And....

```
   Q
   U
 F R E N C H
   E
   N    L
   E L I Z A B E T H
     N            A
   S P O K E      S
                  T O
                  I
                  N E X T
                  G    O
                  S
```

*(164) Next link to queene, Hastings
spoke French to Elizabeth*

And....

```
            C
            O
       Q U E E N E
            R        L       N
     P O E T    L I N K E
       F        Z       X
                A       T O
                B
                E
           H A S T I N G S
                H
                S
```

*(166) Next link to queene,
Hastings poet of
Elizabeth's court*

ANAGRAMS IN THE SONNET IN PERSIAN LADY PAINTING

Line 4: 'are all the Musique, that
my life prolonges'

*(167) Queen is mother of
Hastings, poem truly tells all.*

Line 7: 'Hes teares in sylence,
and my sighes unknowne'

*(169) My name is Hastings, key
shewn here encodes answer in clue*

Line 5: 'With pensive thoughtes
my weeping stagg I crowne,'

*(168) The weeping stagg is
Hastings, now uncover the
wit test in my poem*

Line 8: 'are all the physicke that
my harmes redresse.'

*(170) Hid my Shakespeare title
here. They are my secret playes.*

Line 9: 'My onely hope was in this goodly tree'

(171) Hastings wisely denys poem, to royal mother

FROM THE 'PHAETON' SONNET

Line 1: 'Sweete friend whose name agrees with thy increase'

(172) Hastings set the wit test, few were aware code hides my name in heere

Line 4: 'And green-lockt sommers shadie pleasures cease.'

(173) More riddle clues: Hastings uses Shakepeare as code name

Line 7: 'The dazies sprout, the little birds doo sing,'

(174) Tis true, lie hidd poet Hastings, Elizabeth Tudor's son

THE WILTON MONUMENT

First line: 'Life's but a walking shadow'

(176) As few know Hastings was all but hid

Line 8: 'Hearbes, gummes, and plants doo vaunt of their release.'

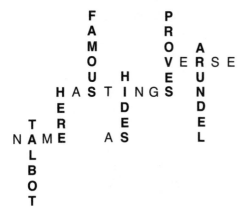

(175) Here verse proves, Hastings hides as famous name, Arundel Talbot.

Capitalised words in the inscription (SHADOW, LIFE, PLAYER, STAGE) together form a non-linear anagram

(177) False poet hid wise royall sage

And....

```
P O E T        F
A     H   W    A
I     R E G A L L Y
D         S    S
               E
```

*(178) The false poet was
paid regally*

The name of Hastings' childhood
home 'Stoake Parke Manor House'
(old spelling)

```
            A   S
                U
                R
                N
        P       A
        O       A
H E R E E       M A S K
        T O O K E
```

*(180) Tooke surname here as
poet mask*

And....

```
            W
        F   A
        A L I A S
        L
        S
P O E T
    H
G R E E D Y
```

*(179) Greedy false poet
was the alias*

**THOMAS EDWARDS envoy
Narcissus 1595**

Penultimate line 'Yet his golden
art might woo us,' *25*

```
    M Y
      O
    T R U T H
            A
            S
        G O T
            I
            N O W
      L     G
    H I D E S
      E
```

*(181) Lie hides Hastings, now
you got my truth* *32*

Index